AF335723

God, Belief, and Perplexity

God, Belief, and Perplexity

WILLIAM E. MANN

OXFORD
UNIVERSITY PRESS

OXFORD
UNIVERSITY PRESS

Oxford University Press is a department of the University of Oxford. It furthers
the University's objective of excellence in research, scholarship, and education
by publishing worldwide. Oxford is a registered trade mark of Oxford University
Press in the UK and certain other countries.

Published in the United States of America by Oxford University Press
198 Madison Avenue, New York, NY 10016, United States of America.

© Oxford University Press 2016

Library of Congress Cataloging-in-Publication Data
Names: Mann, William E., 1940–author.
Title: God, belief, and perplexity / William E. Mann.
Description: New York, NY: Oxford University Press, 2016. | Includes index.
Identifiers: LCCN 2015035304 | ISBN 978–0–19–045920–8 (hardcover: alk. paper)
Subjects: LCSH: Augustine, Saint, Bishop of Hippo. | Abelard, Peter, 1079–1142. | Anselm, Saint,
Archbishop of Canterbury, 1033–1109. Classification: LCC BR65.A9 M3234 2016 | DDC 212—dc23 LC
record available at http://lccn.loc.gov/2015035304

1 3 5 7 9 8 6 4 2
Printed by Sheridan, USA

To Dana

CONTENTS

SECTION III   ANSELM

PERMISSIONS

"The Philosopher in the Crib" (Chapter 1) originally appeared in *Augustine's Confessions: Critical Essays*, ed. William E. Mann (Lanham, MD: Rowman & Littlefield Publishers, Inc., 2006), 1–16. Reprinted by permission of the publisher.

"The Theft of the Pears" (Chapter 2) originally appeared in *Apeiron* 12/1, 1978: 51–58. Reprinted by permission of Walter de Gruyter GmbH.

"Pride and Preference: A Reply to MacDonald" (Chapter 3) originally appeared in *Faith and Philosophy* 23, 2006: 156–168. Reprinted by permission of the publisher.

"The Life of the Mind in Dramas and Dreams" (Chapter 4) originally appeared in *Augustine's Confessions: Philosophy in Autobiography*, ed. William E. Mann (Oxford: Oxford University Press, 2014), 108–134. © by Oxford University Press in 2016. Reprinted by permission of Oxford University Press.

"Augustine on Evil and Original Sin" (Chapter 5) originally appeared in *The Cambridge Companion to Augustine*, 2nd edition, ed. David Vincent Meconi and Eleonore Stump (Cambridge: Cambridge University Press, 2014), 98–107. © 2014 by Cambridge University Press. Reprinted by permission of the publisher.

"Inner-Life Ethics" (Chapter 6) originally appeared in *The Augustinian Tradition*, ed. Gareth B. Matthews (Berkeley: University of California Press, 1999), 140–165. © 1999 by the Regents of the University of California. Reprinted by permission of the publisher.

"To Catch a Heretic" (Chapter 7) originally appeared in *Faith and Philosophy* 29, 2003: 479–495. Reprinted by permission of the publisher.

"Perplexity and Mystery" (Chapter 8) originally appeared in *Metaphilosophy* 29, 1998: 209–222. Reprinted by permission of John Wiley and Sons.

"Abelard's Ethics: The Inside Story" (Chapter 9) originally appeared as "Ethics" in *The Cambridge Companion to Abelard*, ed. Jeffrey Brower and Kevin Guilfoy (Cambridge: Cambridge University Press, 2004), 279–304. © 2004 by Cambridge University Press. Reprinted by permission of the publisher.

Introduction

Augustine, Abelard, and Anselm constitute a formidable A-team of philosophers. This volume presents my essays on some of the quandaries, arguments, and theories that surfaced in these three philosophers' writings. The essays in this volume complement those to be found in my *God, Modality, and Morality* (Oxford University Press, 2015). The two volumes differ, however, in their emphasis. The essays in *God, Modality, and Morality* aim largely at presenting and defending a theistic worldview. Although some of those essays dealt with the views of such historical figures as Plato, Aristotle, Aquinas, Eckhart, Luther, Leibniz, and Kierkegaard, others dwelt exclusively on contemporary issues in philosophical theology. Though the cast of characters in this volume is smaller, the roles they play are varied. Some essays still deal with issues in philosophical theology. Other essays are aporetic in nature, revealing cases of philosophical perplexity, sometimes but not always leaving them unresolved. Still other essays explore the limits of human reason when it comes to matters divine.

Some of the essays criticize the views of fellow workers in the field, workers from whom I have learned much. Other essays press into service the views of contemporary philosophers who would be surprised to find themselves in the company of their patristic and early medieval predecessors. I make no apologies for that. Quandaries and arguments can be perennial, still rightly fascinating successive generations of thinkers. We pay respects to our philosophical ancestors (and our philosophical contemporaries) by taking seriously their contributions to—in some instances, their *initiation of*—those quandaries and arguments.

The discerning reader will note that I have presented the A-team slightly out of chronological order. Augustine (354–430) is the earliest by far, but Anselm (1033–1109) antedates Peter Abelard (1079–1142). I have nonetheless chosen to place the essay on Abelard immediately after the essays on Augustine because the topic of the essay, namely, Abelard's ethics, is heavily indebted to his reading of Augustine.

Augustine

The first five essays are reflections on cases of Augustinian perplexity that surface in the early books of the *Confessions*. In some cases Augustine finds it important to resolve the perplexity because some important tenet of his understanding of the Christian faith depends on its resolution. In other cases, however, when the quandary does not disturb the life of the Christian believer, he is content to leave it unresolved, perhaps as a reminder of the limitations of human understanding.

"The Philosopher in the Crib," for example, examines Augustine's speculation in Book 1 of the *Confessions* that infants may not be as innocent as they seem. The central question here is whether some infant behavior can be motivated by selfish, jealous desires. Recently, arguments have been offered to the effect that infants cannot have any desires or beliefs; the development of those capacities is alleged to occur only in tandem with the development of language. This essay examines one such argument put forward in "Thought and Talk" by Donald Davidson. I suggest that Davidson's argument is less than dispositive. Thus Augustine may have been justified in his speculation. The essay concludes by listing a series of related, unresolved quandaries.

"The Theft of the Pears" presents Augustine's psychologically acute meditation in *Confessions* 2 on his youthful theft of his neighbor's pears. After rejecting a series of possible explanations for why he did what he did, he concludes that he must have stolen the pears simply for the sake of knowingly doing something wrong. This conclusion troubles him. The desire to steal must have a cause, but since he believes that everything that exists is good—a belief that is at the core of his rejection of Manichaean dualism—he cannot find any good that he regards as sufficient to have prompted him to act. The theft is not merely a case of knowing the good but failing to do it: its point is to rejoice in what one knows to be wrong. But that "point" seems pointless.

"Pride and Preference: A Reply to MacDonald" revisits *Confessions* 2, this time in response to Scott MacDonald's "Petit Larceny, the Beginning of All Sin: Augustine's Theft of the Pears." MacDonald and I agree that Augustine's theft was not chosen haphazardly from his catalogue of wrongdoings. We disagree about what the theft illustrates. Central to MacDonald's interpretation are the theses that all sins are cases of preferring lesser goods over greater goods and that all sins are motivated ultimately by pride. Concerning the inverted preference thesis, I argue that preferring a lesser good over a greater good is not a sufficient condition for sinfulness: the condition must be supplemented with a proviso that the preference is contrary to God's commands. MacDonald takes the ultimacy of pride thesis to entail that sinners desire to be *transvaluators*. I argue that this is implausible—most sinners are scofflaws, not moral revolutionaries—and that there is no evidence for the thesis in Augustine.

"The Life of the Mind in Dramas and Dreams" undertakes the task of exploring similarities between one's mental activities while in the theater and while dreaming. In an under-appreciated passage in *Confessions* 3, Augustine identifies (for the first time in history) the paradox of tragedy: why do we respond emotionally to representations of the fates of persons who we know never existed? I discuss Kendall Walton's suggestion, in *Mimesis as Make-Believe*, that our psychological states in response to drama are various kinds of "quasi-attitudes" that are not identical to the mental states we have when dealing with ordinary life. I argue that Walton's suggestion does not fully resolve Augustine's plight. Augustine's description of the soul's power of imagination sheds light on his attitude toward dramas and dreams. His account does not dispel his worries about the persistency of his erotic dreams, disclosed in *Confessions* 10. He would like to disavow responsibility for them, but he never succeeds. If playwrights can be held accountable for the content of their plays, then "dreamwrights" seem responsible for the content of their dreams.

"Augustine on Evil and Original Sin" addresses Augustine's solution to the perplexity that plagued him in his earlier years—how can evil exist in a world created by an omniscient, omnipotent, perfectly good God? In *Confessions* 7 he gives his reasons for rejecting Manichaean dualism. Book 13 emphasizes the doctrine of creation ex nihilo, with its entailment that everything that exists is good. But not all creatures are equally good. Augustine regards sin as the willful abandonment of greater goods for lesser ones, when the abandonment is contrary to God's commands. This essay concludes with a brief discussion of Augustine's handling of two spectacular cases of sin, the devil's defection from God and Adam and Eve's fall.

The sixth and seventh essays delineate and apply some of Augustine's distinctive contributions to moral theory. "Inner-Life Ethics" presents the elements of the theory, elements that can be found scattered in works written by 401. The theory is shaped by Augustine's understanding of Jesus's Sermon on the Mount and Augustine's soul-body dualism. Augustine's dualism is distinctive in claiming that because the soul is superior to the body, the body cannot affect the soul, and that the moral appraisal of an agent's bodily behavior must take account of the state of the agent's soul. Augustine interprets the Sermon on the Mount as emphasizing the moral importance of an agent's intentions: if one intends to do something morally impermissible, one is already morally culpable, even if the intention is never acted upon. The theory is then applied to Augustine's concern over his theft of the pears, his worry about his erotic dreams, and his remarks about lying.

"To Catch a Heretic: Augustine on Lying" examines Augustine's two treatises on lying, *De Mendacio* and *Contra Mendacium ad Consentium*. Augustine's differentiation between statements that are lies from those that are not illustrates the importance of a presence of an intention to deceive. His views on lying are compared with views expressed in Bernard Williams's *Truth and Truthfulness*. One of the surprising consequences of Augustine's views is that a person can lie when telling the truth! In spite of some examples that Augustine regards as poignant, he defends the position that all lying is sinful, even when the consequences of lying would be better than the consequences of telling the truth.

The eighth essay, "Perplexity and Mystery," probes Augustine's occasional attitude of indifference to paradox and his capacity to resolve mystery by responding to Gareth B. Matthews's "The Socratic Augustine" and Peter King's "Augustine on the Impossibility of Teaching." Matthews suggests that, despite Augustine's dogmatic tendencies, he is content to accept some cases of Socratic perplexity as genuine because the phenomena they describe are real. I argue for the alternative view that Augustine is content not to pronounce on some seemingly paradoxical phenomena because they are not relevant to religious dogma. King defends the Augustinian thesis that teaching, construed as causal transmission of knowledge, is extremely mysterious if not impossible. I suggest that much of the alleged air of mystery evaporates once we distinguish between metaphysical dependency and epistemological dependency.

Abelard

One suspects that Augustine and Abelard would have found much to disagree about, especially in metaphysics. In contrast, "Abelard's Ethics: The Inside Story" argues that Abelard understood, incorporated, and in some cases developed more fully an ethical outlook to be found in Augustine's writings. In characterizing sin as contempt of God, Abelard rejects views that maintain that sin is a vice, or a bad deed, or even the will to perform a bad deed. Sin is precisely the *intention* to do evil. Abelard thus distinguishes sharply between acting willingly and acting intentionally. (The justification for the distinction can be found in the difference between Augustine's *De Libero Arbitrio* and his *De Sermone Domini in Monte*.) This essay explores several ramifications of Abelard's intentionalism, including the analysis of intention as a kind of consent, differences between intentions and desires, the role of natural law, ignorance, and mistaken belief.

Anselm

Certain short passages in the history of philosophy, for example, Aristotle's "sea battle," Descartes's *Cogito*, and Hume's claim that one cannot derive values from facts, have rightly inspired thousands of pages of subsequent discussion, for and against. Add to this list of short passages Anselm's so-called ontological argument for God's existence. The first four essays in this section are devoted to exploring the argument. I do not believe that the argument is sound, but I do believe that many attempts to fault it either expose it to an unnecessary vulnerability or miss their target. "Definite Descriptions and the Ontological Argument," for example, argues that it does a disservice to Anselm to transcribe his crucial descriptive phrase, "the being than which none greater can be conceived," into a formal language incorporating Bertrand Russell's theory of descriptions. Russell's theory analyzes definite descriptions in terms of existentially quantified sentences. Applied to Anselm's argument Russell's theory has the consequence of begging the question of God's existence before the argument begins. This essay presents on Anselm's behalf some alternative theories of definite descriptions embedded in free logics, formal languages whose singular terms do not have existential import. The use of such languages frees one then to consider the substantive principles on which the argument may depend.

"The Ontological Presuppositions of the Ontological Argument" presents a reconstruction of Anselm's argument in English, identifying two principles on which the argument depends. The first is the claim that whatever is understood is in the understanding; the second is that for whatever exists solely in the understanding, something greater than it can be conceived. Most of this essay focuses on the first principle. Anselm claims that there is an intimate connection between something's being in the understanding and its being conceived. Moreover, he relies on a distinction between conceiving of something and conceiving that thing to exist. I offer two ways of analyzing the distinction. Neither way provides Anselm with a sound argument for God's existence.

"The Perfect Island" explores the second principle, that is, the principle that for whatever exists solely in the understanding, something greater than it can be conceived. There are at least five versions of that principle, of varying strength. Anselm's argument relies on the weakest of the five. Gaunilo invoked his "lost island" counterexample in an attempt to demonstrate that an argument structurally identical to Anselm's would "prove" the existence of the greatest conceivable island, thus exposing the absurdity of Anselm's argument. But Anselm's argument relies only on the weakest version of the second principle, whereas

Gaunilo's argument requires one of the stronger versions. This essay presents a model in which the weakest version is true while the other four versions are false. Gaunilo's argument is thus not a successful counterexample.

"Locating the Lost Island" replies to Lynne Rudder Baker and Gareth B. Matthews's "Anselm's Argument Reconsidered," in which the authors claim to have produced a sound version of Anselm's ontological argument. Using Gaunilo's "lost island" counterexample, this article explores the question whether an Anselmian argument can prove the existence of the greatest conceivable being without relying on premises that also prove the existence of the greatest conceivable island. A distinctive feature of Baker and Matthews's approach is that it countenances some "objects of thought" that not only *do not* exist in reality but logically *cannot* exist in reality. They then argue that for any conceivable island, a greater island is conceivable, but that there cannot be a conceivable being greater than the greatest conceivable being. Their strategy is vulnerable on two counts. It does not address the possibility that there is no upper limit to greatness in conceivable beings. Nor does it assure us that the greatest conceivable being is even logically possible. Thus their version of Anselm's argument is inconclusive.

Anselm made other significant contributions to the philosophical understanding of Christian belief. "Anselm on the Trinity" presents his attempts to show that the western Christian doctrine that God is one yet threefold in nature is free from contradiction. Two-fifths of the *Monologion* is devoted to this project, along with two shorter works, *On the Incarnation of the Word* and *On the Procession of the Holy Spirit*. In carrying out this project Anselm is aware that he must avoid the heresies of Arianism, tritheism, and modalism. Following Augustine, Anselm models his account of the relations among Father, Son, and Holy Spirit as relations among memory, understanding, and will. In humans these are imperfect and encapsulated capacities. Consistent with Anselm's commitment to God's simplicity, his project cannot allow any such flaws in his conception of God. In *On the Incarnation of the Word*, Anselm reworks an analogy used in Augustine's *On Faith and the Creed*. The Nile is spring, river, and lake, yet there are not three Niles. Anselm realizes that taken literally, the analogy leads to tritheism, or the denial of God's simplicity, and tries to improve on the analogy. However, Anselm is aware that improvement on the analogy can only yield dim, imperfect vestiges of the Trinity, which is a mystery not available to human unraveling.

If this A-team has a captain, it surely is Augustine. His presence permeates these essays in obvious and not so obvious ways. Where he seems absent, as in the essays on the ontological argument, he is still present. Anselm originally wanted to give the *Proslogion* the title "Faith Seeking Understanding," a banner under which Augustine had called believers to marshal their contemplative resources. Anselm takes the *Proslogion* to be the product of such a meditative exercise. But he recognizes, as did Augustine, that contemplation is not always successful. Even when functioning optimally, it sometimes encounters impenetrable mysteries; at other times, it discovers perplexities, some resolvable, some not.

SECTION I

AUGUSTINE

1

The Philosopher in the Crib

Inbecillitas membrorum infantilium innocens est, non animus infantium.
—*Confessions* 1.7.11

At a crucial point in his *Ethics* Peter Abelard juxtaposes two passages from Jerome. The first is Jerome's translation of the Septuagint version of Job 14:4–5: "No one is clean of stain, not even a child of one day, if his life is on earth." The second is from Jerome's commentary on Ezekiel: "As long as the soul remains in the stage of infancy, it lacks sin."[1] It is not Abelard's intent to catch Jerome in an inconsistency regarding the moral probity of children. Abelard in fact enlists both of Jerome's pronouncements in service of a distinction that Abelard is keen to emphasize, a distinction between original sin and individual acts of sin. Original sin is the state or condition in which humanity finds itself as a result of the disobedience of our earliest ancestors. Abelard regards it as a punishment or penalty, reminding us of our distance from God, a distance measured, as Augustine had claimed, by ignorance and difficulty.[2] This is the "stain" (*sordes*) of which Jerome speaks, according to Abelard: children are inescapably born with it.

On Abelard's construal of Jerome's second claim, children are incapable of committing acts that qualify as sinful because they have not yet developed the cognitive wherewithal necessary for sinning. Sinning for Abelard is essentially an intentional activity, and until children acquire the intellectual abilities requisite for formulating intentions, they cannot sin. Abelard's account of sin draws heavily on conceptual apparatus developed by Augustine.[3] It comes as more

---

[1] For text and references, see D. E. Luscombe, ed. and trans., *Peter Abelard's Ethics* (Oxford: Clarendon Press, 1971), 20–23.

[2] For details, see my "Augustine on Evil and Original Sin," in Eleonore Stump and Norman Kretzmann, eds., *The Cambridge Companion to Augustine* (Cambridge: Cambridge University Press, 2001), 40–48. Reprinted as Chapter 5 of this volume.

[3] For elaboration of Abelard's account and its indebtedness to Augustine, see my "Ethics," in Jeffrey E. Brower and Kevin Guilfoy, eds., *The Cambridge Companion to Abelard* (Cambridge: Cambridge University Press, 2004), 279–304. Reprinted as Chapter 9 of this volume.

than a surprise, then, to see Augustine himself worry seriously about the possibility that infants are already capable of sinful acts; indeed, that the phenomenon of infant sinning is widespread. If Augustine's worry is well-founded, then in addition to the gloom of original sin, we must heap onto infants the doom of actual sin. More than that, it appears as though we must also conclude either that the phenomenon of infant sinning undermines the conceptually sophisticated account that Augustine gives or that infants are a good deal more intellectually precocious than we generally believe them to be.

Let us examine the worry that Augustine expresses. Near the beginning of *Confessions* 1.7.11 Augustine cites Job 14:4–5 (LXX), but he does not confine its message, as Abelard would later do, within the ambit of original sin. Instead he embeds it in a discussion of two putative cases of infantile sinning. In the first case, he infers from his adult observations of infants—including, presumably, his own infant son, Adeodatus—how he himself must have behaved:

> Who reminds me of the sin of my infancy, inasmuch as "no one is clean of sin in your presence, not even an infant with a life of one day on earth"? Who reminds me? Is it just any wee little one now, in whom I see what I do not remember about myself? I sinned then in doing what? Was it because I gasped sobbingly for the breasts [that fed me]? For if I were to do that now, not gasping for breasts but for food suitable to my years, I would be derided and most justly rebuked. Thus at that earlier time I did what deserved rebuke, but because I could not understand a rebuke, neither custom nor reason allowed me to be rebuked.[4]

Augustine appears to regard the second case as more shocking than the first:

> I myself have seen and can testify about a jealous little one: he was not yet speaking, but he watched his fellow nursling with a pale and bitter expression.... This is truly anything but innocence: not to endure a brother sharing in a source of milk copiously flowing and even overflowing when he is most needful of its nourishment, the one food so far sustaining his life.[5]

---

[4] *Quis me conmemorat peccatum infantiae meae, quoniam "nemo mundus a peccato coram te, nec infans, cuius est unius diei vita super terrain"? Quis me conmemorat? An quilibet tantillus nunc parvulus, in quo video quod non memini de me? Quid ergo tunc peccabam? An quia uberibus inhiabam plorans? Nam si nucn faciam, non quidem uberibus, sed escae congruenti annis meis ita inhians, deridebor atque reprehendar iustissime. Tunc ergo reprehendenda faciebam, sed quia reprehendentem intellegere non poteram, nec mos reprehendi me nec ratio sinebat.*

[5] *Vidi ego et expertus sum zelantem parvulum: nondum loquebatur et intuebatur pallidus amaro aspectu conlactaneum suum.... Nisi vero et ista innocentia est, in fonte lactis ubertim manante atque abundante opis egentissimum et illo adhuc uno alimento vitam ducentem consortem non pati.*

What is striking about the first case, aside from its tone of misanthropy, is the conjunction of claims Augustine makes about it, namely, that his behavior must have been reprehensible, yet that rebuke would have been unintelligible to him and thus (in some sense) impermissible. Augustine is thus committed to the following thesis:

> (A) It is possible for x's behavior to be reprehensible even though x lacks the intellectual capacity to understand any attempt to rebuke x.

Some might claim that (A) is incoherent, on grounds that x's lack of understanding cancels any literal ascription of reprehensibility to x's behavior. To the extent to which x cannot comprehend someone else's actions as an instance of rebuke, x's behavior, the target of the rebuke, cannot really be deserving of rebuke. In these circumstances x's behavior might be regrettable, or even dangerous, but it cannot be reprehensible.

So the argument might go. It receives support from our legal notions concerning adult criminal insanity: the 1847 M'Naghten definition specifies that a person was criminally insane if "at the time of committing the act, the party accused was laboring under such a defect of reason, from disease of the mind, as not to know the nature and quality of the act he was doing; or if he did know it, that he did not know he was doing what was wrong." It is but a short step from here to the opinion that the insane are not responsible for their actions, and another short step to the subsequent opinion that punishment, or rebuke, would be pointless at best,[6] cruel at worst.

No defender of (A) need deny any of this. (A) simply allows for an occasional decoupling of the reprehensible from the comprehensible; it is silent about where the decoupling might occur. Augustine raises the question whether it occurs in cases of infant behavior. Let us take the two parts of (A) in turn, seeing what considerations Augustine offers for them.

How can the infant behavior described in the first case be reprehensible? It cannot be, for example, that it is a manifestation of the vice of gluttony. Gluttony involves one's knowingly exceeding the deliverance of reason regarding food and drink.[7] It is for this reason that animals cannot be gluttons. Unlike animals, infants are *potential* gluttons. But inasmuch as they have not yet developed the sort of discursive reasoning whose neglect or misuse is necessary to the formation of vices, they cannot be actual gluttons. Babies cannot be innately virtuous, but by the same token neither can they be innately vicious.

---

[6] Pointless if the point were to educate or reform the actor. There might be a point to the punishment or rebuke if it deterred others from behaving as the actor behaved.

[7] See, e.g., Thomas Aquinas, *Summa Theologiae*, 2–2, q. 148, a. 1.

What is wrong in the first case, according to Augustine, is that it cannot be good to resort to tears to try to get what would be harmful if given; to be vehemently indignant at freemen, elders, parents, and many other prudent people for their refusing to cater to one's whims; to try one's best to strike and injure them.[8] The second case adds to this roster the emotion of jealousy. It is easy to use the terms *jealous* and *envious* as if they were synonymous. Here it is important to distinguish the two notions on Augustine's behalf. It is safe to say that the kind of jealousy that he ascribes to the infant is ephemeral, flaring up at the bare perception of the other infant's situation, combining elements of fear (of loss) and resentment (aimed at a perceived cause of loss), liable to dissipate as quickly as it arose. In contrast, envy (*invidia*) would crystallize after Augustine's time into one of the seven deadly sins, that is, a moral vice, a sibling of gluttony, whose establishment requires reason. Although infants cannot possess anything as cognitively complex as the vices, Augustine describes them as already capable of a certain kind of manipulation (using tears to get what they want),[9] indignation (which in the first case is unjustified), the desire to inflict damage on others, and jealousy. He seems to think that these dimensions of the mental life of infants provide a sufficient peg on which to hang a judgment of reprehensibility. We need to ask, however, whether his imputation of even these sorts of capabilities reads too much adult mental structure back into the minds of infants. (In some colonial American portraiture, children look ever so much like miniature adults.) Pressure to ask the question is provided by the second claim Augustine makes about his behavior in the first case, whose generalized version appears in the second half of (A), that he lacked understanding. What sort of understanding did he lack, and is its absence sufficient to deny to him the reprehensible capabilities he claims to have possessed?

Rebuke is essentially a linguistic process or practice. Unlike the raw infliction of physical pain or hardship on persons as a consequence for what they have done, a rebuke is a kind of linguistic performance. It is typically a speech act (though there can be written rebukes) whose illocutionary force is to express sharp criticism of some action or characteristic of the addressee, and whose perlocutionary force, at least in standard cases, is to produce in the addressee appropriate feelings of shame. More than that, rebuke presupposes that the addressee can interpret the speech act for what it is, an expression of criticism designed

---

[8] *An pro tempore etiam illa bona erant, flendo petere etiam quod noxie daretur, indignari acriter non subiectis hominibus liberis et maioribus hisque, a quibus genitus est, multisque praeterea prudentioribus non ad nutum voluntatis obtemperantibus feriendo nocere niti quantum potest . . .?*

[9] Manipulation is not the only use infants have for crying, according to Augustine. Earlier in Book 1 (6.8) he claims that when he did not get his way with his elders, he used crying to take revenge upon them.

to induce shame. I might be able to scold my dog, but it is not clear that I can rebuke or upbraid her.

As an infant, of course, Augustine lacked speech. The very term *infant* derives from the Latin *infans*, whose core adjectival meaning is not having the power of speech. The part of Book 1 in which he discusses the reprehensibility of infant behavior precedes, in exposition and chronology, his famous description (in 1.8.13) of the acquisition of language.[10] In 1.6.8 he describes in vivid terms what he takes his preverbal plight to have been:

> Little by little I became aware of where I was and I wanted to make known my desires to those who might fulfill them. But I could not, since they [the desires] were internal, but those [who might fulfill them] were external, and had no faculty enabling them to enter my soul. So I threw my limbs about and uttered sounds, signs similar to my desires, the few that I could, of the sort that I could, but they were not really similar.[11]

Not yet having mastered the linguistic capacity necessary for speech, baby Augustine cannot have been expected to comprehend a rebuke for what it is. It appears, then, that if Augustine is to stand his ground about the reprehensibility of his infant behavior, he must think that an inability to understand language does not entail an inability to have desires, to feel emotions, and to be manipulative.

To be sure, there are desires, emotions, and manipulative abilities that it would be absurd to ascribe to infants: even the most gifted ones are incapable of desires for social justice, feelings of nostalgia, and telling (or even showing) the truth while counting on the hearer's distrust to lead the hearer to believe the opposite. But the reprehensible capabilities cited by Augustine in the first case are a good deal more rudimentary than these. He says that he was "indignant" at noncompliant adults. That may be a bit of intentional and excusable rhetorical inflation. "Any failure on the part of the caretaker to fulfill those wants will lead

---

[10] A description made famous by Wittgenstein, who used it at the beginning of *The Brown Book* and in *Philosophical Investigations*.

[11] *Et ecce paulatim sentiebam, ubi essem, et voluntates meas volebam ostendere eis, per quos implerentur, et non poteram, quia illae intus erant, foris autem illi nec ullo suo sensu valebant introire in animam meam. Itaque iactabam membra et voces, signa similia voluntatibus meis, pauca quae poteram, qualia poteram: non enim erant veresimilia.*

The infant's plight is how to become linguistically competent from an initial state of noncompetence. But to acquire the competence—in particular, to use signs successfully to communicate what it is that one wants—seems to presuppose an understanding of conventional agreements about what the signs signify. That is, successful use seems to presuppose possession of a language. Put this way, the infant's situation can seem to be hopeless.

to reactive anger, as if (to put it in prematurely complex terms) some right of its own had been slighted."[12] Surely it is not absurd to ascribe reactive anger to infants. Fast on the heels of that ascription comes the imputation of a desire to harm the noncompliant adults. And acquiescence in that imputation will make it seem natural to accept the attribution of the manipulative use of tears, initially as a signaling device, reactively as a way of striking back. As for the episodic jealousy that Augustine describes in the second case, if it is simply a function of fear of loss plus reactive anger, then it seems not beyond the repertoire of infants.

Philosophical friends of the purity of infants will want to stop this train of ascriptions before it leaves the station. But how? I cannot anticipate all the philosophical moves that might be made. I shall consider one, however, that links its denial to the fact that infants lack speech or linguistic capacity in general. Its conclusion is that infants cannot have reprehensible desires or emotions because they cannot have *any* desires or emotions. It would seem that a conclusion as sweeping as this one is required if one is to disbar even very rudimentary desires and emotions. There are two themes that contribute to the construction of an argument to this conclusion. One theme includes the claim that all desires and emotions are propositional attitudes, taking propositions as their contents. A desire, for example, is always a desire *that* some situation obtain. Partisans of this theme would presumably claim that desires *for* something, x, are always analyzable into desires that some proposition about x be true. (Without taking a stance on the desires of infants, Plato does assert in the *Meno* that the desire *for* something is the desire *to* possess it: it is easy to run the desire to possess the thing into a desire *that* one possess the thing.[13]) Partisans could undertake similar maneuvers with respect to emotions. Fear *of* something, for example, might be regimented into fear *that* one will encounter the thing.

The other theme connects propositional understanding to linguistic ability. It alleges that the ability to have propositions as the content of one's propositional attitudes—and thus to have propositional attitudes at all—is dependent upon actual, not merely potential, linguistic competence. One cannot be said to have a propositional attitude if one cannot understand the "that"-clause that is the content of the attitude. And understanding a "that"-clause requires understanding some language in which the clause is expressed. I cannot want the last portion of crème brûlée—or (in the preferred canonical transcription) *that I have* the last portion of crème brûlée—if I do not understand any language that expresses that proposition. Similarly, I cannot fear that the frumious bandersnatch will fasten upon me unless I understand some sentence expressing that proposition.

---

[12] Martha C. Nussbaum, *Upheavals of Thought: The Intelligence of Emotions* (Cambridge: Cambridge University Press, 2001), 192.

[13] *Meno* 77c–d. See also *Symposium* 204d–e.

Taken together, these two themes contribute to an argument whose conclusion is that infants cannot have desires or emotions. The argument takes this form:

(1) If x is an infant, then x lacks actual linguistic competence.

(2) If x lacks actual linguistic competence, then x cannot understand any proposition.

(3) If x has a desire or emotion, then x has a propositional attitude.

(4) If x has a propositional attitude, then there is some proposition that is the content of x's propositional attitude.

(5) No proposition is the content of x's propositional attitude if x cannot understand the proposition.

Thus: (6) If x is an infant, then x has no desires or emotions.[14]

The argument is valid. Even so, it would be of little interest if no one subscribed to it. One subscriber, I suggest, is Donald Davidson. I should say more precisely that Davidson subscribes to a close relative of this argument. The Davidsonian deviations center on his analysis of sentences ascribing propositional attitudes. Davidson prefers trafficking in sentences and utterances rather than propositions. As a consequence, he prefers "thoughts" (which include "desire, knowledge, belief, fear, interest, to name some important cases"[15]) over "propositional attitudes." Taking those differences into account, we can construct a Davidsonian reconfiguration of the argument.

(1) If x is an infant, then x lacks actual linguistic competence.

(2′) If x lacks actual linguistic competence, then x cannot interpret any sentence.

(3′) If x has a desire or emotion, then x has a thought.

---

[14] Its structure is:

(1) $(I \rightarrow L)$

(2) $(L \rightarrow {\sim}U)$

(3) $((D \vee E) \rightarrow A)$

(4) $(A \rightarrow P)$

(5) $({\sim}U \rightarrow {\sim}P)$

Thus: (6) $(I \rightarrow {\sim}(D \vee E))$

[15] See esp., "Thought and Talk," in Donald Davidson, *Inquiries into Truth and Interpretation*, 2nd ed. (Oxford: Clarendon Press, 2001), 155–170; the passage cited is on p. 156. For some background, see also "On Saying That," in the same volume, pp. 93–108. For discussion of Davidson's (and others') views on thought and language use, see Hilary Kornblith, *Knowledge and Its Place in Nature* (Oxford: Clarendon Press, 2002), chap. 3.

(4′) If *x* has a thought, then *x* has "a disposition to utter certain sentences with appropriate force under given circumstances."[16]

(5′) *x* does not have a disposition to utter certain sentences with appropriate force under given circumstances if *x* cannot interpret the sentences.

Thus: (6) If *x* is an infant, then *x* has no desires or emotions.

Because the conclusion of these arguments runs contrary to our ordinary beliefs about infants, we might wonder about the warrant for the various premises. In the first argument it is not clear that we need accept premise (2), despite the rationale suggested for it in the examples involving crème brûlée and frumious bandersnatches. Beings that have actual linguistic competence, we may grant, routinely communicate what they understand by means of some language in which they have facility, whether it be English, Latin, or Punic. They may even occasionally or habitually communicate what they understand to themselves in this fashion. That is, they may think in an acquired language. (We may also grant that there are many things that they understand that they could not understand without having actual linguistic competence, for example, that the perfect active indicative of *fero* is *tuli*.) And so they, and we, may come to think, on analogy to Molière's Monsieur Jourdain, that not only have they been speaking prose all along, they have also been thinking, understanding, entertaining propositions, for exactly as long as they have had the ability to speak prose and precisely because of that ability.

But we need not think this, nor does Augustine: he has the wherewithal to deny premise (2). Let us begin by looking at Augustine's account of how people who do have actual linguistic competence exercise their competence. The account can be stitched together from a pair of memorable passages from Augustine's *Tractates on the Gospel of John.*[17] Linguistic communication is a process involving one person conveying some of his thoughts—we can take "thoughts" here in Davidson's omnibus sense—to another person. If I wish to communicate my thought to you, I select from whatever stock of conventional languages I have at my disposal a language—Augustine's menu includes Latin, Greek, and Punic—that matches a language you can understand. I emit an

---

[16] Davidson, "Thought and Talk," 167.

[17] The two passages, 14.7 and 37.4, are cited by Christopher Kirwan and Peter King, respectively. See Kirwan's "Augustine's Philosophy of Language," in Stump and Kretzmann, *Cambridge Companion to Augustine,* 201; and King's introduction to Augustine, *Against the Academicians and The Teacher* (Indianapolis, IN: Hackett Publishing Company, Inc., 1995), xvi. King's passage, however, has an elision. For the full texts in translation, see, respectively, St. Augustine, *Tractates on the Gospel of John: 11–27* and *Tractates on the Gospel of John: 28–54,* trans. John W. Rettig (Washington, DC: Catholic University of America Press, 1988, 1993).

acoustic blast[18] that cloaks my thought in the tones of that language. You receive the tones, stripping off the acoustic cloaking to lay bare the thought, which is now lodged in your mind. The blast is ephemeral, lasting no longer than the time it takes to travel through the air from me to you. And, in standard cases, it is in some natural language or other. The thought, in contrast, can be more or less permanent, can take residence in your mind without having vacated mine, and is independent of all natural languages.

In terms of this account Augustine can describe the plight of infants. They are adept at emitting acoustic blasts. The problem is that because an infant's stock of natural languages is nil, blast recipients are at a loss to know what thought, if any, has been transmitted. And so the recipients may be inclined to think that because no thought was successfully received, there really was no thought at the transmission source: all there was the audible static. But recall the last sentence in the passage presented earlier from *Confessions* 1.6.8: "So I threw my limbs about and uttered sounds, signs similar to my desires, the few that I could, of the sort that I could, but they were not really similar." It seems initially puzzling to know how to construe the "similar . . . not really similar" claim. The sentence makes sense, however, if we suppose that Augustine is marking out different similarity comparisons. As an infant, he tried to produce sounds that he thought might somehow depict or mimic his desires. The effort to communicate was a failure because the sounds produced failed to match the contours of any natural language.

What the sentence makes clear is that Augustine supposes that he *had* thoughts and desires, even though he was incapable of expressing them. Now is the time to circle back to one of the claims he makes in his commentary on the Gospel of John. It is easy to slide from the claim that some thoughts are independent of natural languages to the claim that some of an individual's thoughts antedated that person's acquisition of a natural language. The slide can seem even smoother if we take into consideration Augustine's doctrine of illumination. In *De magistro,* written eight years before the *Confessions,* Augustine argues that communication through conventional language alone teaches us nothing. If you sound out *syzygy* you have not taught me what a *syzygy* is; in fact, I can only find out that *syzygy* is a genuine term by knowing first what a *syzygy* is. If you tell me that a syzygy is a point in the orbit of a celestial body at which the body is in conjunction with or opposition to the sun, the proposition your words convey to me may be true, it may induce belief in me, and I may be justified in believing that it is true.[19] But I do not, for all of that, *know* that the proposition is true. By

---

[18] The phrase is John Searle's, not Augustine's; see Searle's *Speech Acts: An Essay in the Philosophy of Language* (Cambridge: Cambridge University Press, 1969).

[19] Cf. the discussion of *sarabarae* in *De magistro* 10.33–11.37.

Augustine's strictest lights, the process of linguistic communication described in his Gospel commentary is sometimes sufficient to convey justified true belief but always insufficient to transmit knowledge. The shortcoming is not in the transmitter; it is in the receiver when the receiver lacks *understanding.* Myles Burnyeat has suggested that for Augustine understanding "is of the connections between things, of things only as parts of a whole interrelated system; that is why, like empirical vision, it involves seeing things for oneself."[20] So my justified true belief about a syzygy only becomes knowledge as I come to see how that belief fits in with other relevant (and true) beliefs. But, as Burnyeat emphasizes, I must do the connecting for myself. That implies that I must be capable of seeing the connections. Augustine identifies the source of this capacity for intellectual vision as Christ, whose teaching illuminates the connections to be seen and the minds of those seeking to know.[21] All that Augustine need add to reject premise (2) is that Christ's illumination is represented propositionally in infants, preceding and making possible their acquisition of a natural language. Not many cognitive scientists nowadays will sign on to the Christ-as-the-only-genuine-teacher doctrine. But many of them converge on the opinion that "some capacity to understand the minds of others may be present in babies before they begin to speak."[22]

The vulnerable locus in Davidson's argument is not (2′), the analogue of (2), because (2′) ties actual linguistic competence to actual sentential interpretation, not propositionally representable thoughts: all parties agree that infants are unable actually to engage in sentential interpretation. The vulnerability lies rather with (4′) and (5′). According to (4′), a necessary condition for having a thought is having a disposition to utter certain sentences in certain circumstances. Davidson requires dispositions because it may be that x has never given actual voice to his thought. If I attribute a particular thought to x, Davidson suggests that we could suppose that what I affirm is that x "would be honestly speaking his mind were he to utter a sentence translating mine." Now Davidson recognizes that the conditions underlying the subjunctive conditional do not preclude the possibility that x is not adept in any natural language:

> When I say, "Jones believes that snow is white" I describe Jones's state of mind directly: it is indeed the state of mind someone is in who could honestly assert "Snow is white" if he spoke English, but that may be a state a languageless creature could also be in.[23]

---

[20] M. F. Burnyeat, "Wittgenstein and Augustine *De magistro,*" *Proceedings of the Aristotelian Society,* supplementary volume 61 (1987): 22.

[21] *De magistro* 11.38.

[22] Paul Bloom, *How Children Learn the Meanings of Words* (Cambridge, MA: MIT Press, 2000), 61.

[23] "Thought and Talk," 167.

Davidson's concession to languageless creatures adversely affects (5′). For now it might be that although *x* cannot interpret the relevant sentences, *x* nonetheless has a disposition to utter them. The appearance of paradox here melts away once we see that the subjunctive conditional that underwrites the possession of the disposition does not require the possession of the relevant language. That is, if *x* has the disposition, then *x* would utter the sentences with appropriate force under appropriate circumstances if *x* knew the relevant language.

In order to save (4′) and (5′) from an onrush of languageless thinkers, Davidson appears to raise the standards for what counts as thought. In order to have the *concept* of a thought, according to Davidson, one must already be a language interpreter. Setting aside any doubts we might have about this claim, we can still ask whether it might be that a creature could have, say, a belief while lacking the concept of a belief. Davidson says not:

> Someone cannot have a belief unless he understands the possibility of being mistaken, and this requires grasping the contrast between truth and error—true belief and false belief. But this contrast . . . can emerge only in the context of interpretation, which alone forces us to the idea of an objective, public truth.[24]

An uncharitable soul might parody this argument by suggesting that if it works, then it shows that one cannot have a bee sting unless one knows the difference between a bee and a wasp, a difference that emerges only in the context of entomology. And although Davidson gives the appearance of raising the standards for admission to the community of thoughtful creatures, what he says retrospectively about his essay is more latitudinarian. The essay, he says, "concludes, rather speculatively, that only a creature with a language can properly be said to have a full-fledged scheme of propositional attitudes."[25]

Full-fledged schemes begin life fractionally fledged. The high-flying flock of language interpreters that Davidson envisions began with the pin feathers of simple beliefs, desires, and emotions, some of which, we may presume, predate and indeed are instrumental to the acquisition of language. Perhaps what is called for here is a compromise (and a change of metaphor). I am willing to recognize Davidson's *city beliefs and thoughts,* the more sophisticated, tony siblings of *country beliefs and thoughts,* provided that we not disown the country siblings. City beliefs and thoughts are more articulated than country beliefs and thoughts, presupposing linguistic competence and meshing nicely, one notes

---

[24] "Thought and Talk," 170.
[25] *Inquiries into Truth and Interpretation,* xx.

with an air of admiring suspicion, with Davidson's views on radical interpretation and Davidson's project of providing a truth-theoretical account of meaning.[26] But when we retreat from admiration of the glamorous city beliefs and
thoughts and turn our attention back to country beliefs and thoughts, we find
that step (5′) of the Davidsonian argument is resistible. So, then, is the conclusion. It may be that infants have no city desires or emotions, yet, for all the argument shows, they can have country desires and emotions.

My conclusion at this point is somewhat provisional. If it depends on a thesis to the effect that infants have no desires or emotions, then the case for the
actual sinlessness of infants has not yet been made. But Augustine's account of
sin requires more than a stock of haphazard desires and emotions housed in
the agent. A sin requires the *intention* to do something. Augustine depicts an
intention as a kind of executive decision: having received as input a suggestion
and taking pleasure in what the suggestion suggests, the agent then formulates
an intention by consenting to do what the suggestion suggests. To count as an
intention, the consent must be firm enough that the agent would perform the
action were the opportunity to arise. If the agent consents to do something that
is forbidden by God, then the consent itself is sinful, whether or not the agent
ever has the opportunity to translate it into action.[27]

Described in this way, intentions might appear sophisticated enough to be
beyond the capacity of infants. Yet it does seem tempting to believe, of the two
cases that Augustine presents, that the infants acted intentionally. It is hard to
believe that the infants' behavior was purely accidental or natural; if neither accidental nor natural, then intentional. So two opposing trains of thought run toward
each other: can one of them be sidetracked? Note that one of them makes reference to intentions, while the other concentrates on intentional behavior. The distinction is scarcely noticeable in ordinary parlance. It does matter philosophically.
Reductionistic accounts of intentional action deny that there is any special kind
of mental act properly called an intention; all that is in the mind, we may suppose,
are beliefs and desires. A reductionistic account explains an intentional action by
supposing that it just is an action caused in the right way by relevant beliefs and
desires. Perhaps, then, there can be intentional actions that are the products of the
beliefs and desires that infants are capable of having. But a reductionistic account
in itself is silent on the question *whether* infants are capable of having any beliefs or
desires. Reductionism in itself, in other words, does not provide an answer to the
question whether infants can act intentionally. Nonreductionistic accounts take
intentions to be, as you might expect, irreducible to beliefs and desires, and they

---

[26] See various essays in *Inquiries into Truth and Interpretation*.

[27] See my "Inner-Life Ethics," in *The Augustinian Tradition*, ed. Gareth B. Matthews
(Berkeley: University of California Press, 1999), 140–165. Reprinted as Chapter 6 of this volume.

suppose that intentional actions are the result of such intentions. I believe that Augustine's account of intention is nonreductionistic. I believe, nonetheless, that it also presupposes that intention-forming agents have beliefs and desires; beliefs and desires are implicated in Augustine's notions of suggestion and pleasure. Still, even if we concede that infants have some beliefs and desires, it does not follow from that concession alone that they can form intentions. The gap between the concession and the legitimacy of attributing intentions to infants is especially poignant on Augustine's account. If an intention is like an executive decision, one may be all the more skeptical about whether infants have the cognitive goods necessary to make those kinds of decisions.

I have suggested, with some perplexity, that the case for attributing to infants any intentions, let alone sinful intentions, is neither clearly up nor clearly down.[28] Let me add to this area of perplexity Augustine's remarks on the role that memory has in responsibility. Beginning at *Confessions* 1.6.7 and ending only when he describes his transition to boyhood at 1.8.13, Augustine tirelessly reminds his reader that he cannot remember anything about his infancy. All that he knows about his infantile behavior he acquired from the testimony of his elders and by inference from his own observations of children (1.6.8, 1.6.10, 1.7.12). He claims that his memory is as experientially isolated from his infancy as it is from his prenatal existence (1.7.12). And then he astonishingly wraps up his discussion of his infancy with these words: "But see how I set aside that time: for of what significance is it to me now, when I recall no trace of it?"[29] The natural

---

[28] Referring to the case of the infant jealous of his fellow nursling, Garry Wills says that the case "becomes for [Augustine] almost as much the model of motiveless malignity as his theft of the pears would be in Book Two." See Wills, *Saint Augustine's Childhood* (New York: Viking, 2001), 97. There can be disagreement about how to interpret the theft of the pears, but we need not broach the controversial parts to demur from Wills's assessment. First, as Augustine describes him, the infant is not motiveless; he is motivated by jealousy. Second, whether or not there was an ancillary motive to Augustine's youthful theft of the pears, such as the thrill of participating in a gang, or a deeper, ulterior motive, such as pride, it is clear that Augustine maintains that he stole the pears, *knowing* that it was wrong and *for the sake of doing* something wrong. It is doubtful that even the most zealous friends of the precocity of infants would suppose that infants can have such fiendishly citified thoughts. Everyone would agree that the theft is a paradigm case of an intentional action. But a case like that of the jealous infant is surely its foil.

For a sampling of the sorts of disagreement there can be about interpreting the theft of the pears, see Scott MacDonald, "Petit Larceny, the Beginning of All Sin: Augustine's Theft of the Pears," reprinted in *Augustine's Confessions: Critical Essays*, ed. William E. Mann (Lanham, MD: Rowman & Littlefield Publishers, 2006), 45–69; William E. Mann, "Pride and Preference: A Reply to MacDonald," *Faith and Philosophy* 23, no. 2 (2006): 156–168. Reprinted as Chapter 3 of this volume; and Gareth B. Matthews, *Augustine* (Malden, MA: Blackwell Publishing, 2005), chap. 13, "Wanting Bad Things."

[29] *Sed ecce omitto illud tempus: et quid mihi iam cum eo est, cuius nulla vestigia recolo?* Chadwick translates this as "But of that time I say nothing more. I feel no sense of responsibility now for a

protest is that it *should* be of some consequence to him if, as he has been intimating, he actually sinned at the time. Augustine is no Lockean: he is not claiming that personal identity extends backward in time only as far as memory reaches. On the contrary, he thinks that *he,* the forty-some-year-old person writing the *Confessions,* is the same person as the infant son of Monica and Patricius, about whom he can remember nothing.

Lack of memory hardly seems exculpatory. Think of the blatant inadequacy of the plea, "My behavior at the party last night is of no consequence to me, since I can't remember a thing about it." Is Augustine's dismissal any more defensible than this? For one thing, barring the intercession of Frankfurtian manipulators, I could have behaved differently last night; more particularly, I could have behaved in such a way that I would now have been able to remember last night's behavior. Of course, it might be that my behavior last night was noble and sterling, but a kind of behavior that, for some weird reason, could only have been elicited by my voluntarily undergoing a procedure that has as a side effect my inability to recall anything about last night. Perhaps, then, there are circumstances in which I should comport myself so that I subsequently will not be able to remember what I did. If so, it is not absence of memory in itself that is to be praised or faulted; that depends on how one came to lose it.

So here is a difference between infants and normally functioning adults. Infants, one can safely assume, have no voluntary ability to organize their behavior so that they will subsequently remember some episode from their infancy. The absence of such an ability, however, is not sufficient in itself to exculpate infantile behavior. The inability of infants to act so that they would later remember what they did does not entail an inability to do otherwise than what they do. If we think that being able to do otherwise is a *sufficient* condition for being morally responsible,[30] then infants still seem to be liable to charges of sinful behavior. What would be sufficient to get them off the hook, morally speaking, is an argument to the effect that infants cannot do otherwise than what they do. I do not propose to examine such arguments. Instead, I wish to end by comparing the case of infant responsibility to another perplexing case, brought up explicitly by Augustine. In *Confessions* 10.30.41 Augustine raises the question of whether one can sin in a dream. Is dreaming of sinning itself a kind of sinning? Augustine worries that it might be: in dreams we seem able to entertain suggestions, to take pleasure in them, and to consent to them. We even seem able, on occasion, to employ our reason to resist the blandishments our dreams set before

time of which I recall not a single trace." See Saint Augustine, *Confessions,* trans. Henry Chadwick (Oxford: Oxford University Press, 1991), 10.

[30] Pace the Principle of Alternate Possibilities, which maintains that being able to do otherwise is a *necessary* condition for being morally responsible.

us. Augustine cannot bring himself to believe that sins can occur in dreams. Yet neither can he fully dismiss the possibility. His meditation in this section ends with another remarkable summation:

> And yet, there is so great a difference that when it happens otherwise [from what reason would have consented to], we return, upon awakening, to peace of conscience, and we discover by this difference itself that we have not done what nonetheless we regret has been done in some way in us.[31]

This much becomes clear from the next section of the *Confessions*: Augustine thinks that one would be a better person for not having such dreams; that it takes God's grace to cure one of the sickness of having them.[32] It is also clear that Augustine regards the sickness as something for which the patient is responsible. Although he resists characterizing his dream episodes as cases of sinning, he is also unwilling to regard them as morally indifferent. He suggests that they are lapses of reason where reason might and should have prevailed.

Now let me introduce you to a philosopher, Aurelius, who is, to put it mildly, at least our equal in understanding human psychology, but who applies uncommonly high standards to human conduct, both his own and others'. To be specific, Aurelius believes that infants who act out of anger or jealousy do not meet his standards. Nor does he regard adults who dream of sinning as meeting those standards. How does Aurelius rank these two deviations from his ideal? Is angry or jealous infantile behavior worse than, better than, or about the same as adult sinful dreaming? Aurelius is more tolerant of infants over adults. After all, he points out, adults have had much more time to gain rational control of themselves than infants have had. Thus the adult sinful dreamer has less of an excuse than the infant. And since Aurelius thinks that intending to commit a sin is *already* to have sinned, he discounts the fact that infantile behavior is outward, publicly observable behavior while dream behavior is merely internal. Because Aurelius believes that one can form intentions in dreams, and that intending to sin is to sin, for him not much hangs, morally speaking, on the difference between external behavior and merely internal behavior. Given Aurelius's substantive moral views, his judgment that infantile behavior should be regarded more leniently than adult dreaming behavior is reasonably straightforward.

---

[31] *Et tamen tantum interest, ut, cum aliter accidit, evigilantes ad conscientiae requiem redeamus ipsaque distantia reperiamus nos non fecisse, quod tamen in nobis quoquo modo factum esse doleamus.* For further discussion of the issues raised in this passage, see Ishtiyaque Haji, "On Being Morally Responsible in a Dream," in Matthews, ed., *The Augustinian Tradition*, 166–182.

[32] *Confessions* 10.30.42. In *De Genesi ad litteram* 12.15.31 Augustine claims that the dispensation from such dreams was one of the gifts God bestowed on Solomon; see 1 Kings 3:5–15.

Alas, Aurelius's judgment is not Augustine's. I think that the passages I have cited from *Confessions* 1 and 10 show that Augustine takes a harsher stance toward some specimens of infant behavior than he does toward any specimen of adult dreaming, even though, as you may have noticed, he holds the same substantive moral views held by Aurelius. What accounts for the divergence? I wish that I could say that I knew. But I do not. By my count, then, I am left with four cases of perplexity. Can infants have sinful intentions? Is lack of memory about one's infancy sufficient to exculpate infants from any sinful deeds they may have committed? Can one sin in a dream? Should one regard adult dreams of sinning as less morally serious than infant behavior? I can add a fifth. If preverbal children can have a suite of desires, emotions, and manipulative abilities rich enough to raise suspicions about the purity of their behavior, then should we not take a similar stance toward some of the behavior of some animals? My intuitions incline me to say that animals are *incapable* of sinning. Should I then take a similar stance toward infants? Or should I revise my intuitions about the purity of animals? Or should I look for a relevant difference between the two cases? If the latter, what could that difference be?

I should not end on a note—or five notes—of perplexity. Here, instead, is an invitation to wild, counterfactual speculation. We began with the distinction between original sin and individual acts of sin. Reading Book 1 of the *Confessions* shakes the complacency of Jerome and Abelard's assumption that although infants are subject to original sin, they cannot commit individual acts of sin. It may be Augustine's view that even infants are capable of sinning *because* they are subject to original sin. Now suppose that Adam and Eve had not fallen, and that Cain and Abel were thus born without original sin. What would their infancy have been like?[33]

---

[33] This paper was read at a conference to honor Gareth B. Matthews, held at the University of Massachusetts at Amherst on May 7, 2005. Calvin Normore was commentator. An earlier draft benefited from comments from David Christensen.

2

The Theft of the Pears

One of the most memorable passages in the *Confessions* is St. Augustine's account, in Book 2, of his youthful theft of pears. It is also one of the most philosophically perplexing passages, and not the least perplexed person is Augustine himself. It is the purpose of this paper to unravel some of the snarl that surrounds Book 2. I shall address myself to two questions. First, why does Augustine choose such a seemingly trivial example of a sin? Second, why is he puzzled about the explanation he gives of it? Concerning the second question, I shall not demonstrate that he is genuinely puzzled; I shall assume he is. I think that a reading of Book 2 will bear me out on this issue, but that is not crucial to the paper. For my claim will be that even if he was not genuinely puzzled, he should have been.

I

Early in Book 2 of the *Confessions*, Augustine tells us that he is going to hark back to the past foul deeds of his youth, the "carnal corruptions" of his soul which made him "rotten to the core" in the eyes of God, for in his youth he "wallowed in the mire" of Babylon "as if in cinnamon and precious ointments."[1] Having thus excited our prurient interests, he then produces the following example of a sin in testimony of his depravity:

> There was a pear tree in a garden neighboring on our vineyard, laden with fruit which was tempting neither in form nor taste. In the middle of one night—to which time we exceedingly vile young men had continued our play in the streets, according to our pestilential habit—we

---

[1] St. Augustine, *Confessions* 2.1.1 and 2.3.8. All further references to the *Confessions* in the paper will simply mention the book, chapter, and paragraph numbers. The translations are based on the text in *St. Aureli Augustini Confessionum Libri XIII*, edited by Martinus Skutella (Stuttgart: B.G. Teubner, 1969).

proceeded to shake down and carry off this fruit, and we took away from there a monstrous load, not for our own eating, but rather to throw to the pigs. (2.4.9)

One is inclined to say that if this is the foulest sin that Augustine could muster from his repertoire, then he led an exemplary childhood. Either the language of self-rebuke that Augustine uses is grossly hyperbolic or Augustine did have reason to think that the example is, appearances to the contrary notwithstanding, a specimen of a deed which is not trivial. The *Confessions* is written in the form of an extended prayer, but Augustine intended it to serve a didactic function also (see, e.g., 2.3.5). If so, why did he choose this seemingly banal example? Is it that we are supposed to learn something from its apparent banality?

We may begin by noting that if we are to take the example seriously, then the gravity of the misdeed cannot lie in its consequences: one indication of this is that there is not a word about the consequences of the theft in Augustine's discussion. It is natural then to turn to the motive involved, and it is here that the perplexity increases. For Augustine rebuts a large number of possible motives. He did not steal out of need (2.4.9 and 2.6.12), nor did he want to enjoy the pears (2.4.9 and 2.6.12). The pears were not even very attractive (2.4.9). Hence, his case does not fit the pattern of the typical crime. Normally a man commits a crime because he desires to gain, or fears to lose, one or more of the goods of the lowest order (2.5).[2] Nor did he steal out of pride, ambition, cruelty, lasciviousness, curiosity, ignorance, folly, slothfulness, extravagance, effusiveness, avarice, envy, anger, revenge, fear, or grief (2.6.13). What then is left?

What is left is what does not appear to settle easily with Augustine:

> . . . I did not wish to enjoy that thing I craved for by theft, but the theft itself and the sin. (2.4.9)

> . . . [W]e did that which it pleased us to do for the reason that it was not permitted. (2.4.9)

> Behold, let my heart now speak to you about what it sought there [in the abyss]: that I would be gratuitously evil and that my evil would have no cause except evil. It [my evil] was foul, and I loved it. I loved to sink completely. I loved my defect—not that towards which I defected, but I loved my defect itself. My soul was deformed, and leaping away from

---

[2] For goods of the lowest order Augustine gives as examples material goods which are pleasant to the senses, one's being esteemed, and friendship. He seems to have in mind the hierarchy of goods he expounded earlier in *De libero arbitrio* 2.18–19, in which the lowest goods were those things that are good, that is, God-given, but which can be misused, and which are not necessary for living rightly.

your support, towards destruction, I desired not something that was a disgrace, but the disgrace itself. (2.4.9)

For I threw away the plucked fruit, and was thus a feaster only on iniquity, enjoying the fact that it made me joyful. For if any of that fruit entered into my mouth, the foul deed was the seasoning therein. (2.6.12)

Was I able to enjoy that which was not permitted, not because of anything else than that it was not permitted? (2.6.14)

Since no other explanation fits the case, Augustine concludes that he must have stolen for the sheer sake of stealing.[3]

Augustine intends his readers to extract a philosophical moral from the example. What makes the theft of the pears so morally odious is that the motive of the theft was pure malice. The moral one is supposed to extract is that an extremely bad—perhaps the worst—kind of sin one can commit is one that is motivated by the sheer pleasure of sinning. "A man commits homicide. Why did he do it? . . . Surely he would not have committed homicide for no other reason than to have enjoyed the homicide itself? Who will believe that?" Not even Catiline, a paragon of viciousness, killed for the sake of killing (2.5.11). By implication the foulest kind of murderer would be the one who did kill for the sake of killing alone.

There is further evidence to support the conjecture that Augustine believed that for any particular kind of action, φ, which is sinful, to φ for the sake of φing is always worse than to φ for any other reason or motive. In *Contra mendacium* 7.18, Augustine distinguishes between those kinds of action which are always sins, no matter what the intention of the agent, and those kinds of action whose sinfulness or lack of sinfulness is a function of the agent's intentions. Examples of the former are lying, blasphemy, and significantly, theft. An example of the latter would be conjugal intercourse: if done for the sake of procreation, it is not sinful; if done for the sake of lust, it is sinful. Curiously enough, in the second half of

---

[3] It is true, as Augustine says at 2.8.16, that the fact that he had accomplices was a necessary condition for his committing the theft, but he is careful to insist that that was not sufficient: what more was needed was the pleasure of doing something wrong for its own sake. Robert J. O'Connell places more emphasis than I do on the companionship involved as a necessary condition for the commission of the offense. Just as the theft required *mutual* consent, so did the Fall of Man. See Robert J. O'Connell, *St. Augustine's Confessions: The Odyssey of Soul* (Cambridge, MA: The Belknap Press, 1969), 50. I am inclined to say that Augustine adds the business about companionship as an afterthought, for the reason that he is genuinely puzzled about how one can explain a sin simply by saying that the person sinned for the sake of sinning. I try to uncover the sources of Augustine's puzzlement below. At any rate, the present paper need not compete with O'Connell's account: it can be viewed as complementing it.

Book 10 of the *Confessions* Augustine gives us a whole string of sins whose sinfulness is of this second type. None of the actions in question is intrinsically bad, but in each case what makes it sinful is that the agent does it for the sake of doing it. It is necessary and hence not sinful to eat, but at 10.31.44 (and *Sermo* 51.24) he inveighs against gluttony and gormandizing, which he characterizes as eating for the sake of eating. At 10.33.49–50 he warns against listening to sacred music simply for the pleasure of listening to the sounds. In 10.34.51–53 he suggests that the temptations of the eye lead a man to take delight in visually experiencing beautiful objects. Idle curiosity is to be inquisitive merely for the sake of being inquisitive (10.35.54–57). Vainglory is the desire to be feared, loved, or praised for the pleasure of being feared, loved, or praised (10.36–37.58–60). And in *De nuptiis et concupiscentia* 1.9.16 and *Contra julianum* 5.9.35–38, Augustine says that the motive for conjugal intercourse must be the desire for offspring, and not the desire for the pleasure of the act itself, even though the lustful pleasure is a necessary concomitant of the act.

On the other hand, lying for Augustine is always sinful, no matter what the agent's intentions, and what we would like to know is whether Augustine thinks that the worst kind of lie is one told for the sake of lying. In *De mendacio*, Augustine does distinguish a lie-teller (*mentiens*) from a liar (*mendax*): ". . . the lie-teller is one who lies unwillingly; the liar truly loves to lie and he frequently indulges his soul in the pleasure of lying."[4] But Augustine does not say that his liar is the worst kind of person who tells a lie: in fact, he thinks the liar is only in fourth place. Ahead of him are the man who lies in religious teaching, the man whose lie harms someone and helps no one, and the man whose lie helps someone and harms someone else.[5]

The natural protest here is that Augustine's hierarchical classification puts an unnecessary cramp on things by its failing to appreciate the difference between judgments about the badness (or goodness) of an action and judgments about the character of an agent. All else being equal, the man who tells a lie that helps no one and harms someone from the best intentions shows a better character than his counterpart who tells the same lie for the pleasure of lying. Even if a lie in matters of religious teaching is the worst kind of lie, we might wish to say that the man who lies concerning religious teaching out of the noblest intentions is less despicable than the man who lies concerning religious teaching for the sake of lying. In short, Augustine can have it both ways, by maintaining that to lie in matters of religious teaching is the worst kind of lying action, and that to lie in

---

[4] *De mendacio* 11.18. The translation is based on the Benedictine text printed in *Oeuvres de Saint Augustin: 1ʳᵉ Série: Opuscules: II Problemes Moraux* (Paris: Desclée de Brouwer et Cie, 1948).

[5] *De mendacio* 14.25. There are four more categories after these four, all apparently arranged in order of decreasing seriousness.

matters of religious teaching for the sake of lying is the most sinful kind of lie within the category of lies about matters of religious teaching. So the classification from *De mendacio*, once it is thus amended, does not necessarily tell against the thesis I am imputing to Augustine.

Finally, I wish to cite the following as evidence. In *De sermone Domini in monte*, Augustine says the following:

> Therefore, just as sin is arrived at through three steps—suggestion, pleasure, and consent—so are there three distinctions of the same sin—in the heart, in deed, and in habit.[6] The pleasure before the habit [is acquired] is either nothing or is so slight that it is nearly nothing; to consent to it is a great sin when it is forbidden, and when anyone consents [to it], he commits a sin in his heart. However, if it then proceeds into deed, the craving would appear to be satisfied and extinguished. But afterwards, when the suggestion is repeated, a greater pleasure is kindled, which nevertheless is still much less than that [pleasure] which, by means of constantly repeated acts, turns into habit. For to conquer this is most difficult.[7]

We have not only the distinction between sinning in one's heart (which is, I believe, *intending* to sin in deed) and sinning in deed, but these two are in turn distinguished from sinning habitually. What makes habitual sinning worse than sinning in deed? Augustine links habitual sinning to increased pleasure. His reasoning seems to be that because habits are hard to break, it must be that a habitual performance of an action is more pleasurable to the performer than a non-habitual performance of the same action would have been: why else would habits be so hard to break? (I take it, incidentally, that Augustine's theory is empirically false.) It is but a short step from one's linking habitual sinning to increased pleasure to one's saying that the difference between the habitual sinner and the occasional sinner is that the habitual sinner sins for the sake of sinning itself, and that that is what heightens his pleasure, while the occasional sinner does not, or does not necessarily. And since habitual sinning is the worst stage of sinning, and habitual sinning just in sinning for the sake of the pleasure of sinning, it is natural to expect that Augustine would hold that sinning for the sake of sinning is the most grievous stage of sinning within any category of sinful action.

---

[6] St. Augustine, *De sermone Domini in monte* 1.12.35. The translations are based on the text in *Sancti Aurelii Augustini: De Sermone Domini in Monte: Libros Duos*, edited by Almut Mutzenbecher (Turnhout: Typographi Brepols Editores Pontificii, 1967). See also *In joannis evangelium* 49.3 and *Sermo* 98.6. For an elaboration on the trichotomy of suggestion, pleasure, and consent, see *De sermone Domini in monte* 1.12.33–34.

[7] *De sermone Domini in monte* 1.12.34.

II

We have now seen that Augustine can regard his theft of the pears as a serious sin, since it was a case of sinning for the sake of sinning. But we have still to account for his hesitation, his palpable reluctance, about his explanation of the action.

Augustine is perplexed by the idea that he stole pears just for the sake of stealing pears. It is tempting to think that his perplexity arises out of a philosophical worry about whether and how moral weakness is possible. Augustine, after all, is supposed to be a Platonist, and we all know that Plato denied that it is possible for a man knowingly to do wrong. But if Augustine stole the pears for the sake of doing wrong, then he stole the pears knowing that he was doing wrong, and indeed, just because he wanted to do wrong. But this is surely anti-Platonic, and perhaps that is why Augustine is uneasy about saying that he stole the pears for the sake of doing wrong.

All this is tempting, but I believe that it is mistaken. Augustine is never inclined to doubt that there are people who knowingly do wrong, but, as I shall try to show, he is puzzled about *explanations* of the form "x sinned for the sake of sinning." In his scheme of things, such an explanation turns out odd, but not primarily because he has doubts about the possibility of moral weakness.

Let me display some different issues. None of the following propositions is equivalent to any of the others:

(1) No one ever φs for the sake of φing.
(2) No one ever sins for the sake of sinning.
(3) Explanations of the form 'x φed for the sake of φing' are uninformative.
(4) Explanations of the form 'x sinned for the sake of sinning' are logically odd.

My contention is that Augustine holds views that lead him to (4), and that there is little or no evidence that shows that he holds views that commit him to (1), (2), or (3). About (3) I shall have nothing to say, except that one trusts that Augustine did not lead us through the agony of Book 2 of the *Confessions* because he thought that explanations like "Because I wanted to" are generally trivial. And (1) need not detain us much longer. It is true that Plato espoused (1) as a piece of a priori psychology in the *Gorgias* (466b–470c),[8] but there is no reason to think that Augustine ever held (1).

---

[8] The importance of this passage for an adequate understanding of the Socratic-Platonic thesis that Virtue is Knowledge has been urged by Gerasimos Santas in "The Socratic Paradoxes," *The Philosophical Review* 73 (1964): 147–164.

It may be tempting to think that Augustine did hold (2), or doctrines which entail (2). And if he is committed to (2), that could serve to explain his uneasiness about the way he has characterized his theft, for the characterization is inconsistent with (2). Did Augustine embrace (2)? There is no evidence to suggest that he did. It is true that not even Catiline killed for the sake of killing, but it does not follow that there are no people who sin for the sake of sinning. Indeed, Augustine has described the liar as the person who lies for the sake of lying.

But perhaps Augustine did hold doctrines that entail (2), and perhaps he is dimly aware, in *Confessions* 2, that these doctrines rule out his characterization of the theft? If so, what could these other doctrines be? I am inclined to say that he holds no doctrines which entail (2), but it would be difficult for me to make that case out conclusively. But let me suggest briefly one way in which we can test my inclinations.

There is *one* use of the locution "x φed for the sake of ψing," where x's φing and x's ψing need not be distinct actions, which has the following implications: (a) x φed, and at the time x φed, (b) x knew that he was φing, (c) x φed precisely because he wanted to ψ, and (d) x knew that (he was φing precisely because he wanted to ψ). There are, of course, other uses of the locution which do not have all these implications, but let us focus on this use, which we might call the full-blown use. It is clear that if (a), (b), (c), and (d) are all true of x, then x φed for the sake of ψing. It is clear also that Augustine's claim that he stole the pears for the sake of stealing the pears is an instance of the full-blown use of "x φed for the sake of ψing."

Now suppose we graft onto (2) the implications of the full-blown use of "x φed for the sake of ψing." We would have

> (2′) No one is ever such that (a) he sins, while at the time he sins, (b) he knows that he is sinning, (c) he sins precisely because he wants to sin, and (d) he knows (that he is sinning precisely because he wants to sin).

If (2′) serves to make precise the content of (2), we can ask whether Augustine holds any doctrines which entail (2′). Notice that (2′) is entailed in any *one* of the following theses:

(A) No one ever sins.
(B) No one ever sins knowing at the time that he is sinning.
(C) No one ever sins precisely because he wants to sin at the time.
(D) No one ever sins, knowing at the time (that he is sinning precisely because he wants to sin).[9]

---

[9] "$(x) \sim (Px)$" implies "$(x) \sim (Px \ \& \ Qx)$." If no mules are fertile, it follows a fortiori that no mules are fertile and over eight feet tall. Thus, (A) is a logically sufficient condition for (2′), and so is (B), and (C), and (D).

If Augustine holds either (A), or (B), or (C), or (D), then he is committed to holding (2′), and thus (2). Here I shall leave a question open for Augustine scholarship. I know of no passage in Augustine's works which shows that he accepts any of (A) through (D). Of course he could still hold (2′) without holding any of (A) through (D),[10] but if he does hold any of (A) through (D), he would have sufficient grounds for holding (2′). And if (2′) captures the meaning of (2), he would be in effect denying that there are cases of moral weakness.

I doubt that Augustine ever was inclined to deny the phenomenon of moral weakness, but at any rate, there is a more ready-to-hand explanation for his uneasiness about "I stole the pears for the sake of stealing the pears." If I am right, Augustine assumes that such a statement is a causal explanation, but at the same time, he thinks that it necessarily fails to locate a cause. It is (4) which comes closest to his views. Much of the story is familiar, and I shall sketch it quickly. Everything that is, is good, since everything that is, is created by God. But some things are better than others: some goods are immutable and others are mutable. To sin is to choose a lesser, mutable good in a situation in which one could have chosen a greater, immutable good.[11] Augustine is offering us a definition of what it is to sin: now let us note what happens when we analyze "x sinned for the sake of sinning" in terms of the definition. It becomes "x chose a lesser, mutable good over a greater, immutable good for the sake of choosing a lesser, mutable good over a greater, immutable good." Let us further suppose that the case of "x sinned for the sake of sinning" at hand is a specimen of the full-blown sense of "x φed for the sake of ψing"; a case, that is, relevantly like "Augustine stole the pears for the sake of stealing the pears." In that case we have

> (S) x sinned for the sake of sinning (full-blown) if and only if (a) x chose a lesser, mutable good over a greater, immutable good, and at the time, (b) x knew that he was choosing a lesser, mutable good over a greater, immutable good, (c) x chose a lesser, mutable good over a greater, immutable good precisely because he wanted to choose a lesser, mutable good over a greater, immutable good, and (d) x knew (that he was choosing a lesser, mutable good over a greater, immutable good precisely because he wanted to choose a lesser, mutable good over a greater, immutable good).

---

[10] I can believe that there are no square circles even though I disbelieve that there are no squares and that there are no circles.

[11] See, e.g., *Confessions* 7.12.18 and *De libero arbitrio* 2.18–19.

Let us suppose that (S) is unproblematically the result of rubbing Augustine's definition of sin together with my analysis of the full-blown use of "x φed for the sake of ψing." It is a supposition which Augustine might naturally have made, and it will help to highlight what exactly his worries are.[12] Consider (Sc):

> (Sc) If x sinned for the sake of sinning (full-blown), then x chose a lesser, mutable good over a greater, immutable good precisely because he wanted to choose a lesser, mutable good over a greater, immutable good.

Augustine's puzzlement focuses here. How can a person come to have such a want? For Augustine the question rapidly becomes—What could cause such a desire? It is his inability to answer this question to his own satisfaction that lies behind his puzzlement about his theft of the pears. Why is it that he cannot answer the question satisfactorily?

First, the desire for the lesser good cannot be a result of the agent's mistaken judgment about the relative values of the goods in question, for by hypothesis we are dealing with a case in which the agent knows full well what the correct relative values are.

Suppose then that one claims it is the lesser good itself which causes the desire for the lesser good over the greater good. Augustine tends to regard such a claim as impossible. He is fond of comparing the desires of the soul to the physical forces that operate on bodies. "*Pondus meum amor meus; eo feror, quocumque feror.*"[13] It is natural to go from there to think that the soul is or ought to be attracted by greater goods over lesser goods, just as, to speak anachronistically, the gravitational force between objects A and B will be greater than the gravitational force between A and C (B and C at equal distances from A) provided only that the mass of B is greater than the mass of C. So the claim that it is the lesser good itself which causes the desire for the lesser good over the greater good would make no more sense to Augustine than the claim that it is the mass of C, admittedly less than the mass of B, which causes the gravitational force between

---

[12] Of course we may object to this. Even if my analysis of the full-blown use of "x φed for the sake of ψing" is correct, and even if Augustine's definition of sin is acceptable, (S) will in many cases be false. (S) is studded with opaque contexts—contexts in which the substitution of identicals for identicals will not necessarily preserve truth-value. Thus, for example, a man could know that he is sinning, and Augustine's definition of sinning could be correct, but it would not follow that he thereby knows that he is choosing a lesser, mutable good over a greater, immutable good. Nevertheless, (S) has a certain pedagogical value in its revealing quite clearly the course of Augustine's uneasiness. Thus I blink the fact that it does not follow legitimately.

[13] *Confessions* 13.9.10. See also *De libero arbitrio* 3.1.6–10, *De civitate Dei* 11.28, and the references in Etienne Gilson, *The Christian Philosophy of Saint Augustine* (New York: Random House, 1960), 310, fn. 29.

A and C to be greater than the gravitational force between A and B, even though B and C are equidistant from A.

Augustine is forced to conclude that in cases like these—and his theft of the pears is one such case—it cannot be explained how the desire comes into existence. The desire was caused by nothing, according to Augustine, since everything that is, is good, and a good thing cannot of itself bring about something bad.[14] But to say that the desire was caused by nothing is not to explain it: it is rather to affirm that the desire's existence has no adequate causal explanation.

So Augustine has arrived at the following impasse. That he stole the pears for the sake of stealing the pears is the correct explanation of his action. But the correct explanation turns out, on analysis, to involve a component that Augustine regards as inexplicable. It involves a desire, that is, whose existence cannot be accounted for causally. The generalization from this case is that any instance of purely malicious evildoing—of sinning for the sake of sinning—will have an inexplicable explanation. There are people who sin for the sake of sinning, but why they do so is a mystery.

I have discussed an example at length, and I have shown how one might come to understand why Augustine chose the example and why it puzzles him. I shall conclude by sketching a way in which the example of the theft of the pears may serve to point out a logical tension in Augustine's more global philosophical and theological views. For the admitted fact that he stole the pears for the sake of doing wrong settles uneasily with the combination of his determinism, his anti-Manichaeanism, and his anti-Pelagianism. Against the Manichees, he insists that evil things cannot have a real existence, and that evildoing cannot be caused by anything that exists. The price he pays is high. Confronted with cases of moral weakness, such as his own theft of the pears, he is forced to say that such cases are causally inexplicable: the desires in question are caused by nothing. This of course sits ill with his determinism. But practically anything else he could say would sit ill with his anti-Manichaeanism. The alternative is to deny that there really are cases of moral weakness. But as I hope to have shown, Augustine never seriously entertains that possibility. And to deny moral weakness would be to concede too much to the Pelagians. If I am correct about even a part of this, what began by looking like a badly chosen and silly example in Book 2 of the *Confessions* turns out to lead us into the most global issues in Augustine's philosophy.

[14] See *De libero arbitrio* 2.20.203–204 and *De civitate Dei* 12.6–7.

3

Pride and Preference

A Reply to MacDonald

Scott MacDonald's "Petit Larceny, the Beginning of All Sin: Augustine's Theft of the Pears" is likely to become a classic in the philosophical literature on Augustine on sin.[1] MacDonald offers something he once described Augustine as offering—a "patient and subtle pathology of sin in general and primal sin in particular."[2] The particular account of sin that MacDonald examines is Augustine's account, in Book 2 of the *Confessions,* of his youthful, nocturnal, collaborated theft of pears. I wish to file a dissent from the case that MacDonald makes, a dissent that veers respectfully but sharply from that case.

One of the several merits of MacDonald's essay is that it leads us to distinguish between two questions when trying to understand Augustine's analysis of sin. What makes any action a sin? For any sinful action, what motivates it? According to MacDonald, Augustine's resolution of the theft of the pears requires not just *separation* but *stratification* of the two questions. It is not merely that answering the first leaves the second unresolved. It is that asking the second question "moves us to a deeper level of explanation" (*PL,* 408). There might be those uniformitarians who had hoped to kill two inquisitive birds with one explanatory stone, maintaining that any adequate answer to one question also answers the other. On MacDonald's view, such uniformitarian accounts of Augustine's analysis of sin fail. But not all is lost for the uniformitarian ideal. For it is MacDonald's thesis that Augustine's answer to the first question with regard to the theft of the pears is perfectly general: what makes *it* a sin is exactly the same thing that makes *anything* a sin. In similar fashion it is MacDonald's contention that the answer to the second question with regard to the theft of the pears is also perfectly general,

---

[1] Scott MacDonald, "Petit Larceny, the Beginning of All Sin: Augustine's Theft of the Pears," *Faith and Philosophy* 20 (2003): 393–414; cited hereinafter as *PL.*

[2] Scott MacDonald, "Primal Sin," in *The Augustinian Tradition,* ed. Gareth B. Matthews (Berkeley: University of California Press, 1999), 113.

that is, the same motivation lying behind Augustine's theft lies behind *every* sinful action. One size does not fit all, but two sizes will do.

What makes an action a sin? Sin "consists in the loving of lesser, created goods in preference to God, the highest and immutable good": it is metaphorically "a kind of fornication," literally "giving one's best love inappropriately and unrestrainedly, thereby joining oneself to goods whose value to us is out of all proportion with their real value" (*PL*, 394–395).[3] Call this "the inferior preference thesis."

What ultimately motivates every sinful act?

> [I]mitation of God in the form of prideful self-assertion is at the bottom of all sin. . . . When sinners (irrationally) prefer lesser goods to higher ones, they are in essence determining for themselves how goods are to be ranked relative to one another, disregarding their objective value and rankings. But that is an act of self-assertion, claiming for oneself a power one does not and cannot possess, the power to determine by one's own will the relative values of things. All sinners, then, whatever the species of their sin, insofar as they love something inordinately, exemplify the sort of over-reaching self-assertion that Augustine calls pride. (*PL*, 408–409)

Call this "the pride thesis." Note that the pride thesis contains at least three claims. One is a claim about the *ultimacy* of pride. Particular sins can have a wide variety of motivations appearing on their surface. But underlying them is pride (although this does not preclude pride from manifesting itself on the surface at times), occupying such a fundamental position that there is no further, more fundamental motive that explains pride's presence. Another claim, perhaps entailed by the ultimacy of pride, is a claim about the *ubiquity* of pride. Pride is not just scattered hither and yon among sins. *Every* sin has pride at its heart. And a third is a claim that Augustinian pride essentially involves a particular act of self-assertion, "the power to determine by one's own will the relative values of things."

MacDonald acknowledges that imputing the pride thesis to Augustine is more ambitious than establishing the inferior preference thesis: the evidence is more indirect and the text in the *Confessions* does not proceed in a way one would expect if Augustine's purpose were to get us to see the ultimacy and ubiquity of pride in the commission of sin. In particular, the imputation of the pride thesis requires that we see Augustine as finally rejecting a diagnosis of his theft

---

[3] Compare to *Confessions* 2.5.10 (MacDonald's translation): "Sin is committed for the sake of all these [lower goods] . . . when by virtue of a desire that is inordinate (since these are the lowest sort of good) better and higher things are abandoned. For these [lowest goods], too, have their own delights" (*PL*, 405).

that he repeats several times, namely, that he committed the sin solely for the sake of committing the sin. I shall begin by raising some doubts about the pride thesis. Then I shall focus attention on pursuing the implications of the inferior preference thesis. There is no reasonable doubt that Augustine does believe that when people sin, they pursue a lesser good when they could have pursued a greater good. But we go astray, I shall suggest, if we take the inferior preference thesis as specifying, on Augustine's behalf, what sin *is*. Finally, I shall offer a defense of Augustine's initial diagnosis, that he sinned for the sake of sinning.

My doubts about the pride thesis are textual and philosophical. To begin with the textual ones, let us look at Augustine's *De libero arbitrio,* a work completed shortly before the *Confessions*. MacDonald cites Augustine's account in *De libero arbitrio* of the fall of the devil as a "striking parallel" to Augustine's account of the theft of the pears. As MacDonald presents the passage he takes to be crucial— a passage describing a mind that becomes so pleased with itself that it wills to enjoy its own power in a perverse imitation of God—the passage epitomizes this mental process with an allusion to Ecclesiasticus 10:13: "This is 'pride, the beginning of all sin'" (*PL,* 407). Now, MacDonald's translation of the passage leaves Augustine off in mid-sentence. Augustine's sentence in full is "This is 'pride, the beginning of all sin' and 'the beginning of human pride is apostasy from God'" (Ecclesiasticus 10:12). Augustine might have omitted the Ecclesiasticus 10:12 passage: that he chose to include it suggests that he thought it was consistent with Ecclesiasticus 10:13 and that both passages were consistent with his own interpretive enterprise.

The conjunction of the two passages is puzzling once we note on Augustine's behalf that apostasy from God is itself a sin. If pride is the beginning of *all* sin, then it follows that pride is the beginning of apostasy. But how can pride be the beginning of apostasy while at the same time apostasy is the beginning of pride? I can think of two ways of responding. One is to urge that we not take the term "beginning" literally in the sentence, "the beginning of human pride is apostasy from God." It specifies neither temporal nor logical priority between pride and apostasy but rather *identity*: pride just *is* apostasy from God. The problem with this response is that parity demands that we interpret "pride is the beginning of all sin" similarly. When we do so we get the dubious claim that all sin just is pride. It is hard to know how to evaluate this claim. Our philosophical forebears would have cried "category mistake," alleging that the claim confuses actions with motives. MacDonald's stratification strategy especially must not fall prey to that confusion: sins are inferior preferences; pride is their *ur*-motive. If we suppose that all thefts are sins, as Augustine is inclined to suppose,[4] it still seems

---

[4] See *Confessions* 2.4.9.

that some thefts, like Jean Valjean's theft of a loaf of bread, involve desperation, not pride. And if we claim that even here, prideful self-assertion lurks at a deeper level of explanation beneath the surface desperation, we will not find support for that claim in the flat-footed assertion that sin just is pride. In sum, washing out the term "beginning" in favor of identity denies textual warrant for the ultimacy of pride.

The second way of responding to the Ecclesiasticus passages preserves the literal meaning of the term "beginning" in both verses, but it limits the term "all" in Ecclesiasticus 10:13 so that it now reads "the beginning of all *subsequent* sin is pride." In that case, however, pride loses its primacy: the primal sin is apostasy. Moreover, this interpretation will not sustain the ubiquity of pride thesis. Think of the assertion, "Turning down that job offer was the beginning of all my troubles." Its speaker is most naturally interpreted as making an etiological claim about the initiation of a chain of woeful events, not a claim to the effect that each subsequent woeful event is itself triggered by a new job refusal. On this interpretation of Ecclesiasticus 10:13 all subsequent sins can trace their ancestry back to an initial act of prideful self-assertion—there is no doubt that Augustine holds this view—but it does not follow that every ensuing sin is itself motivated by pride. Clearly, then, the second response does not support the ubiquity of pride, and is therefore at odds with the pride thesis. So, adopt the first response to Ecclesiasticus and you lose the ultimacy of pride. Adopt the second and you lose warrant for the ultimacy and ubiquity of pride. Either way is contrary to MacDonald's pride thesis. Perhaps there is some third interpretation one can give to Ecclesiasticus. My own conjecture is that what we should carry away from this puzzlement is the suspicion that we should not view Augustine as using the biblical text to bolster a philosophical thesis. That suspicion is strengthened by an examination of other Augustinian texts.

First, there is Augustine's procedure in *De libero arbitrio,* the text from which MacDonald draws the case of the devil's fall. In Book 1 Augustine floats the thesis that *libido* or lust "rules every kind of evildoing."[5] In Book 3 Augustine cites with approval the passage in 1 Timothy 6:10 that says that the root of all evil is *avaritia,* or greed.[6] Lust, greed, pride: now we have too many candidates! And greed has a biblical pedigree every bit as good as pride. What to do? One could argue for the *unity of vices.* A strong version of such an argument would have it that "lust," "greed," and "pride" are just three names for the same vice—on analogy to the case of "Venus," "The Morning Star," and "The Evening Star"—and

---

[5] *Clarum est enim iam nihil aliud quam libidinem in toto malefaciendi genere dominari. De libero arbitrio* 1.3.8. The speaker is Evodius, not Augustine, but Augustine shows no subsequent sign of demurring from Evodius's opinion.

[6] *De libero arbitrio* 3.17.48.

that whichever term is most appropriate to use to describe a particular sin depends on the circumstances in which the sin occurred: a weaker version would maintain that lust, greed, and pride are distinct yet inseparable, necessarily coextensive, so that any sin exemplifying one of them ipso facto exemplifies the others. The problem with both these strategies, from MacDonald's point of view, is that they are too egalitarian. They do not accord pride of place to pride. In order to harmonize *De libero arbitrio* with MacDonald's interpretation of the ultimate and universal motivation behind sin, lust and greed must somehow be *subordinated* under the banner of pride.

It counts as some evidence for MacDonald's case that in *De Genesi ad litteram* 11.15.19 Augustine considers the Ecclesiasticus and 1 Timothy passages side by side, proposing that when Paul says that greed is the root of all evil, we should understand greed in a broad and general sense of the term, that is, as not simply the craving for money (as the Greek *philarguria* suggests) but rather as the desire for more than one merits, based on perverse self-love. Augustine adds that this kind of greed is pride, the selfsame pride that brought about the fall of the devil. This passage tells in favor of the opinion that pride either is greed or trumps greed, but one is left wondering about whatever became of lust. Moreover, we still have no warrant for the ubiquity of pride thesis; for all that 1 Timothy 6:10 says, it may be that greed is simply the initial sin that opened the floodgates to all the other sins.

Second, in one of Augustine's anti-Pelagian works, *De natura et gratia*, most likely written in close temporal proximity to the writing of Book 11 of *De Genesi ad litteram*, Augustine explicitly denies the thesis, which he attributes to Pelagius, that all sins are sins of pride.[7] Some sins, Augustine says, are committed by the ignorant, by the infirm, and by those "weeping and moaning": although Augustine does not tarry to identify the latter, I assume that it includes those who act in desperation or under duress.[8] There is no trace here of an inclination on Augustine's part to maintain that in these cases, even though the proximate motive was something else, the motive au fond was nonetheless pride. Indeed, Augustine's gloss here on the Ecclesiasticus 10:13 passage confirms the suspicion that pride is the beginning of all sin only in the sense that it was the historically first sin that brought about the fall of the devil, to which all subsequent sins can trace their ancestry.[9]

---

[7] *De natura et gratia* 29.33.

[8] Aquinas understands Augustine's opinion in this way and endorses it. See *Summa Theologiae* 2–2, q. 162, a. 2, ad 1.

[9] Slightly earlier in the same work Augustine observes that pride is unique in that it can arise from the commission of good deeds (*De natura et gratia* 27.31). But this observation provides no grounds for thinking that every sin has a foundation in pride.

If it was ever Augustine's intention to get us to see that *every* sin, including his theft of the pears, is rooted in pride, he certainly masked that intention. As I read the texts, they do not reveal an author campaigning for the ubiquity of pride thesis.

I turn now to the philosophical doubts I have about the pride thesis. Recall that MacDonald says, apropos of the pride thesis, that (1) the preference for lesser goods over greater goods is irrational and that (2) this very preference is tantamount to a prideful act of self-assertion, claiming for oneself "the power to determine by one's own will the relative values of things." On this account, then, sinners are *transvaluators,* and doomed-to-be-feckless transvaluators at that, since they cannot have it in their power to alter the relative rankings of things in an objective hierarchy of values validated by God.[10] It thus appears that on MacDonald's pride thesis sinners are irrational twice over, irrational in their preferences and irrational in their necessarily futile attempt to restructure an unrestructurable hierarchy of values.

MacDonald's picture of the psychology of sinners is incomplete. According to it, we are to suppose that sinners prefer goods that are inferior to what they could and should prefer. And we are to suppose that sinners are simultaneously engaged in an exercise of transvaluation, asserting that what they prefer is actually better than what the established value hierarchy claims to be more preferable. But if we describe their situation in this way and say nothing more, then it seems as though sinners are *triply* irrational, irrational in their preferences, irrational in their efforts as transvaluation, *and* irrational in holding simultaneously that the good they prefer is inferior and not inferior.

This way of summing up the irrationalities is the observer's way, a way that would be appropriate, for example, for the adult Augustine to follow in examining, retrospectively, his own youthful career. One thing that is missing from it so far, however, is a consideration of the doxastic states he might have been in at the time he was committing the theft. What beliefs might he have had about his preferences and about the implications of his activities? Did he believe at the time of the theft that the good that he preferred was inferior to what he could have and should have preferred? Was he aware that he was engaged in transvaluation?

There are two reasons for assuming that Augustine believed that he was pursuing an inferior good in a culpable way. First, the assumption agrees with Augustine's description. As Augustine says, "Your law, Lord, which clearly punishes theft, has been inscribed on human hearts. Not even wickedness itself can erase it."[11] We need

---

[10] I leave it an open question here whether for Augustine God's "validation" is (1) his unerring intellectual recognition of the hierarchical structure intrinsic to values in creation, (2) his conferring of relative values on created thing by his unimpedible will, or (3) both (1) and (2).

[11] *Confessions* 2.4.9, MacDonald's translation.

only suppose, then, that whatever else cardio-inscription might entail, it confers belief. Second, to suppose that Augustine did not believe that the good he preferred was inferior—here I take "did not believe" to cover the possibility that he believed that the good he preferred was not inferior *and* the possibility that he had no doxastic attitude with respect to his preference—complicates the issue whether his preference was sinful. For on the supposition that Augustine did not believe that the good he preferred was inferior, his case would appear to have been a case of mistake or of ignorance. Depending upon further elaboration of the circumstances, it might have been that his being mistaken or ignorant was itself culpable. But it is not obvious that his *preference* would have been sinful in the absence of a belief that he was preferring a lesser good over a greater good.[12] To suppose that his suboptimal preference was sinful, no matter what his doxastic state, would seem to commit one to supposing that all sins are "strict liability" sins, sins, that is, for which there is no requirement of mens rea. And Augustine is far from supposing *that*![13]

So Augustine, we may assume, believed at the time that the good he preferred was inferior. But inasmuch as he was a sinner, by MacDonald's lights, Augustine was a transvaluator, shaking his fist heavenward, as it were, and claiming the right to promote his favored good to the top of the heap of goods he might have chosen. "As it were": must Augustine have been aware that this was what he was up to? I daresay that many sinners would be surprised to hear that they are transvaluators, and perhaps would even disavow this analysis of their behavior. But as Freud has taught us, an agent's agenda may be hidden from the agent: surprise and disavowal to the contrary notwithstanding, it might be that MacDonald's analysis is correct. I doubt, however, that MacDonald wants to maintain that sinners are *never* aware of their attempts at transvaluation. I believe that MacDonald supposes that the particularly defiant ones—the devil[14] and the youthful, pear-stealing Augustine—are fully aware of their transvaluational proclivities. If so, then the youthful Augustine quite consciously hit the trifecta of irrationality mentioned above: by stealing the pears he was irrational in his preference,

---

[12] There is a remarkably compressed argument in *Meno* 77d–e to the effect that the person who desires bad things, believing that they are good, actually desires good things.

[13] Legal scholars credit Augustine with initiating a condition of mens rea for wrongdoing, although the inspiration may have come from Seneca. See Jerome Hall, *General Principles of Criminal Law*, 2nd ed. (Indianapolis, IN: Bobbs-Merrill, 1960), 79–80.

[14] Well, maybe. Milton's Lucifer says:

> So farewell hope, and, with hope, farewell fear,
> Farewell remorse; all good to me is lost.
> Evil, be thou my good.

> (*Paradise Lost*, Book IV, lines 108–110)

Is Milton's Lucifer a transvaluator?

irrational in his attempt at transvaluation, and irrational in simultaneously believing that his preference was justified and unjustified.

I cannot clear Augustine in juvenile court of all charges of irrationality. I wish, however, to induce a verdict of "not proven" against the charge of transvaluation, inasmuch as the charge is based solely on the imputation of pride. If you look in the *Oxford Latin Dictionary* under *superbia,* the term for "pride," you will find its primary meaning is "lofty self-esteem, disdain."[15] You will *not* find that the *OLD* goes on to say "invariably accompanied by a desire to determine the relative values of things." Now of course one cannot expect a dictionary to trace out all the necessary connections of a term. But because I am a native user of English and have never associated the English term, "pride," with an impulse toward transvaluation, I am emboldened to suggest that there is no necessary connection between pride and a desire to determine the relative values of things. Surely a person can take pride in her accomplishments without at the same time asserting some sort of power to redefine the standards against which her accomplishments are gauged. Indeed, recognition of and acquiescence in the fixed standards is frequently a source of the pride.

This leads me to suggest an alternative interpretation of Augustine's theft of the pears. Distinguish between a revolutionary and a scofflaw. A revolutionary seeks to establish a new regime. A scofflaw seeks not to overturn the existing system—it may in fact be to his advantage if everyone else were to conform to it—but to *flout* it. MacDonald's youthful Augustine is a revolutionary. But if Augustine had been a transvaluational revolutionary, he would not have regarded his action as a sin, let alone as an instance of sinning for the sake of sinning, except in a scare-quotational sense of "sin." So I suggest that Augustine is a scofflaw. Do not, however, sell my Augustine short. Ordinary scofflaws disobey the law because they see some advantage therein to themselves and because they think or feign to themselves that the law they transgress is not *that* important. As Augustine takes pains to point out, no advantage accrued to him by means of his theft, nor did he anticipate any. And he insists that the law he flouted is no petty, merely conventional human law, like an ordinance forbidding parking on the wrong side of a two-way street. So although Augustine's theft may not have been the action of an ordinary scofflaw, it was the action of an out-of-the-ordinary scofflaw. What makes his theft out of the ordinary? If I understand MacDonald correctly, the case is supposed to be salient for Augustine in part because its agent seems to aim at no good whatsoever. The action's lack of any apparent good then is supposed to force us to see what we might miss in most cases of sin—cases in

---

[15] You will also find that *superbia* can be used to allude to a variety of *pear,* the superbus! More grist for MacDonald's mill?

which an inferior good is sought—because when an inferior good is detectable, we tend to be satisfied with its presence as fully accounting for the sin. That is, the presence of the inferior good interferes with our being able to perceive what drives every sin, pride. The theft of the pears, on MacDonald's account, is salient because it removes that interfering factor.

MacDonald thus claims that Augustine subsequently denies what Augustine initially proposes about the theft, that it is out of the ordinary because it is sinning for the sake of sinning. I wish to reinstate Augustine's initial proposal, but before I do, I want to examine briefly the inferior preference thesis.

Recall how the inferior preference thesis was expressed: sin "consists in the loving of lesser, created goods in preference to God," and that to sin is to give "one's best love inappropriately and unrestrainedly, thereby joining oneself to goods whose value to us is out of all proportion with their real value" (*PL*, 394–395). We can discern two conceptions of sin here:

(A) x sins if and only if x prefers a lesser good over God.
(B) x sins if and only if x prefers a lesser good over a greater good.

Given that God is the highest good, (B) entails (A). But only one of the two conditionals contained in (A) is obvious, namely,

(A′) If x prefers a lesser good over God, then x sins.

To whom does (A′) apply? I suspect that it is a rare sinner whose sin can correctly be described as preferring a lesser good over God. Perhaps Scarpia, who sings "Tosca, mi fai dimenticare Iddio!" But Scarpia's character is thereby shown to be shocking in its depravity. So while we may grant that (A′) is true, it leaves many sinners unaccounted for.

As for the other conditional contained in (A),

(A*) If x sins, then x prefers a lesser good over God,

it is questionable whether (A*) is generally true. A contemporary Dives might have a set of preferences such that he prefers accumulating wealth over aiding the needy, but nevertheless ranks God over Mammon. Dives thus sins (by omission, at least) even though there may be no lesser good that he prefers over God. One might try to salvage (A*) by maintaining, in the right tone of voice, that in this case, Dives really does prefer wealth over God. I shall not attempt to resolve the status of (A*), choosing instead to point out that if (A′) gives us too narrow a notion of sin and (A*) is questionable, then, since they are jointly entailments of (B), we should suspect that there is something wrong with (B).

As it stands, (B) is too inclusive to give us a characterization of sin. Consider the poor soul, call him "Oompah," who dedicates his life to preserving and propagating the music of John Philip Sousa. Oompah cheerfully acknowledges that Mozart's music is better than Sousa's, but persists in his obsession with Sousa nonetheless. Whenever he could have listened to the *Sinfonia Concertante*, he finds himself cuing up "Stars and Stripes Forever." There is much to find wanting in Oompah, but I for one am unwilling to call his passion sinful. Oompah is incontinent, to be sure, but incontinence is not the same thing as sinfulness. (B) at best identifies the former, but it does not pin down the latter.[16] In his classic "How Is Weakness of the Will Possible," Donald Davidson offers this definition of incontinence:

> In doing x an agent acts incontinently if and only if: (a) the agent does x intentionally; (b) the agent believes there is an alternative action y open to him; and (c) the agent judges that, all things considered, it would be better to do y than to do x.[17]

Davidson's definition does a tolerably clear job of explicating the inferior preference thesis, as encoded by (B), but it cannot be taken as a definition of sin (and thus neither can the inferior preference thesis). Oompah the Sousaphile provides one counterexample: here is another that cuts more deeply. Leibniz is famous for having argued that in creating this world God must have created the best possible world. As far as I can tell, Augustine is no Leibnizian; he stakes out no claim that God must create the best.[18] One reason that a person might have for demurring from that claim is provided by the thought that there may *be* no best possible world. It might be that for *any* world God chooses to create, there is a better possible world that God could have created. If so, and if the inferior

---

[16] MacDonald prefaces the expression of (B) with the remark that "sin is a kind of fornication," but it is hard to know the cash value of the remark since fornication itself is a kind of sin.

[17] Donald Davidson, "How Is Weakness of the Will Possible?" in *Moral Concepts*, ed. Joel Feinberg (Oxford: Oxford University Press, 1969), 93–113; the definition appears on p. 94. Davidson later suggests a modification:

> In doing x an agent acts incontinently if and only if: (a) the agent does x for reason r, and (b) the agent has a reason r^l that includes r and more, (c) on the basis of which the agent judges some alternative y to be better than x.

The ingredients for the modification appear on p. 111; I have regimented them into the format of the original definition.

[18] For further discussion of this point, see my "Augustine on Evil and Original Sin," in *The Cambridge Companion to Augustine*, ed. Eleonore Stump and Norman Kretzmann (Cambridge: Cambridge University Press, 2001), 43. Reprinted as Chapter 5 of this volume.

preference thesis adequately delineates the notion of sin, it would seem to follow that omniscient, omnipotent God sins no matter what world he chooses to create and perhaps also sins if he chooses *not* to create (if it plausible to think that some of the worlds God might have created would have yielded a better state of affairs on balance than the state of affairs of his not creating any world).

Clearly something has gone wrong. The simplest diagnosis is to suggest that the inferior preference thesis gives, at best, a necessary consequence of, but not a sufficient condition for, an action's counting as a sin. In claiming that (B) was too inclusive to capture the notion of sin, I supposed that incontinence was a genus, of which sin is a species. The simplest and most obvious way to provide the differentia is to suggest that what makes an action a sin is its violation of a divine command or edict, like the prohibition against theft, presumably inscribed on human hearts in indelible ink but obviously not hardwired into the human will. That is, we can enhance (B) in this fashion:

(B′) x sins if and only if (1) x prefers a lesser good over a greater good and (2) x's preference is contrary to a command of God.

In the absence of a divine command regarding artistic tastes, (B′) enables Oompah the Sousaphile to avoid the charge of sinning (but not the charge of incontinence). (B′) also shows that God does not sin in creating a less good world than he might have created, for he violates no divine command in doing so.[19] Can God, unlike Oompah, be cleared of a charge of incontinence? If the sequence of better and better possible worlds is infinite, then there is no the best world among them, and it cannot be weakness of will for one not to choose what one knows does not exist.

Since I am disinclined to say that pride lurks at the bottom of every sin, disinclined to regard Augustine's theft of the pears as a case of transvaluational activity, and disinclined to think that the inferior preference thesis gives a sufficient account of sin, I owe you some account of why Augustine chose the theft as his flagship case of sinning, and why he seems to find the theft both repellent and perplexing.

---

[19] Beware the proposition, "God created a less good world than he might have created." Aquinas in effect claimed that it was true in one sense and false in another. It is true that God could have created a world populated by better components than this world. But it is false that God could have done a better job of ordering the components that he has actually decided to bring into existence. For citations and discussion, see Norman Kretzmann, "Goodness, Knowledge, and Indeterminacy in the Philosophy of Thomas Aquinas," *The Journal of Philosophy* 80 (1983): 631–649; and Norman Kretzmann, "A Particular Problem of Creation: Why Would God Create This World?" in *Being and Goodness: The Concept of the Good in Metaphysics and Philosophical Theology*, ed. Scott MacDonald (Ithaca, NY: Cornell University Press, 1991), 229–249.

Sinning for the sake of sinning is perplexing enough, by Augustine's lights. Some truly heinous acts are nonetheless at least intelligible because they are instrumentally rational, given the goals of the agent, such as Catiline's killing people just to keep in practice.[20] Other actions may have no purpose other than their own performance—thus not rising to the threshold of instrumental rationality—but nevertheless be blameless, such as whittling on a lazy summer afternoon. But by categorizing his theft of the pears as sinning for the sake of sinning, Augustine blocks the attribution to his action of either instrumental rationality or blameless recreation. Augustine knew full well that what he was doing was forbidden, so the action cannot be subsumed under the categories of ignorance or mistake. How then can sinning for the sake of sinning be made intelligible?

Consider an analogy. Suppose that some modern-day Croesus spends several million dollars for a Monet painting at auction and then sets fire to it. Appalled by his action, we seek an explanation. Here is a transcript of an imaginary interview.

INTERVIEWER: Do you have any idea of Monet's importance?

CROESUS: Of course. I have an MFA and I concentrated on the French Impressionists. In fact, I'm fortunate enough to have acquired two other Monets for my private collection.

I: Ah, so you wanted to drive up the value of those two paintings by reducing the number of surviving Monets in the world.

C: Heavens no. I don't believe that the economics of the art-world works that way. The number of Monets was already small enough to guarantee an inelastic demand curve. As far as I can tell, I took a financial loss by burning the painting.

I: Then you must really have disliked that particular painting.

C: Surely you jest. The use of the pallette, the spontaneous brushwork, the dynamism . . . you've seen reproductions of it. It really was one of Monet's finest.

I: Perhaps you harbor some disapproval of Monet's character?

C: No, he seems to have led an exemplary life. Now Caravaggio, that's another story.

I: Was this some sort of publicity stunt?

C: You should know better than that. The only reason the public knows that I burned the painting is that one of my employees leaked the news to the press, to my chagrin. The only witness to the burning was my friend, Midas.

I: So you did it to impress Midas, as if you were one of those nineteenth-century tycoons who lit their cigars with one-hundred-dollar bills?

---

[20] *Confessions* 2.5.11.

c: No, not really. It's true that had Midas not been there to give me moral support, I wouldn't have burned the painting. But I didn't do it in order to impress him; friends don't need to impress friends.[21]

I: Then I'm at a complete loss to explain your action. In addition to being barbaric, it now seems utterly senseless.

c: That was the point: I wanted to do something aesthetically dreadful just for the sake of doing something aesthetically dreadful. It was barbaric, it was utterly senseless, and I did it for that reason alone.

I: I presume it hasn't escaped your attention that as a person of considerable financial power, your action appears to the general public as an arbitrary but arrogant and prideful assertion of that power.

c: I regret that the public has that perception. I wasn't proud of what I did at the time, and I'm certainly not proud of it now. In fact, I've recently established a foundation whose aim is the preservation and restoration of works of art.

I: You said earlier that the sole reason you burned the painting was to do something aesthetically dreadful. That's not to offer a reason; that's to confess that your action had no reason.

I submit that by making appropriate transformations in the dialogue above, we can convert it into Augustine's adult interrogation of his adolescent self. And, just as our interviewer is continually frustrated in trying to understand the springs of Croesus's action, I offer the conjecture that the adult Augustine is frustrated, *remains frustrated, and intends his reader to come away frustrated,* in trying to comprehend his youthful theft. Why is that? Let me gesture toward an answer.

Plato famously claims that virtue is knowledge and that all wrongdoing is the result of ignorance. Contrary to Plato, Augustine presents a case in which he knowingly engages in wrongdoing. Plato is not without his defensive resources. One species of ignorance reveals itself in mismeasurement, for example, in estimating incorrectly the value of a commodity, or in discounting the future too steeply.[22] Augustine's case appears tailored to rebut that charge of ignorance. In particular, the theft resists description as a bad deal, the trading of a superior commodity for inferior goods. For if the sole point of the theft was to commit the theft itself, it was not the goods that were sought after; the pears, to recall, were thrown to the pigs. If, as Augustine famously claims in his own right, all evil is non-being, then sinning for the sake of doing evil is sinning for the sake of—nothing. Thus Augustine's point is that his theft of the pears is an example of

---

[21] Gareth B. Matthews probes the psychodynamics of gang activity in *Augustine* (Malden, MA: Blackwell Publishers, 2005), chap. 13, while pointing out that Augustine "never withdraws his insistence that his pleasure lay in committing the act itself" (p. 121).

[22] See *Protagoras* 356a–357e.

complete senselessness, a brute slap in the face of Plato's rationalistic optimism. In response to a question I raised earlier, his theft *cannot* be made intelligible. This surd provides repulsion and perplexity enough.

Having staked out an interpretation according to which Augustine believes that he sinned for the sake of sinning, I am obliged to respond to what I believe is MacDonald's most profound reason for disallowing the interpretation: the interpretation would deny Augustine "the conceptual leverage he needs to overturn his Manichaean convictions":

> [H]e comes to see that all of God's creatures are good and that sin, the first and fundamental evil in creation, arises from creaturely free choices that aim essentially (and inordinately) at genuine goods, things in which it is wholly appropriate to take some measure of delight. To allow that there are sins in which sinners aim at no good, sins in which sinners find no recognizable delight, would undermine the foundations of Augustine's theodicy and thereby the entire edifice of his Christian intellectual enterprise. (*PL,* 402)

We enter into waters deeper than can be fathomed here. I can offer only the sketchiest of sketches of an alternative understanding of Augustine's anti-Manichaeanism.

The baseline assumption is that everything that exists is good because everything that exists either is God or is created by supremely good God. To be sure, some created things are better than others. In *De libero arbitrio* Augustine classifies the human will as an intermediate good, higher than any material object because the former but not the latter is necessary for living rightly, but lower than the virtues because while the virtues cannot be misused, the will can.[23] The will is misused when it chooses, freely and culpably, a lesser good over a greater good. What the will cannot do is choose a created *thing* that is utterly devoid of goodness: if the thing were utterly devoid of goodness, it would not exist. But Augustine's anti-Manichaeanism does not rule out the possibility of one's *choosing* in a way that is, objectively speaking, devoid of goodness even though both the instrument of choosing and the object chosen must be good to some degree. Perhaps in all such cases the agent feigns to himself that there is a kind of goodness in the choosing, the thrill of doing something forbidden for its own sake. Thus, to recall MacDonald's subjective constraint on motivation,

---

[23] *De libero arbitrio* 2.19.50.

> If an agent S voluntarily performs some action (Φs), then there must be something, D, in or about Φing that delights S and (for that reason) moves S to Φ. [*PL*, 399]

I maintain that Augustine's anti-Manichaeanism is fully compatible with his allowing, as a legitimate substituend for the variable, "D," the phrase, "the prospect of sinning for the sake of sinning." Augustine's will is an intermediate good. Its freedom, the very gift that enables its possessor to live rightly, carries with it the liability of choosing wrongly, very wrongly. Augustine's anti-Manichaeanism does not make sinning for the sake of sinning metaphysically or psychologically impossible. It does not require that one choose something in creation that has positively evil existence. But Augustine's anti-Manichaeanism, coupled with his conception of the will, does allow for the liability that one will choose wrongly just for the sake of choosing wrongly.[24]

[24] An early version of this paper benefited from comments from David Barnett, Sin yee Chan, David Christensen, Mark Moyer, Derk Pereboom, and Adam Wager. A later version was read at the symposium "Augustine on Wanting Bad Things" at the American Philosophical Association's Pacific Division meeting in Pasadena in 2004; co-symposiasts were Scott MacDonald and Gareth B. Matthews. William Hasker saved me from a couple of blunders in an even later version.

4

The Life of the Mind
in Dramas and Dreams

Dramas and dreams traffic in unrealities. They are fabrications, mere representations, images of things and events that in turn may also be unreal. They are common, not rare. In the *Confessions* they perplex Augustine. He finds dramas a source of curious but not especially worrisome perplexity. Dreams—in particular, his erotic dreams—are perplexing and worrisome. Although the two sources of perplexity are separated by some two hundred pages, they are, I suggest, connected in ways that Augustine might not have fully seen. Attempts to resolve them raise important questions about the structure and activity of the human mind.

In discussing Augustine's perplexity, I shall look at some views held by contemporary philosophers on kindred topics. I do this in the belief that one way of paying respect to our philosophical ancestors is by using contemporary instruments to examine and perhaps to cast new light on their contributions to philosophy. There are wonderful recordings of the *Goldberg Variations* performed on the harpsichord. But I would not want to deny to performers the dynamic possibilities enabled by the piano.

Augustine at the Theater

Soon after going to Carthage at the age of seventeen Augustine became "captivated by theatrical shows."

> They were full of representations of my own miseries and fueled my fire. Why is it that a person should wish to experience suffering by watching grievous and tragic events which he himself would not wish to endure? Nevertheless he wants to suffer the pain given by being a spectator of these sufferings, and the pain itself is his pleasure. What is

this but amazing folly? For the more anyone is moved by these scenes, the less free he is from similar passions. Only, when he himself suffers, it is called misery; when he feels compassion for others, it is called mercy. But what quality of mercy is it in fictitious and theatrical inventions? A member of the audience is not excited to offer help, but invited only to grieve. The greater his pain, the greater his approval of the actor in these representations. If the human calamities, whether in ancient histories or fictitious myths, are so presented that the theatregoer is not caused pain, he walks out of the theatre disgusted and highly critical. But if he feels pain, he stays riveted in his seat enjoying himself.[1]

This passage is the earliest statement of what has become known as "the paradox of tragedy,"[2] although to speak of *the* paradox may underestimate its resources. Augustine's passage adverts to no fewer than three paradoxical phenomena.

Why is it that a person should wish to experience suffering by watching grievous and tragic events which he himself would not wish to endure? . . . The greater his pain, the greater his approval of the actor in these representations. There are certain sorts of unpleasant feelings, such as anxiety, fear, anger, and grief, that people in general try to avoid. Yet many of these same people actively seek out and eagerly take in spectacles on the stage that they believe will evoke these feelings in them. Moreover, they seek out these spectacles not *in spite* of their belief but *because* of it. Offered a choice between seeing a performance of *King Lear* and a performance of *As You Like It*, many will opt for *King Lear*. An even higher percentage of people, I suspect, would choose *Romeo and Juliet* over *Romeo* ☺ *and Juliet* ☺, a rewritten version in which the star-crossed lovers survive.[3] Call this the *anomalous psychological phenomenon*. Given its widespread occurrence, it calls out for explanation.

But what quality of mercy is it in fictitious and theatrical inventions? A member of the audience is not excited to offer help, but invited only to grieve. Emotions like fear and compassion are closely tied to action. People who find themselves in the

---

[1] *Confessions* 3.2.2. Here and elsewhere I use the translation of *Confessions* by Henry Chadwick (Oxford: Oxford University Press, 1991), with modifications as noted. The passage appears on pp. 35–36. This volume will be cited henceforward as "Chadwick."

[2] See, e.g., Kendall L. Walton, *Mimesis as Make-Believe* (Cambridge, MA: Harvard University Press, 1990), 255–259. Walton cites David Hume's essay "Of Tragedy" (1741–1742). Augustine seems to have anticipated the paradox some 1,344 years earlier.

[3] On this point I am indebted to Tyler Doggett and Andy Egan, "How We Feel about Terrible, Nonexistent Mafiosi," *Philosophy and Phenomenological Research* 84 (2012): 277–306. See also Walton, *Mimesis as Make-Believe*, 258.

vicinity of a dangerous animal will tend to flee; people seeing others in danger will tend to come to their aid. But only a boor watching a production of *Romeo and Juliet* would rush onto the stage to dash the vial of poison from Romeo's hand. A similar phenomenon occurs in dreaming—and so here is one commonality between dramas and dreams:

> I dream I am about to be attacked by a tiger: I feel the emotion of fear, but I don't make a move—I just lie there. The belief has triggered my affective system, but it has left my motor system in a state of passivity.[4]

Call this disconnection between affective and motor systems the *diminished response phenomenon.*[5]

If the human calamities, whether in ancient histories or fictitious myths, are so presented that the theatergoer is not caused pain, he walks out of the theater disgusted and highly critical. "Fictitious myths" are at no disadvantage vis-à-vis tragic representations based on history. *Romeo and Juliet* does not suffer in comparison alongside *Richard the Third*. Oedipus, Antigone, Queen Dido, King Lear, Anna Karenina, and Willy Loman have two things in common: their fates have inspired feelings of fear and sorrow in countless audiences, and none of them ever existed. It can seem perplexing enough to explain how the nonexistent can affect the existent. But the perplexity is heightened when we ask how it can be that what never existed can affect members of the audience who *know* it (*what* "it"?) never to have existed. This is the *phenomenon of nonexistence* associated with the paradox of tragedy.

Having identified these puzzling phenomena, Augustine drops the subject. Perhaps his lack of further interest is explained by the fact that unlike his perplexity about time, in which he finds himself inescapably immersed, Augustine can simply avoid the theater. Henry Chadwick comments that Augustine deplored the theater, "largely because of the frequently erotic content of the shows, but also because of the fictional character of the plays, fiction being, to his mind, a form of mendacity."[6] Set aside plays with erotic content: the paradox of tragedy remains unresolved. It would be hard for Augustine in particular to maintain that fiction that is known to be fictional by its consumers is mendacious. In *De mencacio* 2.2, written shortly before the *Confessions*, Augustine had maintained that jokes, for instance, are not lies. Even though the jokester does not speak the

---

[4] Colin McGinn, *Mindsight* (Cambridge, MA: Harvard University Press, 2004), 102.

[5] Some physiological states count as responses but not as motor responses. Watching a horror movie may induce an elevated pulse, tightening of one's grip on the theater seat, gasping, but not bolting and running.

[6] Chadwick, 36.

truth, he lacks an intention to deceive, which Augustine takes to be essential to mendacity. Suppose that a group of actors decides, as a cruel hoax, to re-enact on the street a violent murder scene that is part of a play that the group performs in the theater. The street re-enactment is identical in speech and movement to the stage performance. The bystanders believe that what they are witnessing is a real-life murder. Thus their motor systems, along with their affective systems, are appropriately engaged. The actors have succeeded in deceiving the bystanders. Had those same actors performed the same sequence of events in the theater, they would have had no intention to deceive. (Nor would any such intention have been successful, even on an audience populated by the very same bystanders.) Theatrical tragedies, like jokes, do not succeed by deception.

There is more than one variety of mendaciousness. Even if the actors and playwrights do not deceive—by passing off fable as truth, for example—they might mislead their audiences by commending base actions as things done by noble personages. This complaint had been made by Plato in Book X of the *Republic*.[7] In Book 2 of *The City of God* Augustine cites with approval Plato's banishment of all poets from the ideal city on grounds that they attribute all sorts of immoralities to the gods, thus either mocking beings alleged to be moral exemplars or commending their immoral behavior as models we should emulate.

So might begin a discussion of the morality of art. I wish to shift the lens, however, away from Augustine's attitudes *toward* the theater, and onto his attitudes while *in* the theater. Let us focus in particular on Augustine's psychological attitudes. His language implies that his beliefs, desires, emotions, and moods occurring in the theater were on all fours with his ordinary beliefs, desires, emotions, and moods. As he sees, that implication leads to a series of puzzles.

Let us suppose that he is watching a play that includes a scene of Dido's committing suicide. He is made miserable by the scene. Of course, that was the whole point of his going to the theater. Had the scene not made him miserable he would have demanded his money back. But no less of an authority than Plato tells us that no one desires to be miserable.[8] Hence either Plato is mistaken or Augustine is not really made miserable. This dilemma is occasioned by the anomalous psychological phenomenon.

Let us suppose further that Augustine knows that he could forestall his impending misery, not by doing anything as boorish as dashing on stage to prevent Dido from self-immolation, but simply by leaving the theater. Yet he chooses to stay, "riveted in his seat." His choice illustrates the diminished response phenomenon. It is natural to suppose that, as a corollary of Plato's axiom, one will

---

[7] Plato, *Republic* 605c–e.

[8] *Meno*, 78a. I do not suggest that Augustine was aware of this dialogue.

seek to avoid situations that make one miserable. Once again, either Plato is mistaken or what Augustine experienced was not misery.[9]

It does not appear, moreover, in the case we are supposing, that Augustine would have the belief that he is grieving about an actual, historical occurrence, for which regret and mourning might be appropriate. We might rightly mourn the senseless, real-life murder of Leon Klinghoffer while taking in a performance of John Adams's opera, *The Death of Klinghoffer*. But shortly before his discussion of the theater Augustine reports that he wept more over the death of Dido than over his own spiritual death. If he had thought that Dido had really existed, then his mourning more for her death than for his own spiritual "death" would not indicate an emotional evaluation that is out of order, for as the *Confessions* attests, unlike Dido's death, Augustine's spiritual death is reversible. What makes his mourning absurd and objectionable for him is that it occurs in tandem with the belief that Dido never existed.[10] The puzzle bequeathed to us in this case by the phenomenon of nonexistence is to explain how Augustine can believe that Dido is a mythical character through and through while at the same time mourning her demise.

Kendall Walton has argued that there is less to the paradox than meets the eye. The way to dissipate the air of paradox, on Walton's account, is to get clear about the psychological states of theatergoers. One bracing feature of this account is its implications for the furniture and structure of the mind. In particular, the account denies the assumption that the mental states of theatergoers are identical in kind to the mental states they have when dealing with ordinary, non-fictional life.[11] On Walton's view, when Augustine reports that he experienced grief upon taking in a staging of Dido's death, he is mistaken or he is not speaking literally.[12] If he is mistaken, he has misidentified or misdescribed his mental state: the feeling he had in the theater was not ordinary grief, not like the grief he felt, described so eloquently in the *Confessions*, over the death of his unnamed friend and, later, the death of his mother.[13] Following Walton's lead, we can call his emotional response to Dido's death "quasi grief."

---

[9] One might try to argue that the misery theatergoers experience is voluntarily undergone for their moral edification. That may be true for some theatergoers. But it is hard to believe that it applies to all.

[10] *Confessions* 1.13.21, in Chadwick, 15–16.

[11] See *Mimesis as Make-Believe*, esp. chaps. 5 and 7; and Kendall Walton, "Spelunking, Simulation, and Slime: On Being Moved by Fiction," in Mette Hjort and Sue Laver, eds., *Emotion and the Arts* (Oxford: Oxford University Press, 1997), 37–49. Views similar to Walton's are explored by Tyler Doggett and Andy Egan in "Wanting Things You Don't Want," *Philosophers' Imprint* 7, no. 9 (2007): 1–17; and their "How We Feel about Terrible, Non-Existent Mafiosi."

[12] "Must we declare Aristotle wrong in decreeing that tragedies should evoke fear and pity? Not unless we naively insist on a literal-minded reading of his words." Walton, *Mimesis as Make-Believe*, 249.

[13] *Confessions* 4.4.7–4.7.12 and 9.12.29–9.12.33, respectively, in Chadwick, 56–60 and 174–176.

To illustrate the notion of a quasi emotion, let us return briefly to the example of the cruel hoax staged by thespians on the street. The perceptual input, we have supposed, is the same in all relevant respects for the bystanders on the sidewalk as it is for the audience in the theater. The difference in motor output between the bystanders and the audience—flight versus fascination—must be explained. The bystanders' cognitive default setting is credulity: they have no cues to suggest to them that what they are experiencing is not what is really happening. Knowledgeable theatergoers, in contrast, know that what they are experiencing is not what is really happening. It does not follow that their default setting is incredulity. (The magician's conjuring tricks trigger incredulity by flaunting the seemingly impossible. Successful tragedy, in contrast, depends on the Aristotelian assumption that "the poet's function is to . . . describe a kind of thing that might happen, i.e., what is possible as being probable or necessary."[14]) It is rather that theatergoers willingly invoke their imaginative capacities. This participation by imagination is a species or specimen of "make-believe." The term "make-believe" can mislead. Theatergoers do not make up a battery of *beliefs*. One's beliefs are not as easily manipulated by the will as one's imagination is. *Pace* Coleridge, one may not find it easy to engage in "the willing suspension of disbelief," nor is that required: imagining is just different from believing and disbelieving. The mental engagement of theatergoers is an exercise in imagination, construed not as a kind of detached counterfactual speculation, but as an activity that mobilizes their emotions.[15] On Walton's account, the bystanders feel fear while the theatergoers feel quasi fear. The difference between quasi fear and fear is not, or need not be, a difference in intensity. The two emotions may even be phenomenologically identical; that is what makes misidentification and misdescription easy and pervasive. Nonetheless, they are two emotions,[16] differentiated by their causal ancestry.

---

[14] *Poetics* chap. 9. I refrain from launching into a comparison between Augustine's views about the theater and Aristotle's views on fear, pity, and catharsis for two reasons. The subject of catharsis in Aristotle's *Poetics* is, as Alexander Nehamas puts it, "altogether overwhelmingly difficult." See Nehamas, "Pity and Fear," in *Essays on Aristotle's Poetics*, ed. Amélie Oksenberg Rorty (Princeton, NJ: Princeton University Press, 1992), 303. Other essays in the same collection amply attest to Nehamas's observation.) And there is utterly no reason to believe that Augustine was aware of the *Poetics*.

[15] In "Spelunking, Simulation, and Slime" Walton adopts the language of mental simulation to characterize the imaginative engagement undertaken by those who interact with artworks: "Appreciators simulate experiences of being attacked by monsters, of observing characters in danger and fearing for them, of learning about and grieving for good people who come to tragic ends, of marveling at and admiring the exploits of heroes" (46–47).

[16] "The experience of fictionally . . . grieving for Anna Karenina may itself be counted an emotional one, although one's emotion is not grief for Anna" (*Mimesis as Make-Believe*, 255). Quasi emotions are not ersatz emotions. For that reason, throughout this essay I contrast quasi grief, not with "real" or "genuine" grief, but with ordinary grief.

Supposing this account to apply to Augustine's case, we could say that he experienced quasi grief over Dido's death. Experiencing ordinary grief would have betokened confusion between Augustine's cognitive and affective attitudes. He knows that no one has died. Not Dido, who never existed; not the actress on stage, who will be taking curtain calls when the play has ended.[17] So he knows, or should know, that ordinary grief is uncalled for.[18] Once this supposition is granted, we can see how it deals with the components of the paradox of tragedy.

The anomalous psychological phenomenon depicts theatergoers as craving to have experiences of suffering. It does not require allegiance to Walton's theory to point out that this phenomenon is not really so bizarre. Not to weep as Butterfly dies would be a symptom of a psychological abnormality. And, as Lorenz Hart observed, sometimes in affairs of the heart it is "a pleasure to be sad."[19] Aside from this observation, however, Walton's theory implies that the suffering that Augustine experiences is simply not ordinary grief.

The difference in causal ancestry between an emotion and a quasi emotion helps to explain the diminished response phenomenon. The nonintervention of theatergoers watching the murder of Banquo in *Macbeth* is not like the inaction of witnesses to the murder of Kitty Genovese in New York in 1964. No moral stigma hangs over the heads of theatergoers; no special sociological theory is needed to explain their group behavior. Unlike the witnesses, the theatergoers know that no actual violence is taking place. Instead, they are spectators whose imaginations are absorbed in the appreciation of a well-crafted tale of fictional violence.

Finally, Walton's theory allows us to pay respects to nonexistent characters without supposing that they exert some sort of causal influence over us. To maintain that Augustine experienced ordinary grief over the death of Dido while simultaneously believing that she never existed either confers too much power on Dido or imputes too little rationality to Augustine. But there need be nothing odd or untoward about his investing quasi grief over Dido's fate, for her fate is a "kind of thing that might happen": had it happened, Dido's plight would have been the occasion for ordinary grief.

I propose to set aside critical examination of Walton's theory,[20] choosing instead to see to what extent it might be compatible with Augustine's

---

[17] I am assuming without justification that in Carthaginian theaters, feminine roles were played by women, and that thespians took curtain calls.

[18] Seeing a tragedy might, per accidens, trigger grief, not for the fictional character portrayed on stage, but for a lost loved one.

[19] Richard Rodgers and Lorenz Hart, "Glad to Be Unhappy." See also Plato, *Philebus* 47e–48a.

[20] If quasi emotions are just whatever fills the functional role of simulating ordinary emotions while satisfying the diminished response phenomenon, then it is not clear that we cannot account for them by appealing to items in our standard psychological storehouse. These include standing

philosophical psychology. I shall sketch one aspect of Augustine's psychological theory, namely, his remarks on imagination. I shall draw selectively on *De Trinitate* 11 and *De Genesi ad litteram* 12, works written later than the *Confessions*, but which amplify positions that Augustine held earlier. These two sources present Augustine's account of perception of material objects, an account that is closely bound up with imagination. Having this account before us will help in diagnosing Augustine's perplexity about his dreams.

Augustine on Imagination

At the end of Book 10 of *De Trinitate*[21] [hereinafter cited as *Trin.*] Augustine sets the stage by giving pride of place to three mental powers in humans, memory, understanding, and will, claiming for them that their structure and function imperfectly image God's triune nature. He does *not* claim that these three powers, as central and impressive as they may be, collectively exhaust the structure of the human mind. To put it in a way that he might not fully approve, the human mind is both immeasurably weaker yet more complicated than the divine mind. Weaker, because its memory is incomplete, its understanding imperfect, and its will easily corrupted. More complicated, because humans, unlike God, are embodied creatures in need of some bodily apparatus that allows them to experience the material world. The apparatus includes the organs of sense that allow for touch, taste, smell, hearing, and vision. The sense modalities provide the anchor for Augustine's account of imagination. Augustine concentrates his remarks on vision, claiming that the account he gives of it will apply, *mutatis mutandis*, to the other senses (*Trin.* 11.1).

Visual perception involves three elements, the specific thing seen, the specific instance of seeing it, and the will either to (continue to) see the thing or to avoid seeing it. The instance of seeing the thing is "the form of the body impressed on this sense" (*Trin.* 11.2). This account begins as a causal theory of perception might begin. But it is a causal theory with two twists. First, Augustine insists that the bodily form is numerically distinct from the form that is impressed on the sense—call this the "sensual image"—just as

---

emotions, moods, and occurrent emotions directed at a situation other than the situation that triggers the emotion (e.g., reading Augustine's account of his friend's death might occasion our grieving for one of our friends). It should also be noted that sometimes ordinary fear elicits diminished response; one is "frozen with fear." I hope to discuss these issues elsewhere.

[21] Secs. 17–19.

the form of a signet ring is distinct from the form that it impresses on wax (*Trin.* 11.3). It is not simply that one person's instance of seeing a triangle is distinct from another person's. It is also that the imagistic contents of the two acts of seeing are distinct from each other and from the bodily form of the figure that is seen. These images are, as it were, visual tropes. Augustine offers empirical evidence for this numerical diversity, citing the phenomena of afterimages and double images arising from letting one's eyes go out of focus (*Trin.* 11.4). He has good reason to regard his energies as well-invested in this issue, but in order to make good on that claim we have to look at what he says more explicitly in *De Genesi ad litteram* [hereinafter cited as *Gen. litt.*].

In *Gen. litt.* 12.6.15–12.7.16 Augustine distinguishes among three kinds of vision. There is vision through the eyes (bodily vision), through the spirit (spiritual vision), and by a grasping of the mind (intellectual vision). He takes pains in particular to offer an explanation of spiritual vision, conceding that his use of the term, "spiritus," is special:

> **Spiritus** "A power of the soul, inferior to the mind, where the likenesses of bodily things are expressed."[22]

The definition is carefully crafted. It stipulates that spirit is an immaterial power, a "power of the soul," whose function is to broker transactions between the soul and the material world. Augustine calls this power "inferior to the mind": it records sensual images but is powerless to understand or interpret them; that is a function belonging to the mind.[23] Finally, although Augustine uses the verb *imprimere* in *Trin.* 11.2 to characterize the relation that holds between the thing seen and its image in the spirit, he chooses *exprimere* in the *Gen. litt.* 12.9.20 definition. The sequel of *Gen. litt.* 12 demonstrates that the choice is apt.

Gen. litt. 12.16.32 makes explicit a position rooted in works written earlier than the *Confessions*:[24]

> **Superiority** Every spirit is (without doubt) superior to every body.[25]

---

[22] *Vis animae quaedam mente inferior, ubi corporalium rerum similitudines exprimuntur* (*Gen. litt.* 12.9.20).

[23] The spiritual images interpreted by the mind need not be one's own. Augustine points out that Joseph was able to interpret the Pharaoh's dream images for him.

[24] See *De immortalitate animae* 16.25 and *De musica* 6.5.9–15.

[25] *Spiritus omnis omni est corpora sine dubitatione praestantior*. See also *Gen. litt.* 12.24.50–51.

Fast on the heels of **Superiority** Augustine adds a principle about productive causation:

> **Production** That which produces is superior in every way to the thing from which it produces something.[26]

Notice now that if the bodily form produces the sensual image, then by **Production** the bodily form—and hence the body of which it is the form—is superior to the thing from which it produces the image, that is, the spirit. But this consequence contradicts **Superiority**. So Augustine cannot consistently allow that sensual images are caused by material bodies.

How then does the sensual image come to be? Augustine's answer is clear: "[T]he body does not produce the same image in the spirit, but the spirit itself produces it within itself."[27] This is the second twist to Augustine's causal theory: the spirit, not the bodily form, is the cause of its sensual images. This second twist helps to explain the first one, for if the spirit fabricates its own images, it cannot be maintained that those images are numerically identical to the corresponding bodily forms. Moreover, if this account is Augustine's considered opinion, it justifies the shift from *imprimere* in *Trin.* 11 to *exprimere* in *Gen. litt.* 12. The use of *imprimere* in tandem with the simile of a signet ring's impression on wax encourages one to believe that the bodily form is the agent and the spirit the patient. That temptation is somewhat diminished by the **Spiritus** description of bodily likenesses being *expressed* in the soul. That this account is his considered opinion is confirmed later, at *Gen. litt.* 12.24.51: "For the body does not perceive, but the soul through the body, which is, if you please, a messenger, used [by the soul] to form in its own self that which is announced from the outside."[28]

Let us call Augustine's *spiritus* imagination. His description of the power, articulated in subsequent sections of *Gen. litt.* 12, reveals that even if imagination is inferior to the mind, it has a lot of work to do in the life of the soul. As we have seen, it functions to create images of bodily things, images that are then stored in memory. When we recall some material object or situation, the active recollection takes place in the imagination, with memory supplying it with the appropriate images.[29] Imagination enables us to think about things already known by

---

[26] *Omni enim modo praestantior est qui facit ea re, de qua aliquid* (*Gen. litt.* 12.16.33).

[27] *Eandem eius imaginem non corpus in spiritu, sed ipse spiritus in se ipso facit* (*Gen. litt.* 12.16.33).

[28] *Neque enim corpus sentit, sed anima per corpus, quo velut nuntio utitur ad formandum in se ipsa, quod extrinsecus nuntiatur.*

[29] *Trin.* 11.6 and 11.11 claim explicitly that the image represented in imagination is not numerically identical to the image stored in memory; the latter can stay in existence when the former ceases to exist by agent inattention.

acquaintance but presently absent, about things known to exist but with which the knower is not acquainted,[30] and about nonexistent things or things not known to exist. Augustine acknowledges that it is also the host of "various forms of the likenesses of bodies, from wherever they come, turned over in the soul, neither of our own doing nor with our will."[31] Finally, it is the function of imagination to order our thoughts *before* we perform some sequential bodily action and to monitor the sequence *as* we act.[32] We might add that it is also supplies the stuff of which dreams are made.

Augustine Asleep

In *Confessions* 10.30.41–10.36.59 Augustine describes the ways in which the physical senses have tempted him to pleasure, beginning with touch. Here the temptation is sexual, a temptation he has now managed to suppress in his waking life.

> But in my memory of which I have spoken at length, there still live images of acts which were fixed there by my sexual habit. These images attack me. While I am awake they have no force, but in sleep they not only arouse pleasure but even elicit consent, and are very much like the actual act. The illusory image within the soul has such force upon my flesh that false dreams have an effect on me when asleep, which reality could not have when I am awake. {How could it be that then I am not myself, Lord my God?} Yet how great a difference between myself at the time when I am asleep and myself when I return to the waking state. Where then is reason which, when wide-awake, resists such suggestive thoughts, and would remain unmoved if the actual reality were to be presented to it? Surely reason does not shut down as the eyes close. It can hardly fall asleep with the bodily senses. For if that were so, how could it come about that often in sleep we resist and, mindful of our avowed commitment and adhering to it with strict charity, we give no assent to such seductions? Yet there is a difference so great that, when it happens otherwise than we should wish, when we wake up we return

---

[30] Augustine supplies the example of Alexandria, which he never visited.

[31] *Unde unde neque id agentibus neque volentibus nobis variae formae corporalium similitudinum versantur in animo* (*Gen. litt.* 12.23.49).

[32] *Gen. litt.* 12.23.49. Augustine cites the example of speech: every syllable must be marshaled by imagination to ensure that it occurs at the proper time. Cf. *Confessions* 11.27.35.

to peace in our conscience. From the wide gulf between the occurrence and our will, we discover that we did not actively do what, to our regret, has somehow been done in us.[33]

We discover that we did not actively do what, to our regret, has somehow been done in us. Genital arousal is something against which he can offer successful resistance when awake and, given his vows of celibacy, something he takes himself to be required to resist. But his dreams resulting in nocturnal emissions are episodes he cannot avoid; hence, episodes for which he would like to disown responsibility. Although he treats the case as an isolated skirmish in a larger campaign against the temptations of the senses, it is far from clear that he is entitled to dismiss it so quickly. (Indeed, as we shall see, he returns to the case years later.) There are several considerations, some of which are central to Augustine's views, that tell against summary dismissal.

Does the problem extend further than Augustine realizes? Would it make a difference whether Augustine's dream partner is a real person known from his waking life? Or whether the dream is incestuous in nature? That is, are some dreams worse, morally speaking, than others? If the answer is Yes, then it seems hard to resist the consequence that the issue Augustine raises extends well beyond tactile sensations. Suppose that I dream of sideswiping another motorist into a bridge abutment because he cut me off in traffic. Should I, when I waken, discover, to my relief, that I did not actively do what has somehow been done in me?

The natural answer at this point hinges on two theses. One thesis, call it the **No Action Thesis**, is that nothing actually happens while one dreams. Dreamers do not *do* anything although, of course, they dream of doing all sorts of things. The other thesis, the **Character/Action Thesis**, maintains that there is an important distinction between judgments about one's actions and judgments about one's character. The theses can be deployed in the following way. "When Augustine dreamed of sexual dalliance or I dreamed of vehicular mayhem, neither of us actually committed what we dreamed of committing. Invoking a distinction emphasized recently by Ernest Sosa, we can say that people sometimes

---

[33] *Confessions* 10.30.41, in Chadwick, 203. The sentence in curly brackets replaces the corresponding sentence in Chadwick's translation; the Latin text is *Numquid tunc ego non sum, domine deus meus?* The ramifications of this passage have been discussed in Gareth B. Matthews, "On Being Immoral in a Dream," *Philosophy* 56 (1981): 47–54; William E. Mann, "Dreams of Immorality," *Philosophy* 58 (1983): 378–385; Ishtiyaque Haji, "On Being Morally Responsible in a Dream," in *The Augustinian Tradition*, ed. Gareth B. Matthews (Berkeley: University of California Press, 1999), 166–182; and Jesse Couenhoven, "Dreams of Responsibility," in Philip Cary, John Doody, and Kim Paffenroth, eds., *Augustine and Philosophy* (Lanham, MD: Lexington Books, 2010), 103–123.

commit wrongdoings *in their dreams* but not *while they are dreaming*.[34] It should be acknowledged, however, that dreams can occasion feelings of regret or even guilt, not because the agent has wronged anyone, but because the dreams themselves disclose attitudes and tendencies that are alien to the self-image held by the conscious agent. Dreams can thus be a symptom that the agent's true character is not what the agent would ideally like it to be."

There is something right about both theses invoked in the previous paragraph, but it is not clear that what is right about them is sufficient to dispel the concern raised by Augustine. The No Action Thesis is correct insofar as dreams exhibit the diminished response phenomenon, that is, the motor system does not respond, typically, to dream imagery. But Augustine's dream is not typical in this respect. His dream imagery interacts with his genital arousal. He of all people cannot impute the dream imagery to bodily arousal, for that would violate the most signature consequence of the **Superiority** and **Production** principles. But, on the assumption that moral responsibility can be ascribed to dreams, if his imagination is the instigator of his erotic images, it is hard not to hold his imagination morally responsible. We will investigate the issue of moral responsibility shortly. Before we do that, however, we should ask whether the No Action Thesis extends to mental activity. Do dreamers have occurrent beliefs, desires, emotions, and intentions while they dream? Or do they simply dream of having these states? Phenomenology tells in favor of the first view. In favor of something approaching the second view is the diminished response phenomenon. It may be tempting to concede something to both views by ascribing quasi states to dreamers.[35]

The following, at least, seems uncontroversial, and is enough to introduce an examination of the Character/Action Thesis. Let us say that dreams present the dreamer with *scenarios*. These scenarios are fabrications of the imagination, a mental faculty that can operate whether the agent is conscious or unconscious, and whether reason is online or offline. In some of these scenarios the dreamer is, phenomenologically speaking, a passive observer; in others, an

---

[34] See Ernest Sosa, "Dreams and Philosophy," in his *A Virtue Epistemology: Apt Belief and Reflective Knowledge*, vol. 1 (Oxford: Clarendon Press, 2007), 4. Sosa mobilizes this distinction as part of a project of combating skepticism, a position encouraged, he believes, by one's having the wrong view about dreams.

[35] Acceptance of the concession might be conditional on getting clear on the status of quasi belief. McGinn, for example, claims that in dreaming, "I have *quasi*-fear, *quasi*-belief, et cetera," as a result of "fictional immersion" in dreams, a notion that is "familiar to us in more diluted forms, as in our response to fictional works of different types—theatrical productions, films, novels, and so on." See *Mindsight*, 103; italics in original. Sosa claims that his view on dreams is "virtually the opposite" of McGinn's, and characterizes his view in this way: "When we watch a movie, however, we undergo phenomenal experiences without being at fault for failing to take them at face value. We use them

active participant. The scenarios occasion in the dreamer various sorts of mental states that either are or mimic doxastic, emotional, and volitional states. Of immediate interest are the dreamer's "volitional" states, states that seem like acts of willing but that do not engage the motor system. Do they provide enough of a peg on which to hang judgments of moral appraisal, and not just psychopathological assessment? Can a dreamer do something *wrong while* dreaming, and not just something disgusting, degrading, or shameful *in* a dream? The Character/Action Thesis does not pronounce one way or the other here, for it does not by itself tell us what counts as a case of wrongdoing.

More work for quasi attitudes? The etiology of sin as described in Augustine's commentary on the Sermon on the Mount is pertinent to dreaming and seems to have been on his mind when he described his erotic dream (*images . . . not only arouse pleasure but even elicit consent*). To sin is to consent to a pleasurable suggestion that one do something forbidden.[36] Suggestions, according to Augustine, arise ultimately from the bodily senses, either directly, in contemporaneous sensual experience, or indirectly, from images of previous experiences stored in memory and supplied to imagination. Are dream suggestions quasi suggestions? At a minimum, suggestions involve imagery. If suggestions are simply images, bidden or unbidden, and nothing more, then it is hard to see what the notion of a quasi suggestion could amount to. Suggestions as bare images would seem to be pre-attitudinal. But perhaps Augustine's suggestions are more complex. Perhaps they are, as befits their name, *suggestive*, presenting to the person who entertains them an invitation to suppose something. In that case the imagery would come, so to speak, in an irrealis mood, something of the form "Suppose this were to happen."[37] It is unclear in this case what the difference between an ordinary suggestion and a quasi suggestion could be. If there is psychological space for quasi suggestions, let us leave the task of charting the space to the friends of quasi attitudes.

Is dream pleasure quasi pleasure? Augustine's description seems to suppose that dream pleasure is ordinary pleasure, but, as we have seen, the friends of

rather in an exercise of 'make-believe'. . . . What is important for epistemology . . . is that in dreaming we do not really believe; we only make-believe." See "Dreams and Philosophy," 8. I conjecture that with regard to quasi beliefs, McGinn regards them as a species of belief while Sosa does not, lest they give skepticism too much of a purchase.

[36] *De sermone Domini in monte* 1.12.34 [hereinafter cited as *Serm. Dom.*]. For details, see my "Inner-Life Ethics," in *The Augustinian Tradition*, ed. Gareth B. Matthews (Berkeley: University of California Press, 1999), 149–150. Reprinted as Chapter 6 in this volume.

[37] "Irrealis" is not a typographical error. It is "a general term applying to verb moods associated with unreality (i.e., where the proposition expressed is, or may well be, false)." Rodney Huddleston and Geoffrey K. Pullum, eds., *The Cambridge Grammar of the English Language* (Cambridge: Cambridge University Press, 2002), 88.

quasi attitudes will urge that descriptions need not be taken at face value. (Do audiences take ordinary pleasure or quasi pleasure upon seeing Doctor Bartolo's schemes thwarted in Rossini's *The Barber of Seville*? A case can be made for quasi pleasure here.)

Finally, what of dream consent? Augustine provides a subjunctive analysis of consent: to consent to a pleasurable suggestion is (1) not to repress the associated desire, but (2) to satisfy it were the opportunity to arise (*Serm. Dom.* 1.12.33). Expressed in this way, consent implicates intentional behavior, but exactly how needs to be clarified. The context in which Augustine offers this analysis makes it clear that he places special emphasis on clause (2). It is consent that entails an *intention to act* that is already sinful, even when and in spite of the possibility that events never provide an opportunity so to act. But if we shift our attention instead to clause (1), we find a second kind of morally compromised consent, call it "fantasy consent," the intentional elaboration on, rather than suppression of, a pleasurable suggestion to do something (the agent believes to be) sinful. Clause (1) can come apart from clause (2). A person can indulge in fantasy consent without ever taking steps to act on it: if opportunity were to arise, the person might refuse to act on it.

It is tempting to think that the distinction between action consent and fantasy consent is just what is wanted to make an ordinary consent–quasi consent distinction; and then maintain that dreamers give only quasi consent to their dream suggestions. It is helpful here to examine the action consent–fantasy consent distinction in light of the features we encountered with quasi emotions. If, as the friends of quasi attitudes maintain, quasi emotions are genuine emotions but not ordinary emotions, then quasi consent should be genuine consent but not ordinary consent. Second, if quasi emotions can be as intense as ordinary emotions, then, on the assumption that ordinary consent can admit of degrees of intensity, the same should be possible for quasi consent. Finally, since quasi emotions exhibit the diminished response phenomenon, we should expect the same of acts of quasi consent.

It is clear that fantasy consent exhibits the diminished response phenomenon. We would like to know whether fantasy consent is like quasi consent in being a kind of consent distinct from ordinary consent. Paradigm cases of fantasy consent occur in agent-centered daydreams, in which the daydreamer more or less consciously shapes the narrative content of his fantasy. Insofar as he has conscious control over the fantasy, its elements may involve descriptions of intentional action that he, the daydreamer, undertakes in the fantasy.[38] It may

---

[38] It is the element of conscious control that distinguishes fantasies from delusions and hallucinations.

be true, nonetheless, that were the elements of the fantasy actually to materialize, the daydreamer would reject doing what he consented to doing, and that he knows this while he is fantasizing. Such a fantasy seems thus to contain episodes of quasi consent. Were those episodes cases of ordinary consent, the "fantasy" would not be a fantasy. It would be a plan for a course of action, no matter how unlikely its success. In contrast, the daydreamer's construction of his fantasy is a more or less intentional exercise. His consciously imagining himself doing what he knows he would not do is thus a combination of intentional action (the construction of an imaginary scenario) and quasi intentional activity (the acts of quasi consent the daydreamer gives in the fantasy).

Notice that daydreams can be *more or less* voluntarily constructed. Some that are initially endorsed can become transformed into something obsessive, morbid, or delusional. The daydreamer's rehearsing them may thus be a matter of reluctant or even unwilling consent. The language used in the previous two sentences suggests that fantasy consent is a degreed phenomenon. If the language is taken at face value, it gives license to the notion that acts of consent could be arrayed on a continuum of intensity between 0 and 1, with 0 representing, say, unwilling consent (the sort of consent one might give to an armed mugger demanding one's money) and 1 denoting utterly ecstatic endorsement. But the language need not be taken at face value. A case can be made for the view that consent is binary: either one consents to something or one does not; the rest is separable emotional entanglement. Since for Augustine consent is so closely bound to intention, the question arises whether intentions in turn are binary, like an on-off switch, or degreed, like a switch with a rheostat.[39] We need not take a stand here, for both accounts agree on what is important for our present purposes, namely, that acts of consent (and intentions) can display variability in intensity. The accounts disagree about how to explain the variability; how to answer the question about what can get intensified. I suggest a provisional, one-size-fits-all answer in terms of degrees of *willingness*, with the notion of willingness to be understood as remaining neutral between binary and degreed accounts of consent. If John consents enthusiastically and Mary consents halfheartedly, their acts of consent, whether binary or degreed, exhibit different degrees of willingness.

Such is the case to be made for the claim that fantasy consent is (a kind of) quasi consent. We began this excursion by considering the role of quasi consent as it might play out in daydreams. We should exercise some caution in assuming

---

[39] A similar and perhaps connected issue is whether belief is binary or degreed. See, e.g., David Christensen, *Putting Logic in Its Place: Formal Constraints on Rational Belief* (Oxford: Clarendon Press, 2004).

that the lessons learned from daydreams apply, *mutatis mutandis*, to dreams. It seems as though they should. As McGinn puts it,

> It would be odd if the faculties recruited in dreaming were not already exploited during waking life—as if the relevant faculties only spring into operation when the rest of the mind has shut down. Isn't it more natural to suppose that daydreaming and night-dreaming share their psychological architecture (or building blocks)?[40]

But McGinn also calls attention to a significant difference between the two: "One obvious way in which dreams differ from mere reveries is the connection to emotion: we can be afraid in a dream in a way we never are when merely daydreaming."[41] There are two other differences that are especially relevant to Augustine's concern over his oneiric states. Daydreams are (for the most part) under our voluntary control, whereas dreams are not. We are the impresarios of our daydreams, initiating, directing, altering, and terminating them to suit our whims. Things are different with dreams; to be convinced of this one need only think of nightmares. (The difference in voluntary control helps to explain why we can be afraid in dreams but not in daydreams.) Finally, reason is engaged—or at least not disengaged—in the narrative structure of daydreams. Reason can allow imagination to run wild but subject to the consideration that a daydream is not a collage of disconnected images. Reason's presence in dream sequences can be a good deal more feckless.

The previous discussion suggests three strategies, any one of which Augustine might call upon to free his dream from a charge of sinfulness. It appears that none of them is obviously successful, especially, in two out of three cases, by Augustine's own lights. I shall go on to consider a fourth way out, rejected by Augustine himself.

Does quasi consent help? In a word, no; in two more guarded words, not obviously. To consent to do something forbidden is already to have done something forbidden, according to Augustine. He concedes, moreover, that his erotic dream images elicited consent. Even if dream consent is not ordinary consent but rather quasi consent, it is still a kind of consent. In order to defend Augustine against a charge of wrongdoing we would need an explanation that exempts quasi consent from moral appraisal. Perhaps one can be constructed. The construction would have to overcome the following case in favor of ordinary consent. In ordinary dreams dreamers are unaware that what they are experiencing

---

[40] *Mindsight*, 75.
[41] *Mindsight*, 97–98.

is not really happening. They are thus relevantly like the bystanders witnessing a hoax murder. There is no doubt that the bystanders' intentions—to flee, to dial 911, and so on—are ordinary, despite the unreality of what they are witnessing. By parity of reasoning, then, dreamers who actively participate in their dreams do form ordinary intentions. The intentions are (almost always) transitory, evaporating upon awakening, but transitoriness is not unique to quasi consent. Ordinary intentions can also be unstable, subject to change or abandonment as one acquires more knowledge or uncovers a lack of perseverance. Augustine acknowledges as much when he says that *the illusory image within the soul has such force upon my flesh that false dreams have an effect on me when asleep, which reality could not have when I am awake.* "I would not do it when awake" simply does not entail "I did not intend it while asleep." The materials for the entailment are not to be found in Augustine.[42]

The involuntariness of dreams. Augustine can avoid the theater, but he cannot do without sleep, and with sleep comes loss of control. Although indisputably true, this observation is not one to which Augustine can help himself easily. The reason why is rooted in the same book of the *Confessions* that contains the sinful dream passage. Four times in Book 10 Augustine implores of God, "Grant what you command and command what you will" (*Da quod iubes et iube quod vis*). This one sentence seems to have precipitated the Pelagian controversy over the necessity of divine grace for personal salvation. Without going into the ramifications (and calcifications) of the controversy that lay ahead, I offer the following observations about Augustine's thrice-repeated plea. Pelagius saw in it an assertion of our helplessness, an assertion that was at odds with biblical injunctions to perfect ourselves. Modern readers may see here a prefiguration of the Kantian dictum that "ought" implies "can": that in order for a person to be held morally accountable for doing something, it must have been within the person's power to avoid doing that thing. I suggest that Augustine's plea for divine help is aimed only indirectly on what he now *does*. It focuses more directly on the deficiencies of the person he has *become* by his own previous choices. Those choices have built up sinful habits and tendencies he would like to extinguish but over which he has had only partial success. What he now does or is sorely tempted to do is symptomatic of the presence and power of these habits and tendencies.

Augustine could scarcely be clearer about this than in the case of dreams. The first two invocations of "Grant what you command . . . " occur in *Confessions* 10.29.40, framing a plea for continence. The second of those two invocations is

---

[42] One could deny that quasi consent is a kind of consent, thus breaking the analogy to quasi attitudes and attitudes. Even so, there would remain the further task of showing that whatever quasi consent is, it is insulated from moral appraisal.

followed two sentences later by the first sentence of the sinful dream passage: *But in my memory of which I have spoken at length, there still live images of acts which were fixed there by my sexual habit [consuetudo].* The third occurrence of "Grant what you command . . . " appears in *Confessions* 10.31.45, in Augustine's report of his struggle with gluttony. In summation he says that "I struggle every day against uncontrolled desire in eating and drinking. It is not something I could give up once and for all and decide never to touch it again, as I was able to do with sexual intercourse."[43] The final occurrence is embedded in Augustine's discussion of his prideful craving for praise (*Confessions* 10.37.60). In all these cases Augustine implores God to help him in his campaign to extirpate the vices and temptations that Augustine built up earlier in life by his unbridled sexuality, gourmandizing, and ambition. He realizes that the fact that he cannot presently avoid having these weaknesses and, in some cases, acting on them, does not insulate him from a charge of wrongdoing. Any plausible defense of the Kantian dictum must trim its sails to this tack, lest the alcoholic be allowed to argue successfully that he cannot be held responsible for the accident since he was in no condition to avoid it.

The role of reason in dreams. According to Plato,

> When the rest of the soul—the rational, gentle, and ruling part—slumbers . . . then the beastly and savage part, full of food and drink, casts off sleep and seeks a way to gratify itself. You know that there is nothing it won't dare to do at such a time, free of all control by shame or reason. It doesn't shrink from trying to have sex with a mother, as it supposes, or with anyone else at all, whether man, god, or beast. It will commit any foul murder, and there is no food it refuses to eat. In a word, it omits no act of folly or shamelessness.[44]

The passage does not make clear whether Plato thinks that reason is *always* offline when a person dreams. But it suggests a possible avenue of escape from responsibility for what happens in dreams. When reason slumbers, there can be no deliberation. Without deliberation there can be no choice, no consent, no intentions. If, as Augustine suggests, the moral appraisal of dreams depends on

---

[43] *Confessions* 10.31.47, in Chadwick, 207.

[44] Plato, *Republic* 571c–d, translated by G. M. A. Grube, revised by C. D. C. Reeve, in *Plato: Complete Works*, ed. John M. Cooper (Indianapolis, IN: Hackett Publishing Company, 1997), 1180. This passage is the only occasion on which Plato comes close to raising what Gareth B. Matthews has called the "moral dream problem." Plato introduces the quite different "epistemological dream problem"— how can we tell whether we are now wakefully experiencing things or asleep dreaming of them?—in *Theaetetus* 158b–c. See Matthews's *Augustine* (Malden, MA: Blackwell Publishing, 2005), 65–75.

the presence in them of these sorts of reason-dependent mental activities, then a dream in which reason is absent does not make it to the threshold of moral criticism, for much the same reason that the actions of a wild animal do not.

In reply, we can begin by noting that Augustine is aware of the phenomenon of lucid dreams, dreams in which dreamers are or become aware that they are dreaming. One might think that what makes a dream lucid is the online presence of reason. This thought does not receive unqualified support from Augustine. The lucid dream he discusses is one in which he is aware that he is dreaming, aware that his dream includes images representing one of his friends, yet tries, nonetheless, to persuade his friend that neither of them is actually there![45] If lucidity does require the presence of reason, it apparently does not require too much reason. While Plato's verdict about the territorial claims in the case of Reason v. Dreaming remains elusive, Augustine is willing to allow reason a fairly robust role: *Surely reason does not shut down as the eyes close. It can hardly fall asleep with the bodily senses. For if that were so, how could it come about that often in sleep we resist and, mindful of our avowed commitment and adhering to it with strict charity, we give no assent to such seductions?* We are to infer, I suppose, that Augustine's erotic dreams occur only when reason slumbers, and that if reason were always present to his sleep such dreams would not occur. Later in life Augustine interpreted 1 Kings 3:5–15 as recording God's granting to Solomon wisdom powerful enough to stand guard even over Solomon's sleep.[46] Alas, Augustine has not been similarly empowered. May we infer, then, that on those occasions when reason is absent, Augustine's dreams of dalliance are free from a charge of wrongdoing? Apparently not, according to him. When reason is dormant, habits can take over. The value of habits is that they allow for the routinization of repetitive patterns of behavior, which leaves the cognitive faculties free for other tasks (or free to slumber). Even though habits can be hard to break, the behavior that results from them can still be subject to moral appraisal if they were formed voluntarily.[47]

The dream self and the waking self. Recall these two sentences embedded in the passage we have been examining: *How could it be that then I am not myself, Lord my God? Yet how great a difference between myself at the time when I am asleep and myself when I return to the waking state.* Augustine entertains the thought that, appearances to the contrary notwithstanding, the self in his participant dream is not the same self as the self dreaming that he is the participant. The reason he offers for doubting or denying the identity is that there is such a great difference

---

[45] *Gen. litt.* 12.2.3.

[46] *Gen. litt.* 12.15.31.

[47] For Augustine's awareness of the moral gravity of sinful habits, see *Serm. Dom.* 1.12.34–36.

in the will between the two selves. There is a more general issue at stake here concerning the identity of selves, not only in dreams but in other sorts of fictive exercises. On Augustine's behalf we might search for some relation between the self *having* the dream and the self *in* the (participant) dream that falls short of numerical identity. At the same time, in order to preserve the phenomenologically well-entrenched notion of a participant dream, we would like the relation to be more intimate than, say, the relation between spectator and actor. What Jon Elster suggests about daydreaming and fiction may be helpful when extended to dreaming:

> In addition to our immediate personal experience we often enjoy the vicarious experience provided by daydreaming, reading novels or writing them. In fanciful exaggeration we may say that the vicarious experience belongs to a parallel self, one that runs its course alongside the main self. In non-fanciful language, of course, the fictional self is embedded in the main self. When I am daydreaming, *I* am daydreaming. Yet the fanciful language can serve the function of pointing to the importance that satisfaction by proxy can take on.[48]

Elster's descriptive imagery offers cold comfort to Augustine. It would distress him to have his dream self described as "parallel" to his waking self when he would like to believe (if spatial imagery is apt) that it is orthogonal. And, to be sure, when I am dreaming, *I* am dreaming, but that tautology does not address the issue of the relation between the self that is dreaming and the self in the dream. It does not help to describe the fictional self as "embedded" in the main self without knowing more about what is entailed by embedment. Two alternatives suggest themselves. One is that the fictional self is created by the main self; nothing more (or less) than a concatenation of images that is entirely the product of the main self's imagination. The other is that the fictional self has a kind of existence independent from the main self, emerging on some occasions unbidden by the main self.

Let us hear the case against the second alternative. The *Confessions* bears witness to his intellectual struggle against Manichaeism, a dualistic religion which supposed that counterpoised to a good God is an equally powerful force of evil, and that the cosmos is an arena in which these two forces continually do battle. In *De duabus animabus*, a work that antedates the *Confessions*, Augustine attributes to Manichaeism the view that this dualism is evident in individual

---

[48] Jon Elster, introduction to *The Multiple Self*, ed. Jon Elster (Cambridge: Cambridge University Press, 1986), 17.

persons: each person has two selves, or souls, one good, one evil. It is not clear whether Augustine's depiction of Manichaeism on this issue is accurate. What is clear is his antipathy to such a view. A star example of that antipathy can be found in Augustine's description of the conflict of will that he experienced immediately prior to his conversion:

> "Let them perish from your presence" (Ps. 67:3) O God, as do "empty talkers and seducers" of the mind (Titus 1:10) who from the dividing of the will into two in the process of deliberation, deduce that there are two minds with two distinct natures, one good, the other bad. . . . {It was I who was willing, I who was unwilling; I was I.}[49]

Augustine's insistence that division of the will does not entail division of the self undercuts the reason he offers for thinking that he is not his dream self.[50] To describe the difference as a difference between selves is to invite a charge of Manichaeism.[51]

The first alternative suggested by Elster's notion of an embedded self is, to adopt Elster's language, a "vicarious" self or a "proxy." Ordinary proxies are real people, deputized or authorized by another real person to act as that person's agent. Dream proxies are not real people; they are not nearly as robust as their real, dreaming creators. They are utterly dependent on their host for their existence and their activity. If their actions can be imputed to anyone, it must be to their host. The notion of a vicarious person carries along with it the notion of vicarious liability, that is, the liability that a host may have for actions committed by the host's agent, summed up by the phrase, *qui facit per alium facit per se*, he who acts through another acts through himself. It appears that if Augustine is to avoid a charge of responsibility for his dream activities, then he must deny either that the actions (including quasi actions) of his dream proxy are imputable to him, or he must deny that the notion of vicarious liability applies to dreams.

I claimed in the previous paragraph that if the actions of a dream proxy are to be imputed to anyone, it must be to the dreamer. The claim stands in need of defense from two lines of attack, coming from opposite directions. One might maintain, on Augustine's behalf, that dreams—including his offending

---

[49] *Confessions* 8.10.22, in Chadwick, 148. The bracketed sentence replaces Chadwick's translation, reading the Latin text as *ego eram, qui volebam, ego, qui nolebam; ego ego eram.*

[50] And, as he observes, if there are as many selves as there are incompatible desires in a person, why stop at *two* selves? See *Confessions* 8.10.23–24.

[51] It would be fairer to Augustine's convictions (but less elegant English) to translate the Latin *me* in the critical sentence not as "my*self*" but simply as "me": "Yet how great a difference between me at the time when I am asleep and me when I return to the waking state."

dream—are like tics, things that just happen to people. I can think of no conclusive argument against the claim. At the same time, I do not find it persuasive. The claim would be more credible when applied to dreams that are chaotic and disconnected from the dreamer's character and experience. Inasmuch as Augustine regards his erotic dream as too closely connected to his character, I doubt that he would find the claim plausible.

The other line of attack takes its departure from a consideration of various kinds of agency—evil geniuses, angelic messengers, mad scientists, and the like—bent on informing or deceiving us by means of implanting dreams. Augustine has no case to make against the possibility of such oneiric interventions.[52] If they are possible they can certainly contain suggestions that engage the dreamer's imagination. But, apart from the fact that Augustine displays no inclination to think that his erotic dream is implanted by an external agency, a dream's having such an origin does not absolve the dreamer from responsibility for what goes on in the dream. It is up to the dreamer whether or not to take pleasure in and to consent to what the dreams suggest. If this were not so, if the interventions immobilized or compelled the dreamer's will, then the interventions would be more like brainwashing than dreaming. And, as we have seen, for Augustine sin resides in the will, not the imagination.

Prospects are dim, then, for Augustine successfully dissociating himself from his dream proxy. Can he dissociate himself from his proxy's actions? It is not sufficient simply to plead unconsciousness in an effort to defeat a charge of vicarious liability. Jones may have slept as soundly as a baby while his agent, Smith, carried out the crime ordered by him. Nor will it help the defense to claim that sleep is a chronic and unavoidable state to which Jones is prone. Nor will it help for Jones to claim truthfully that the order he gave Smith was given on impulse, as a result of Jones's irascibility, and that had he been awake at the time, he would have rescinded the order. Augustine's plight parallels Jones's. Augustine realizes that the actions of his dream proxy are the expression of his concupiscence, a character flaw he voluntarily acquired or nurtured. Like Jones, Augustine may regret what happened, but he cannot avoid liability for it.

To sum up, it is not obvious that Augustine is entitled to claim that when he wakes up he returns to peace in his conscience. His internalism forces him to regard consent to sin as already sinful. The assimilation of dream consent to quasi consent, even if otherwise unobjectionable, does not exempt quasi consent from moral appraisal. The absence of reason from some dreams only serves to highlight the influence of vicious habits. His anti-Pelagianism undermines an appeal to the involuntariness of dream episodes. His anti-Manichaeism

---

[52] See, e.g., *Gen. litt.* 12.21.44.

prevents him from dissociating himself from his dream self. Worse yet, just as plays have playwrights, dreams have *dreamwrights*. As we have seen, Augustine has no reason to believe that he is not the author of his dream. We have also seen that Augustine—at the latest, by the time he came to write *The City of God*—believed that playwrights were capable of corrupting their audiences by staging scenes of immoralities.[53] In participant dreams the audience, a principal actor, and the dreamwright are one and the same person. If the analogy of dreams to plays holds, then Augustine should worry that his dream fabrications are genuinely sinful in virtue of their corrupting effect on him.

Sinful dreams revisited. At least a decade later Augustine returned to the problem of erotic dreams, convinced, it would appear, that he had an argument to show that they are morally harmless:

> Now if the images of these corporeal things, which I have necessarily thought of in order to say what I have said, were to appear in sleep as vividly as do real bodies to those who are awake, there would follow that which in waking hours could not happen without sin. For who, at least when speaking of this matter and by the necessity of the subject saying something about carnal intercourse he has had, is able to refrain from thinking about the subject of which he is speaking? Moreover, when the image that arises in the thought of the speaker becomes so vivid in the dream of the sleeper that it is indistinguishable from actual intercourse, it immediately moves the flesh and the natural result follows. Yet this happens without sin, just as the matter is spoken of without sin by a man wide awake, who doubtless thinks about it in order to speak of it.[54]

Augustine supposes that a person who confesses to having sinned is not sinning yet again while confessing, even though the person is necessarily experiencing again the images which contributed to the sin. It is convenient to divide Augustine's analogy into three parts.

The Assumption maintains that thoughtful speaking is necessarily accompanied by mental imagery, the same sort of imagery that occurs in dreaming.

---

[53] This attitude toward some works of fiction is not confined to North African bishops. Responsible parents monitor their children's television watching and Internet activity. Many individuals and organizations, including the National Organization for Women, objected to the publication of Bret Easton Ellis's book *American Psycho* (1991) on grounds that it was an unrelenting depiction of sadistic violence against women.

[54] *Gen. litt.* 12.15.31, trans. John Hammond Taylor, in *St. Augustine: The Literal Meaning of Genesis* (vol. 2), vol. 42 of *Ancient Christian Writers*, ed. Johannes Quasten, Walter J. Burghardt, and Thomas Comerford Lawler (New York: Newman Press, 1982), 198–199.

The Claim maintains that there are contexts, such as confessing, testifying, and sermonizing, which make it permissible for a speaker to talk about the speaker's sexual activity.

The Inference allows that since the imagery that occurs in these conscious, verbal contexts is relevantly similar to the speaker's dream imagery, it follows that the speaker's dream was not sinful.

The Assumption is controversial; a full discussion of its merits would take us well beyond our present confines. For present purposes we can grant it to Augustine. The Claim is surely on more secure ground than The Assumption. But The Inference is defective in two ways. To be sure, there are contexts in which it is permissible for one to discuss one's sexual activity. But there are also contexts, ranging from gossiping through boasting to betrayal, in which the same verbal activity ranges from questionable to downright wrong. Augustine has not given us reason to think that dreaming erotic dreams is as innocuous as sermonizing about them. Moreover, if sinfulness is a function of consent, the absence of such consent in retelling does not imply that consent was absent in dreaming.

Summing Up

The paradox of tragedy is a paradox whose enjoyment can lead to expeditions into the thickets of ontology and philosophical psychology. These expeditions are not on Augustine's itinerary. Perhaps he regarded energies devoted to the resolution of this paradox as exercises in idle curiosity, a kind of sin related to vainglory.[55] He realizes, however, that he cannot so easily dismiss scrutiny of sinful dreams. He finds himself snared by the quarry; the irony is that the quarry is of his own making. I do not believe that he ever found a way of freeing himself.

[55] See *Confessions* 10.35.54–10.39.64.

5

Augustine on Evil and Original Sin

Before his conversion to Christianity, Augustine conceived of God as a supremely good being who is "incorruptible, inviolable, and immutable" (*Confessiones* 7.1.1 [hereafter *conf.*]). At the same time, he was aware of the existence of evil in the world, evil that can be divided into two major classes. First, physical objects have limitations and defects. In particular, the limitations of living things result in hardship, pain, illness, and death. Secondly, there are people who behave wickedly and whose souls are characterized by such vices as pride, envy, greed, and lust.

It would seem that a supremely good God would prevent or eradicate as much evil as he possibly could. The problem of evil, then, is to see whether and how it might be both that God exists and that evil exists. Before his conversion, Augustine grappled with this problem for a number of years and found some intellectual satisfaction in the solution offered by Manichaeism. Manichaeism taught that the world is an arena in which two opposing cosmic forces incessantly contend, one good, the other evil. If one concentrates on the attributes of incorruptibility, inviolability, and immutability, it does not seem impossible for there to be two beings having those attributes in common while occupying opposite ends of the moral spectrum. Manichaeism thus offered a straightforward solution for the problem of evil: God is doing the best he can against evil, but finds himself facing an independent opponent as formidable as he.

Although Manichaeism is dualistic, the dualism is confined within a thoroughgoing materialism. Goodness is identified with corporeal light; evil with physical darkness. The youthful Augustine found this feature of Manichaeism unobjectionable because he antecedently had had difficulty understanding how anything could exist without being corporeal (*conf.* 5.10.19, 7.1.1 2). It was, he says, as if God were a boundless ocean completely permeating the finite sponge of the created world (*conf.* 7.5.7). Taking the metaphor a step further, we can offer on behalf of the Manichaeans the observation that the same sponge is also awash with a supremely toxic fluid; indeed, that the two fluids together not only permeate but constitute the sponge.

With his conversion to Christianity Augustine came to think that a proper solution to the problem of evil must depart radically from the Manichaeans in its conceptions of God and evil. He came to see God as a spiritual, not a corporeal, being. Augustine thus rejects Manichaeism's materialistic dualism but embraces a different dualism between corporeal and spiritual beings, with God, angels, and human souls falling into the latter class.

God's incorporeal nature is not sufficient to dispel Manichaeism, for a persistent Manichaean might hold that there is still an ultimate, invincible source of evil, be it corporeal or incorporeal. This alternative is denied by Augustine's insistence that God is rightfully sovereign over all other beings. Even if the attributes of incorruptibility, inviolability, and immutability do not preclude their multiple instantiation in antagonistic forces, sovereignty does: no being can be supremely sovereign if there is another being over which it cannot prevail.

God's sovereignty over all other things is grounded in the fact that he created them. Two features of Augustine's account of creation are especially important to his resolution of the problem of evil: that God creates *ex nihilo,* out of nothing; and that everything that God creates is good. It is instructive to distinguish Augustine's claims about creation from Plato's influential account.

In the Platonic dialogue bearing his name, Timaeus argues that the demiurge or divine artisan creates because not to create would betoken a character fault—envy—that a perfect being cannot possess. But freedom from envy does not dictate what kind of universe the demiurge will create. Being supremely good, the demiurge cannot tolerate creating anything less than the best; he wants everything to be as much like himself as possible. So the demiurge imposes order on initially discordant matter, producing a universe that is as good as the nature of its matter allows.[1] There are three components of Plato's account to which Augustine does not give allegiance.

The first feature flows naturally from the artisan analogy that governs Timaeus's creation account; it also comports with Parmenidean strictures against non-being. Matter existed in some inchoate form before the process of creation, providing the raw material on which the demiurge worked. The demiurge's creative performance was thus constrained by the nature of the raw material at hand, about which the demiurge had no say. Augustine rejects this account of creation as fabrication because of its presupposition that matter is coeval with God. In creating the world, God brought into existence not only its material inhabitants but also the very material of which they are made.

---

[1] Plato, *Timaeus* 29e–30b.

1. For they [your works] have been made by you out of nothing, not out of you, not out of something that is not yours or that existed previously, but out of "concreated" matter, that is, matter created simultaneously by you, since you gave form to its formlessness without any interposition of time. For although the matter of heaven and earth is one thing and the form of heaven and earth another, you nevertheless made both of them simultaneously—the matter, indeed, entirely out of nothing, but the world's form out of unformed matter in such a way that form followed matter with no gap in time. (*conf.* 13.33.48)

2. Thus when I ask of you, from whence the whole of creation has been made, which, even though good of its kind, is nevertheless inferior to the creator so that the one is always immutable and the other mutable you will not speak falsely if you respond that you confess it to be made entirely from non being. (*Contra Secundinum Manicheum*, Sec. 8)

These passages enunciate the doctrine of creation *ex nihilo*. They also imply that God cannot create anything equal to himself. Because every created thing has its origin in non-being, it is mutable. But God is essentially immutable, and any immutable being is superior to any mutable being.

The second and third components of the Timaeus account of creation arise from these two questions. Why did the deity create anything? Why did the deity create this universe? Plato's answer to the first question is "An essentially flawless being cannot be envious" and to the second question, "A supremely good being cannot create anything less than the best." The two responses do not present equivalent doctrines. The first does not entail the second. The demiurge is free from the charge of envy so long as he creates something and is not subsequently envious of what he creates. If that standard of performance is all that is required, then a cynical demiurge might fill the bill by creating a crew of miserable creatures envied by no one. Plato's second response sets a much higher standard. Only the best will do for a supremely good being. Even so, the second response does not entail what the first entails, for the second response does not entail that the demiurge will create anything. The first response supplies that ingredient. The two responses together entail that the demiurge created this world and that this world is the best world the demiurge could have created.

Augustine endorses neither of these views. We can examine his doctrines by seeing what he has to say about God's will in creating and about the goodness of the created world. Concerning God's will, this text is important:

3. Thus if they were to say "What determined God to make heaven and earth?" one should respond to them that those who desire to become acquainted with God's will should first learn about the power of the human will. For they seek to know the causes of God's will when God's will itself is the cause of all

the things there are. For if God's will has a cause, it is something that takes precedence over (*antecedat*) God's will, which is sinful to believe. Therefore to one who says "Why did God make heaven and earth?" one should respond "Because he willed." For God's will is the cause of heaven and earth, and thus God's will is greater than heaven and earth. But one who says "Why did God will to make heaven and earth?" seeks something that is greater than God's will; but nothing greater can be found. (*De Genesi adversus Manichaeos* 1.2.4)

This passage relies on a causal principle—every cause is superior to its effects—that, together with the thesis that nothing is superior to God's will, precludes God's will from having any cause. For Augustine the explanatory buck stops here. To put it another way, Augustine finds nothing in God's nature that entails that God must create.

It is not evident that Augustine thinks that if God decides to create, then God must create the best world that he can. Creation is indeed very good (*De Genesi ad litteram imperfectus liber* 13.3 [hereafter *Gn. litt. imp.*], echoing Genesis 1:31), created out of the "fullness of [God's] goodness" (*conf.* 13.2.2, 15). Augustine adds that God will not create a thing unless he knows that it is good (*De civitate Dei* 11.2.1 [hereafter *civ. Dei*). At the same time, however, he offers the following observations. No created being had a claim against God to be created (*conf.* 13.2.2–3). If Augustine endorses the more general thesis that no being, actual or possible, had such a claim, then it follows that God would have wronged no actual being in omitting to create it and that God has wronged no potential but non-actual being in omitting to create it. God did not create out of any need, nor to perfect any deficiency in himself (*conf.* 13.4.5). God thus knowingly creates a good world, but Augustine's remarks do not entail the Timaeus thesis that this world is as "good a world as God could create." Perhaps naively, perhaps slyly, Augustine characterizes Plato's doctrine simply as the doctrine that the most accurate explanation for the world's creation is that good works are made by a good God (*civ. Dei* 11.2.1). Aquinas would later distinguish between a world's being composed of the best possible parts and a world's having the best possible order among its parts, even if the parts themselves are not the best. Aquinas argued that the created world must be as good as possible in terms of the order imposed on it by God, but that it need not be populated by the best possible components. I have not found Aquinas's distinction in Augustine's writings. If Augustine does regard the created world as best in either of Aquinas's senses, that regard is not a prominent part of his philosophy.

But Augustine does insist that every creature is good insofar as it exists (*De natura boni* 1 [hereafter *nat. b.*]). How, then, is there evil?

Augustine deploys his answer in two stages. First, although every creature is good, some creatures are better than others. That every creature is good

Augustine regards as a consequence of God's creative activity. Insofar as corporeal things exist at all, God has bestowed upon them some degree of measure, number (or form), and order (*De libero arbitrio* 2.20.54 [hereafter *lib. arb.*]; *nat. b.* 3). Organisms and artifacts possess these features to a high degree, but even the comparatively simpler materials out of which they are composed have some degree of measure, number, and order: if that were not so, these raw materials would be literally nonexistent (*lib. arb.* 2.20.54). So for Augustine the predicate "good" is not like the predicate "average." Even if all the children of Lake Wobegon are above average, it is mathematically impossible for everyone to be above average. Yet everything can be and is good in virtue of having measure, number, and order.

Some good things are better than others (*civ. Dei* 11.22). Augustine sometimes seems prepared to regiment all cases of x's being better than y into cases of x's having more measure, number, and order than y (*nat. b.* 3). But he leaves the project's details mostly blank. Thus, for example, he is eager to put forward the thesis that some things, even when corrupted, are still better than other things that remain uncorrupted. According to human estimation, at least, corrupted gold is better than uncorrupted silver, and corrupted silver is still better than uncorrupted lead (*nat. b.* 5). It may be that Augustine believes that human estimation is capricious in this matter. But there is nothing capricious, in his estimation, about the claims that a rational spirit corrupted by an evil will is still better than an uncorrupted irrational spirit, and that any spirit, no matter how corrupted, is better than any uncorrupted body (*nat. b.* 5). In support of the latter claim Augustine says that as a runaway horse is better than a stationary stone and a drunken sot is better than the excellent wine he imbibed, so the lowest, most depraved soul is better than light, the noblest of corporeal things (*lib. arb.* 3.5.12–16).

This is the imagery of a rhetorical master. More prosaic minds seek instruction about how to justify the claim behind the images. The trio of measure, number, and order suggests that betterness might track increased structural integrity or complexity. But since many of us find our paradigm examples of structural integrity and complexity in material objects, we will need guidance on how to apply the trio to sustain Augustine's comparative judgments between spiritual and material beings. The situation is especially puzzling because Augustine regards God, the supreme spiritual being, as supremely simple, having no metaphysical complexity whatsoever.

No creature, then, is evil, in spite of the fact that some creatures are worse than others (*nat. b.* 14). The word "evil," when predicated of creatures, refers to a privation, an absence of goodness where goodness might have been (*conf.* 3.7.12). If we are audacious enough to enquire why God allows such privations to occur, we are apt to be reminded of the following points. First, creatures have a natural tendency toward mutability and corruption, an unavoidable liability of their having been created *ex nihilo*. Secondly, we are subject to perspectival prejudices, failing to see how local privations, especially the ones that affect us, contribute to the good of the whole. The distinctive twist that Augustine puts on this now familiar point is that for him the assessment of the good of the whole is more diachronic than synchronic. One who laments the passing away of particular ephemeral things should realize that to wish that they might last forever is to wish that not they but some other kind of being existed. Moreover, their passing away ushers in new, good creatures. Finally, there is order and beauty to be found in this very dynamic passage, analogous to the way in which speech is made possible by the coming to be and passing away of phonemes, or music by the sequential production of notes (*lib. arb.* 3.9.24–25, 3.15.42–43). Thirdly, "God owes nothing to anyone" (*lib. arb.* 3.16.45). On the contrary, anything that exists owes its entire existence to God's grace.

But "evil" is sometimes predicated of the choices and actions of creatures possessing reason. The second stage of Augustine's treatment of the problem of evil begins here, presupposing, however, the results of the first stage.

4. As I have said, therefore, sin is not a desire for naturally evil things, but an abandonment of better things. And this itself is evil, not that nature which the sinner uses evilly. For evil is to use a good evilly. (*nat. b.* 36)

5. But perhaps you are going to ask since the will is moved when it turns away from an immutable good to a mutable good, from whence does this movement arise? It [the movement] is actually evil, even though a free will is to be counted among the good things, since without it no one can live rightly. For if that movement, that is, the will's turning away from the Lord God, is without doubt a sin, how can we say that God is the author of the sin? Thus that movement will not be from God. From whence then will it come? If I respond thus to your querying—that I do not know—perhaps you will be disappointed; but nevertheless I would respond truly. For that which is nothing cannot be known. (*lib. arb.* 2.20.54)

Sin is not a desire for naturally evil things, according to passage 4. Augustine's claim must be interpreted *de re*—there are no naturally evil things that could serve as objects of sinful desires—rather than de dicto. For *de dicto*, there might well be benighted souls who desire what they take to be naturally evil things, and such a desire would be sinful for Augustine. Passage 4 leaves unexplained what might constitute a case of abandonment of better things. Even if gold is intrinsically better than silver, my desiring a silver chalice over a gold one could hardly count as sinful. Augustine sometimes stipulates that the thing desired must be forbidden to the desirer by justice (*Gn. litt. imp.* 1.3). Since justice is derived from God's eternal law (*lib. arb.* 1.6.50), an object of a sinful desire is something in fact forbidden to the desirer by God's edicts. On some occasions Augustine takes pains to say that the sinfulness of the desire resides not in the desire itself but in one's consent to it (*De continentia* 2.3–5), where consent involves either forming an intention to act in accordance with the desire or, at a minimum, failing to suppress the desire.

As passage 5 indicates, Augustine is fond of describing sin as the will's turning away from God, a culpable rejection of the infinite bounty God offers in favor of an infinitely inferior fare. Passage 5 also conveys the message that what makes the rejection culpable is that it is freely chosen by the agent's will. Described as the free rejection of an infinite good, however, the sin is not just culpable. It is staggeringly irrational: from a cost-benefit viewpoint, the worst deal imaginable. Attracted by the Platonic thesis that all error is due to ignorance, one might then probe for some cognitive defect in the anatomy of every sin. On many occasions we might find a cognitive defect, but it is no part of Augustine's brief that we always will.

Retrieve the last sentiment expressed in passage 5, namely, that the cause of the will's movement away from God is unknowable non-being. Compare it with the remark in passage 3 that "those who desire to become acquainted with God's will should first learn about the power of the human will." We may extract the following parallels. Just as God's will in creating has no cause, so a human's will in sinning has no cause. This feature is one aspect of the power of the human will, but perhaps not the only one. If God can knowingly choose to create a world that is not the best world he might have created, in either of Aquinas's senses mentioned above, then one can argue analogously that humans can have a clear perception that one good is superior to another, yet freely choose the inferior good. In some cases, perhaps, such as choosing silver over gold, the choice may lie below the threshold of sinfulness. In other cases, however, involving the choice of what justice forbids, the threshold is knowingly and culpably passed. Another aspect of the power of the human will is to reject the verdict of reason.

One might wonder whether the latter "power" is more liability than asset. Augustine offers the following answer. Material objects, as a class, are good but can be put to evil use and are not necessary for living rightly. In contrast, some spiritual goods, namely, the virtues of justice, prudence, fortitude, and temperance, are necessary for living rightly and cannot be used wrongly. There is another class of goods, intermediate between material goods and the virtues, which are spiritual, necessary for living rightly, but capable of being used wrongly. In this class are the faculties of will, reason, and memory (*lib. arb.* 2.18.49–19.52). A genuinely free will necessarily carries with it the liability to sin. But without having freedom of choice, with its built-in liability, humans would lack the capacity to choose to live rightly.

There are two cases of sinful choice that dramatize for Augustine the sheer willfulness of sin: the devil's defection from the ranks of the angels; and Adam and Eve's choosing to eat the forbidden fruit in the Garden of Eden. The devil's case serves as a template to which the psychology of many human sins conforms. In answer to the question why the devil rejected the blessed life open to all angels, Augustine cites the motive of pride (*superbia*), which he defines as "the love of one's own excellence" (*De Genesi ad litteram* 11.14.18 [hereafter *Gn. Litt.*]) and a "desire for perverse elevation" (*lib. arb.* 14.13).

Pride is also the initial evil impulse behind the Fall of Adam and Eve (*Gn. litt.* 11.5.7; *civ. Dei* 14.13). The devil's tempting of Adam and Eve did not coerce their Fall, for if the temptation had been coercive, then their punishment would be unjust. Adam and Eve voluntarily succumbed to the temptation because of their prideful fascination with the thought that they would become like God. Augustine takes this similarity between the two cases to warrant the claim that sin entered the created world through pride. At the same time he is careful to insist that pride is not a component in all sins; as he points out, some sins are committed in ignorance or desperation (*De natura et gratia* 29.33).

Adam and Eve's Fall ushered into the world original sin, which is not an event but rather a condition (*De peccatorum meritus et remissione* 1.9.9–12.15 [hereafter *pecc. mer.*]). It is the condition imposed by God as punishment on Adam and Eve for disobedience. According to Augustine, the condition includes dispossession from a naturally perfect environment, the loss of natural immortality, and the acquisition of susceptibility to physical pain, fatigue, disease, aging, and rebellious bodily disorders, especially sexual lust (*Gn. litt.* 11.32.42; *civ. Dei* 14.16.19). The condition is not only pathological, it is inherited, infecting every descendant of Adam and Eve. The condition is innate, not acquired; as Augustine puts it, it is transmitted by propagation, not imitation (*pecc. mer.* 1.9.9–12.15). Augustine's view, then, is that our first ancestors squandered their patrimony and our inheritance and—as if that were not bad enough—thereby contracted a suite of infirmities that is passed on to all their progeny.

The infirmities are physical: Augustine appears not to think that the penalties of original sin include any intrinsic diminution of the soul's active abilities, such as the capacities to reason and to will. Although he nowhere considers the point, Augustine has reason to reject that possibility. One can argue that an alteration of the soul's native abilities would be tantamount to the creation of a new species. It is awful enough to be told that we are at present disadvantaged because of the misdeeds of our ancestors. It would be monstrous to be told that our kind was created as a punishment for misdeeds perpetrated by superior beings of a different species. Even so, the physical infirmities have made it harder for humans to exercise their souls' abilities correctly. According to Augustine, all sinful souls suffer from two penalties, ignorance and difficulty (*lib. arb.* 3.18.52). Ignorance, not inborn stupidity: humans now lack the kind of noetic intimacy with God enjoyed by Adam and Eve, an intimacy, however, insufficient to guarantee the maintenance of righteousness, in either Adam and Eve's or the devil's case. Difficulty, not impossibility: it is no part of Augustine's message that humans have been shattered by the Fall. A full reconnaissance of this terrain would have to include an excursion into Augustine's anti-Pelagianism. But, as Augustine makes clear in the *Retractationes* (1.9.6), he takes his anti-Pelagianism to be fully consistent with this analogy. Suppose that our blessedness consisted in eloquence, so that every grammatical gaffe were a sin. Even then no one would fault an infant for initial ignorance, for the infant has not yet either culpably neglected eloquence or culpably allowed it to be lost once acquired. Nor would we fault an adult who continues to find eloquence difficult. We would reserve censure for those who do not even make the effort and for those who, having achieved some proficiency, backslide into inarticulateness (*lib. arb.* 3.22.64).

6

Inner-Life Ethics

You have heard that it was said, "You shall not commit adultery." But I say to you that every one who looks at a woman lustfully has already committed adultery with her in his heart.

—Matthew 5:27–28, RSV

When Jimmy Carter acknowledged that he had on occasion lusted in his heart, his candor prompted public reactions closer to uncomprehending derision than to shock or sympathy.[*] Perhaps the scoffers did not catch the allusion to the Sermon on the Mount. Perhaps they thought that worrying about one's impure thoughts is symptomatic of a fretfully repressed, neurotic personality. One presumes that if the scoffers had turned their attention to Jesus's identification of lustfulness with adultery *accompli,* they would have regarded it most charitably as a robust specimen of hyperbole, useful, perhaps, for proselytizing purposes but quite literally false. Even as authoritative a source *as The New Jerome Biblical Commentary* offers this deflationary account of Jesus's pronouncement:

> Since adultery is a serious matter, a wrong of injustice as well as of unchastity, acts that lead to it can also be morally seriously wrong, e.g., alienation of affection. Jesus' words here are to be taken strictly in connection with adultery. They do not condemn any thinking about sexual matters such as would be involved in the study of medicine or simple velleities. [As for the passage] *has already committed adultery with her in his heart:* This teaches the truth of experience that when a person has seriously decided to commit a wrong the moral evil is already present, even though it can be increased by further action.[1]

[*] I thank David Christensen, Christopher Kirwan, Scott MacDonald, and Gareth B. Mathews for helpful comments on earlier versions of this essay. I also thank the University of Vermont for furthering this essay with a 1993 Summer Research Grant.

[1] Raymond E. Brown, Joseph A. Fitzmyer, and Roland E. Murphy, eds., *The New Jerome Biblical Commentary* (Englewood Cliffs, NJ: Prentice Hall, 1990), 642.

Consider some male, married ogler. The commentary extracts the following points from Matthew 5:27–28 as applicable to his case. (1) What makes his lustful looking wrong is that it is a symptom or an instantiation or an amplification of some other state, such as alienation of affection, that really is wrong. But (2) mere wishful thinking on his part is no more morally objectionable than the sort of clinical scrutiny that takes place in an anatomy course. (3) Should he decide to (try to) commit adultery, the decision is evil, but the evil exemplified by the decision is not identical to the wrongness that would be realized by the action. Finally, (4) should the wrongful action be attempted or actually committed, that would increase the evil of the decision.

The first thing to be said about points 1–4 is that their ordinariness makes it hard to see how Jesus could ever have impressed anyone as a great moral reformer. The second thing to be said is that, in spite of their ordinariness, each one of the four points is arguably false. If that is so, then the attribution of points 1–4 to Jesus does Christian ethics a double disservice. One authority for whom points 1–4 are false is St. Augustine. Augustine discerned a revolutionary moral outlook in the Gospels and sought to give philosophical articulation to that outlook. Although he wrote no systematic treatise in ethics, nothing that could compare in ambition to Aristotle's *Nicomachean Ethics* or in systematic unification to Kant's *Grundlegung* or Mill's *Utilitarianism,* he cast an enormous shadow over subsequent Christian ethical theorizing, both through and beyond the Middle Ages. What he bequeathed to his successors was not a tidy set of normative principles but rather a provocative framework of concepts and vivid examples from which distinctive normative judgments might issue. Augustine's posterity was thus left with some freedom to speculate about the ways in which the framework might be fleshed out; perhaps, with some caution, even about how the bones of the framework might be differently reconstructed. I will present one arrangement of them, hoping to forge connections between the components without giving the appearance of forging the connections. I will then examine three of Augustine's most distinctive discussions of moral cases, attempting to show how the cases fit into the Augustinian framework. Virtually all the important components of the framework can be found scattered throughout works written by the year 401. Although I shall have occasion to refer to later works, the fact remains that, had Augustine lived no longer than John F. Kennedy, his contribution to normative ethical theory would have been largely the same.

Theory

Body and Soul

Augustine has no doubt that soul and body are two categorically different things. Human bodies are three-dimensional objects composed of the four elements, whereas human souls have no spatial dimensions (*De quantitate animae* 1.2, 5.9). His opinion in *De quantitate animae* 13.22 is that the soul is "substantia quaedam rationis particeps, regendo corpori accommodata," a kind of substance, participating in reason, fit for ruling the body. Humans are composed of both body and soul (*De quantitate animae* 1.2; the opinion is sustained in *City of God* 13.24). Although he is clearly a dualist, Augustine is not preoccupied, as Plato and Descartes are, with explication of the metaphysics of the mind-body problem. Augustine thinks that it suffices for his purposes as Christian apologist and ethicist that soul and body are metaphysically distinct, that to be a human is to be a composite of soul and body, and that the soul is superior to the body.

The superiority of soul to body is grounded in Augustine's hierarchical classification of things into those that merely exist, those that exist and live, and those that exist, live, and have intelligence or reason (*De libero arbitrio* 2.3.7–6.13). Bodies by themselves merely exist. An animal is animate in virtue of possessing an anima, or soul, the kind of soul that confers on the animal the abilities to take on nourishment, to grow, to reproduce, and to perceive (*De libero arbitrio* 1.8.18). But animals do not possess reason (*De libero arbitrio* 1.7.16). In addition to having the same life functions as animals, humans possess reason. Augustine seems not to be content to rest the superiority of human reason over animal functioning simply on the claim that humans have what animals have plus something else (*De libero arbitrio* 2.3.7), for immediately after making the claim he offers a different argument for the superiority of reason. Perhaps he saw that his initial argument is less than persuasive. If x has properties P and Q while y has properties P, Q, and R, it does not follow either that y is superior to x or that the constellation of properties P, Q, and R is superior to the ensemble of P and Q. Augustine needs to find something intrinsic to reason that confers superiority on it over both mere existence and the functions of the soul that humans share with animals. It is true that reason enables humans to know that they are perceiving, to analyze perception into its proper and common sensibles (*De libero arbitrio* 2.3.8–9), to discern the existence of an "interior sense" (*De libero arbitrio* 2.3.8, 4.10),[2] and to distinguish (1) what is sensed, (2) the act of sensing, and (3) the capacity to sense (*De libero arbitrio* 2.3.9). But Augustine does not allow these discriminative abilities to clinch the case for the superiority of reason. For he must disallow the principle to which one would most likely appeal if one cited the ability to discriminate:

If x is cognizant or is capable of being cognizant of y, then x is superior to y.

---

[2] The interior sense is reminiscent of Aristotle's "sensus communis."

Human reason can become cognizant of wisdom, which we can construe as the eternal truths lodged in the divine mind, but human reason is not superior to wisdom. The principle to which Augustine in fact does appeal is different:

If x judges or is capable of judging y, then x is superior to y.[3]

Human reason is fit to judge whether corporeal objects, the bodily senses, and the interior sense are defective or functioning correctly and in virtue of that fact is superior to them (*De libero arbitrio* 2.6.13). At the same time, the judge of whether human reason itself is functioning properly is wisdom. To the extent to which human minds discover the immutable truths contained in wisdom, they function properly. Error and mental vacillation are the result of imperfect minds failing to grasp or retain wisdom (*De libero arbitrio* 2.12.34).

The relative judgmental superiority of the rational soul over physical objects and nonrational organic functions is partly an epistemological superiority, but one that is grounded in a thesis about the soul's metaphysical superiority over physical objects. If we weave together various doctrines from *De immortalitate animae* and *De quantitate animae*,[4] we can produce the following Augustinian fabric. Whatever is indivisible is superior to whatever is divisible (*De quantitate animae* 11.17); any parcel of matter, no matter how small, is divisible ad infinitum (*De immortalitate animae* 7.12); therefore, whatever is indivisible is superior to any parcel of matter. The soul is capable of comprehending incorporeal things (*De quantitate animae* 13.22); only incorporeal things are capable of comprehending incorporeal things (*De quantitate animae* 13.22–14.23); therefore, the soul is an incorporeal thing. Moreover, the soul's incorporeality gives it epistemological access to other incorporeal things. If we suppose further that Augustine would accept the thesis that every incorporeal thing is spatially indivisible, then it follows that the soul, qua spatially indivisible, is metaphysically superior to any body.[5]

At times Augustine depicts the relation between soul and body as one of instrument user to instrument used (*De quantitate animae* 23.41; *De moribus ecclesiae catholicae* 27.52; *De musica* 6.5.9), at other times as one of artisan to the material on which the artisan works (*De immortalitate animae* 16.25; *De musica* 6.5.8), at still other times as master to servant (*De moribus ecclesiae catholicae*

---

[3] See also *De musica* 6.4.6.

[4] *De quantitate animae* was written no later than a year after *De immortalitate animae* was (387–388).

[5] It does not follow that the soul, qua immortal, is superior to the body. Augustine argues for the immortality of the soul in *Soliloquia* 2.19.33 and *De immortalitate animae*, passim, but does not claim that the soul's immortality in itself makes it superior to matter. He takes the natural indestructibility

5.8; *De musica* 6.5.13). Augustine would be the first to insist that these analogies are deficient in some respects. A pianist can trade pianos, a potter can start afresh with a new mound of clay, a master can fire a servant, but we cannot put aside our bodies. Nor does Augustine express the contempt for or disgust with the body that was characteristic of the Pythagoreans and Plato. Mindful of Paul's remarks on the Resurrection (1 Corinthians 15:35–58), Augustine believes that we exist most completely as embodied souls (*De moribus ecclesiae catholicae* 4.6; *De Trinitate* 15.7.11 appears to endorse the stronger claim that we are essentially embodied souls). After all, one cannot be a flourishing pianist without any piano whatsoever. One can love and depend on one's piano even if it needs constant tuning and maintenance. And surely one might hope that in the keyboard afterlife, one's battered spinet will become transformed into a celestial Bösendorfer. Nevertheless the analogies do reflect Augustine's belief that the soul is superior to the body. If it were true that there is some appropriate sense according to which instruments cannot bring about effects in their users, worked-on matter cannot affect artisans, and servants cannot affect masters, then the analogies would be apt expressions of Augustine's metaphysical doctrine that the body cannot affect the soul. Augustine appears to regard this doctrine as a straightforward consequence of the soul's superiority over the body. He thus maintains, for example, that, with regard to sense perception, physical modifications to the body's sense receptors do not cause the soul to have sensory experiences. If the body could affect the soul in these ways, then in that respect the soul would be passive to and dependent upon the body, and in that respect the soul would not be superior to the body.[6] It is rather that the soul, in the process of monitoring the body, is able actively to take notice of the physical modifications and produce in itself the appropriate sensations.[7] It is then also capable of making judgments about the sensations that have thereby been produced.

Perhaps it has occurred to you that Augustine's hierarchical soul-body dualism, with its one-way-only causation, has normative implications. We are not inclined to blame the piano for the wrong notes plunked by the pianist. If we find ourselves praising the piano for its beautiful tone, we may on reflection come to

of matter as evidence that the soul too must be naturally everlasting, since the soul is superior to matter (*De immortalitate animae* 7.12). To avoid circularity, Augustine must then base the soul's superiority on grounds independent of its immortality, grounds such as its indivisibility and causal activity (see below). It is consistent with this position to hold, nevertheless, that any particular physical object is an ephemeral combination of indestructible matter.

[6] I am indebted to Scott MacDonald for reminding me of the importance of this point.

[7] See, e.g., *De immortalitate animae* 16.25; *De musica* 6.5.9–15; *De Genesi ad litteram* 12.16.32–33. Note that it would be hard to square Augustine's account with a Humean theory of causation as constant conjunction between events.

think that the praise is more accurately directed to its maker. The legal doctrine of *respondeat superior* reflects our belief that in many cases what a servant does while in the employ of a master can and should be imputed to the master. Even if we have reservations about Augustine's dualism, we can recognize something plausible about these features of Augustine's analogies in matters of morality. It may be that an agent's bodily motions are always relevant for our assessing the agent's moral responsibility, but they surely are not always dispositive. There are cases in which the resolutions of the soul and the motions of the body come apart. It can happen that the gyrations of the body are simply the product of brute physical forces that do not have any authorization from the soul. As I tumble down the stairs my body may assume the posture of an arabesque. But I have not performed an arabesque; neither (relevant) skill nor will were lodged in my soul. Or it can happen that what the soul does competently authorize does not issue in the right bodily motions. You might decide to arise, only to discover that Lilliputians have tied you down while you slept. Because we are all susceptible to these sorts of dislocations between the soul's commands and the body's executions, we think it important to know, in morally serious cases, whether another person's behavior is an example of such a dislocation. In morally serious cases the condition and activity of the soul can make the moral difference, say, between culpable negligence and innocent mistake, murder and accidental homicide.

If the only application to ethical theory of Augustine's dualism were merely to point out the importance of mental states in assessing moral responsibility, then we would be justified in paying scant attention to it. For virtually any materialistic account of the relation between mind and body, short of ham-fisted versions of eliminative materialism or behaviorism, also allows for the existence and moral relevance of beliefs, desires, intentions, and motives. Augustine's distinctive dualism leads him, I suggest, to a more radical view about the locus of moral assessment. It is relatively noncontroversial to claim that the moral appraisal of an agent's performance should sometimes consider the agent's mental states in order to assess the agent's physical deeds. It is much more controversial to claim that moral appraisal should focus primarily—perhaps exclusively—on the agent's mental states themselves, attending to the bodily behavior only insofar as that behavior might be evidence for the state of the agent's soul. Such a claim is essential to what we might call "inner-life ethics."[8] Augustine's views constitute a fairly extreme version of inner-life ethics. Thus, for example, in *De continentia* 2.3–5 Augustine puts forward three theses intended to apply to all sins, and in particular to the sins cited in Matthew 15:19: "For out of the heart come evil thoughts, murder, adultery, fornication, theft, false witness, slander."

---

[8] I am indebted to Arthur Kuflik for this term.

> The necessity-of-consent thesis: No specimen of bodily behavior counts as an example of sin unless it is preceded or accompanied by the soul's consent to the sin.[9]
>
> The sufficiency-of-consent thesis: To consent to sin is itself to commit a sin, even though the consent may never result in any outward, bodily behavior.[10]
>
> The guilt thesis: According to the laws of God, consent is sufficient to establish moral guilt for the very sin to which consent is given.[11]

The necessity-of-consent thesis maintains that there are no strict liability sins, that is, no sins that one commits merely by moving one's body in a certain way, irrespective of the state of one's soul. The sufficiency-of-consent thesis alleges that a certain state of the soul, consent to commit a sin, is all that is needed for one to have committed a sin. From the point of view of the sufficiency-of-consent thesis it is irrelevant to the fact that a sin has been committed (as opposed to our coming to know that a sin has been committed) that the sin was never translated into bodily action, for lack of opportunity. What the guilt thesis contributes is the contention that the moral guilt that attaches to the inner sin is guilt for having committed the same sin as the one to which one has consented. If Jones intends to kill Smith, then the guilt thesis attributes to Jones moral guilt for murder, not attempted murder or conspiring to commit a felony or any other substitute sin, even if Jones never carries out the intention. To put it provocatively, the sufficiency-of-consent thesis and the guilt thesis entail that Jones can be morally guilty of murder without killing anyone or without even trying to kill anyone.

The remarkable nature of Augustine's views can be brought out by contrasting them with the four points extracted from the *New Jerome*

---

[9] "They do nothing through the agency of the body that they had not first spoken in the heart," but "He has not yet spoken who has not consented by an inclination of the heart to the suggestions occurring in the heart from whatever sensory impressions" (*De continentia* 2.3; re-emphasized several times throughout *De continentia* 2.3–5). Thus, for example, genital arousal is not a transgression of continence if the arousal is involuntary (*De continentia* 2.5).

[10] "So also the other evil deeds of men, which no bodily movement brings about, and of which every bodily sense is unaware, have their secret guilty agents; even consent in thought alone—that is, an evil word of the interior mouth—defiles them" (*De continentia* 2.4). Immediately preceding this passage, Augustine had rung the changes on the list given in Matthew 15:19 with a series of rhetorical questions, all of the form, "Even if the agent is not successful in carrying out the sin in question, is he not guilty of that very sin nevertheless?"

[11] "Even if he has not acted by means of his hand or some other part of the body, he has acted nevertheless because he has now decided in thought that the act itself is to be done; he is guilty of the act according to the divine laws, even though it is hidden from the human senses" (*De continentia* 2.3).

commentary. (1) Lustful looking is wrong, not merely because of its connection to alienation of affection or any other state extrinsic to the looking itself. It is wrong precisely for the reason Jesus said it was wrong: it is a genuine commission of adultery *in corde*. (3) As a consequence of the response to (1), the evil exemplified by the decision to commit adultery is the same as the evil realized by the overt action. (4) As a consequence of the response to (3), the commission of the action does not increase the evil of the decision.[12] If there were any common ground between Augustine and the *New Jerome* interpretation, it would have to reside in point (2), which alleges that there is nothing especially wrong with wishful thinking. I shall give reason to believe that Augustine would deny point (2) also. The Augustinian theses make it clear that consent is an important concept for Augustine's inner-life ethics. To see how Augustine might have arrived at these theses, we need to understand the fundamentals of his normative theory, including the notion of consent.

Happiness, Love, and Goods

Augustine takes it as axiomatic that everyone wishes to be happy (*De beata vita* 2.10; *De moribus ecclesiae catholicae* 3.4). Genuine happiness requires love for and possession of a good that is supreme, eternal, steadfast, and inalienable from the lover (*De beata vita* 2.11; *De moribus ecclesiae catholicae* 3.5, 6.10). Only God can fill this bill. Thus Augustine connects the quest for human happiness to the divine commandment to love God with all one's heart, soul, and mind (Matthew 22:37; Deuteronomy 6:5; see *De moribus ecclesiae catholicae* 8.13). Following in Plato's footsteps, the Stoics had attempted to unify the virtues by identifying them with prudence or ways of being prudent. As if in reply, Augustine redefines the virtues of self-control, courage, justice, and prudence as ways of loving God: self-control is keeping one's love of God unblemished, courage is maintaining love of God in the face of adversity, justice is loving God undividedly, prudence is loving God in such a way that one chooses to further that love and avoids hindering it (*De moribus ecclesiae catholicae* 15.25, 25.46). In fairly swift order, then, Augustine attempts to incorporate the attractive pagan ethical notions of *eudaimonia* and the *aretai* into a Christian ethical framework.

God commands us not only to love him but also to love our neighbors as ourselves (Matthew 22:38). Augustine links the two commandments of

---

[12] For a dissenting opinion, see Christopher Kirwan, *Augustine* (London: Routledge, 1989), 75–76.

love in the following way. We love ourselves properly only when we love God more than we love ourselves. When we love God more than ourselves, we want to attain the supreme good that only God can bestow. Although the following step is not explicitly taken by Augustine, it appears to be well-nigh irresistible and connects love of God to neighborly love: when we love God more than ourselves, we want to attain the ends that he seeks to attain by following the commands that he gives us, including the command to love our neighbors as ourselves. When we do love our neighbors as ourselves, we want them also to attain the supreme good as much as we want ourselves to attain it (*De moribus ecclesiae catholicae* 26.48–49; see also *De doctrina Christiana* 1.26.27). Recognizing that they, like us, are embodied souls, we will endeavor to care for their physical well-being, which is the function of human mercy, and their spiritual well-being, which is the function of moral education (*De moribus ecclesiae catholicae* 27.52–28.55). We should note that, if this portrayal of Augustine's analysis is correct, then the analysis has the consequence that, since fulfillment of the second commandment essentially includes wanting our neighbors to love God as we do, fulfillment of the second commandment depends logically on fulfillment of the first, even though both commandments could be temporally fulfilled simultaneously (*De moribus ecclesiae catholicae* 26.51). Although nothing of importance in this essay hangs on it, I shall assume that Augustine believes that genuine neighborly love can only flow from love of God.

Because God is the creator of all things, everything that exists is good. This thesis lies at the heart of Augustine's rejection of Manichaeanism (see, e.g., *Confessions* 7.12.18–13.19; *De natura boni contra Manichaeos* 1). Nevertheless, some things are better than others: the soul, for example, is superior to the body. Augustine offers a threefold hierarchy of created goods in *De libero arbitrio* 2.18.47–19.51. The highest goods are those goods without which we cannot live rightly and which we cannot use evilly (if we possess them at all): Augustine's examples are the virtues. The intermediate goods are goods without which we cannot live rightly but which we can use evilly (or well). Augustine describes these goods as "powers of the mind" (*potentiae animi*). The only example overtly identified by Augustine is the power of making free decisions, or free will, although it is reasonable to assume that he also meant to include reason and memory as intermediate goods (see *De libero arbitrio* 2.19.51).[13] The lowest goods are goods without which we can live rightly and which can be used either well or badly. The lowest goods thus include things that are neither virtues nor

---

[13] Augustine constructs an analogy between the three intermediate goods of will (as love), memory, and understanding and the three persons of the Trinity; see *De Trinitate* 15.20.38–23.43.

powers of the mind. Augustine's examples include bodily health, strength, and beauty, the bodily senses, political freedom, friends and family relations, political institutions, honor, praise and popularity, and worldly possessions (*De libero arbitrio* 1.15.32; 2.18.49).

Enjoyment and Use

Augustine's distinction between enjoyment (*frui*) and use (*uti*) helps to connect his soul–body metaphysics and his ontology of goods to his inner-life ethics. To enjoy a thing is to love it for its own sake. "Use" is a term of art for Augustine. To use a thing is to employ it as a means for obtaining something loved, subject, we shall see momentarily, to two limitations. In *De diversis quaestionibus* Augustine had characterized vice as the desire to use what should be enjoyed and to enjoy what should be used (*De diversis quaestionibus* 30). In the somewhat later Book 1 of *De doctrina Christiana,* however, he drops mention of a desire to use what should be enjoyed, singling out only the desire to enjoy things that should be used as comprising a sort of slavish, inferior love (*De doctrina Christiana* 1.3.3). Notice, then, that, if the omission is significant, Augustine depicts vice as a kind of second-order desire, a desire to love for its own sake what should be used. The omission is significant and can be explained on the reductive hypothesis that Augustine came to think that a desire to use what should be enjoyed is an incoherent desire and that he added to that thought the further thought that, although incoherence is a cognitive failing, it is not a vice. The type of incoherence exhibited by such a desire does not preclude people from having the desire. It will, however, deter a suitably informed, rational person, who has made the relevant, obvious inferences from his correct beliefs, from forming or maintaining such a desire. To see how the desire is incoherent in this sense, we must investigate Augustine's concept of use more fully.

One limitation Augustine places on the concept of use is that one cannot properly be said to use something, x, to obtain something else, y, that one loves, if y is not worthy of being loved; such a "use" is really a case of abuse (*De doctrina Christiana* 1.4.4). Augustine offers the following argument for the limitation. If a person uses x badly, then x benefits no one. If x benefits no one, then x is not useful. But if x is useful, then x is useful by being used. Thus, if x is used, then x is useful. Thus, if x is not useful, then x is not used. Therefore, according to Augustine:

> If a person uses x badly, then that person does not use x. (*De diversis quaestionibus* 30)

Setting aside objections to the soundness of the argument, we can note that Augustine is urging, in effect, that we take *uti,* or at least his use of it, to function as a success verb.[14] The following principle,

> If a person who loves y uses x to obtain y, but y is not worthy of being loved, then that person uses x badly,

along with the conclusion of the *De diversis quaestionibus* 30 argument, yields the limitation put forward in *De doctrina Christiana* 1.4.4.

If everything that exists is good, we might think that everything has a claim to being loved, and so we may wonder how it is that an object can be unworthy of a person's love. Recall the hierarchy of goods sketched in *De libero arbitrio* 2. Although everything that exists is good, some things are better than others. It is natural to infer not only that everything that exists is worthy of being loved *simpliciter* but also that the strength of our love should be proportionate to the worthiness of the beloved object. Proportionality fails, according to Augustine, when a person attempts to use a superior good merely as a means to obtaining an inferior good: such an attempt inverts the order of goods and invests in the inferior end a love that is disproportionately high compared to the love one has for the superior means (*De diversis quaestionibus* 30). Augustine appears to subscribe to this version of the principle cited above:

> If a person who loves y uses x to obtain y, but y is less worthy of being loved than x is, then that person uses x badly.

The second limitation Augustine imposes on the concept of use is that it must presuppose a capacity for reasoning in the user. To use a thing requires having knowledge, both about the end to which the thing being used is a means and about the thing as a means to that end (*De diversis quaestionibus* 30). It is important to note that Augustine specifies knowledge, not belief. If one acted on the basis of false or unjustified beliefs about means or end, then one would be using a thing badly, which, given the first limitation, would really not be using the thing at all. Knowledge about means and ends depends on a rational soul.

---

[14] Augustine could consistently maintain that there are other uses of *uti* according to which it does not function as a success verb. Think of an analogous situation in English. A: "He answered the question incorrectly." B: "Then he didn't answer the question at all." C: "Of course he *answered* the question: he didn't simply leave that part of the examination blank." I am inclined to think that there are circumstances in which B's response is appropriate and circumstances in which C's response is appropriate.

Thus Augustine claims that if we speak strictly we cannot say that animals use anything.

The only thing that should be enjoyed is God, the Trinity of Father, Son, and Holy Ghost (*De doctrina Christiana* 1.5.5, 33.37).[15] All created things, including one's own rational soul and the souls of others, should be used, in a way that exemplifies the two commandments of love, in order to achieve enjoyment of God (*De diversis quaestionibus* 30; *De doctrina Christiana* 1.22.20–21, 35.39). We are now in a position to explain why Augustine would have thought that a desire to use what should be enjoyed is an incoherent desire. It is not that no one has such a desire. It is rather that, once one traces out the implications of the desire, one will see it to be unintelligible. Since God is the only being who should be enjoyed, such a desire would be a desire to use God.[16] But it is impossible to use God, for at least two reasons. First, recall that, for Augustine, use entails knowledge. To use God, then, entails that one possess knowledge about God sufficient to establish that God is a suitable means to some superior end. There can be no such knowledge. Virtually any knowledge about God entails knowing that God is not the sort of being who can be used. So a desire to use God is incoherent because it entails having adequate knowledge of God when adequate knowledge of God entails knowing that God cannot be used. Second, to use anything for whatever purpose entails taking it as inferior means to obtain a superior end. Because nothing can be superior or even equal to God, so to "use" God is to use God badly, which is in turn not to use God at all. Once again, a desire to use God, the only being who should be enjoyed, is incoherent.

If the reductive hypothesis is correct, then it is Augustine's considered opinion that every human vice can be explicated as a desire to enjoy what should be used. It does not follow that whenever one enjoys a created good one is thereby expressing a vice. Even though God is the only being who should be enjoyed, and even though God cannot be used, Augustine maintains that there are things that should be enjoyed and used (*De doctrina Christiana* 1.3.3). There is no incompatibility here, as long as Augustine is interpreted as saying that God is the only being who should be enjoyed without any eye to use, whereas created goods should not be enjoyed without also using them licitly as means to achieve

---

[15] In *De diversis quaestionibus* 30, Augustine suggests that some invisible, incorporeal things, such as beauty, are fit to be enjoyed. In *De diversis quaestionibus* 46.2 he argues that the Platonic Ideas are eternal but depend for their existence on God's mind. In enjoying beauty, then, we are enjoying what is, from our point of view, an aspect of God.

[16] Of course, desire contexts are opaque. I may want to be the discoverer of the Pharaoh's tomb while not wanting to be the first victim of the Pharaoh's curse, even though the two definite descriptions have (or will have) the same reference. If we are seeking to show that a particular desire is genuinely incoherent, however, it is fair to treat the desire context as if it were transparent.

enjoyment of God. There is nothing wrong with finding oneself enjoying what one is using, or with enjoyment supervening on use, but there is something wrong with one's seeking to enjoy a good instead of seeking to use it. Augustine illustrates the distinction repeatedly; here are two examples. Pleasure generally accompanies the nourishment necessary to sustain one's body, but desiring to eat and drink solely for gustatory relish rather than sustenance is sinful (*Confessions* 10.31.44). When it brings us closer to God, we use sacred music properly; when we delight more in the singing than in what is being sung about, we do not (*Confessions* 10.33.49–50).[17]

Two Trichotomies

Augustine discerns a crucial difference, then, between enjoying something and desiring to enjoy it. The sketchy delineation of vice as a kind of second-order desire in Book 1 of *De doctrina Christiana* is not accidental. The picture on which the sketch is based is displayed more fully in *De sermone Domini in monte*. In commenting on Jesus's pronouncement on adultery in Matthew 5:27–28, Augustine says that any sinful action is the product of three events or processes in the soul: suggestion, pleasure (or delight), and consent (*De sermone Domini in monte* 1.12.34). Memory and the bodily senses are the sources of suggestion. It is not clear whether Augustine thinks that a suggestion always has propositional content, but if it does the proposition will typically be expressed in the subjunctive rather than the optative mood. We may suppose that a nascent adulterer begins by musing about what it would be like to sleep with some person. The next three sentences describe a generic process that splits, as we shall see in the next section, into two species. Pleasure can ensue from the suggestion, although there is nothing in Augustine's description that precludes the possibility of pleasure arising simultaneously with the suggestion. If, as in the present case, the content of the suggestion is something sinful, the person should repress taking pleasure in the enjoyment of the suggestion. If the person consents to the suggestion, then a sin has been committed: the sufficiency-of-consent thesis has been fulfilled.

Before we examine more closely Augustine's notion of consent we should look at another trichotomy that follows on the heels of the suggestion-pleasure-consent trichotomy. A person can sin in the heart, in deed, or in habit

[17] For other examples, see William E. Mann, "The Theft of the Pears," *Apeiron* 12 (1978): 52–53 [chapter 2 of this volume]. Note that many if not all of the ingredients of the doctrine of double effect are nascent in Augustine's discussion of use and enjoyment.

(in *consuetudine; De sermone Domini in monte* 1.12.35).[18] Augustine's contrast between sinning inwardly (in the heart) and sinning outwardly (in deed) is familiar enough by now. Habitual sinning is a less familiar notion, about which Augustine makes the following claims. Habitual sinning arises from the repeated commission (in deed) of illicit acts. Subsequent suggestions to commit the same type of sin are accompanied by a more intense level of pleasure. The habitual sinner thus derives greater pleasure in the commission of the sinful act than does the casual sinner. It is the latter fact that explains why evil habits are hard to break (*De sermone Domini in monte* 1.12.34). The habitual sinner has acquired a vice. If we unite the *De sermone Domini in monte* theory of habit with the *De doctrina Christiana* thesis about vice, we can say that it is Augustine's view that the desire for the heightened pleasure that supervenes on repeatedly enjoying what should be used is what makes the vice a vice and also makes it difficult to extirpate.

The Grammar of Consent

What is it to take pleasure in a suggestion? Is it that one derives pleasure from mentally entertaining the content of the suggestion? Or does the content of the suggestion lead one to think that acting to fulfill the suggestion would bring pleasure? In similar fashion, what is it to consent to a suggestion? Is it merely to continue to entertain the content of the suggestion? Or is it to take steps to act on the suggestion, preparing to bring about what it suggests? Augustine's version of inner-life ethics allows for positive answers to all four alternatives, although not necessarily regarding the same case. At *De sermone Domini in monte* 1.12.33 Augustine provides a counterfactual analysis of consent: if one consents to a pleasant suggestion, then one would realize the suggestion if the opportunity were to arise. So construed, this conception of consent is tantamount to intention. The intention is to perform a certain action, given the opportunity, namely, the very action specified by the content of the suggestion. If φ is a variable ranging over types of action, then we can depict what might be called action-consent in this way:

A person action-consents to the suggestion that s/he φ only if s/he intends to perform the action φ given the opportunity.

----

[18] For further discussion of this passage see Christopher Kirwan's "Avoiding Sin: Augustine against Consequentialism," in *The Augustinian Tradition*, ed. Gareth B. Matthews (Berkeley: University of California Press, 1999), 183–194.

But Augustine's discussion of the suggestion-pleasure-consent trichotomy also alludes to another notion of consent. While entertaining the suggestion of an adulterous liaison, a person might never come to formulate an intention to commit adultery yet continue to fantasize nevertheless about the suggestion. The person consents to the suggestion in this case by failing to repress it, by giving it full play in the imagination. We could call this notion "fantasy-consent":

> A person fantasy-consents to the suggestion that s/he φ only if s/he does not repress the suggestion but takes continued pleasure from the contemplation of φing.

It need not follow that the person who fantasy-consents believes that acting to fulfill the fantasy would bring pleasure. The two notions of taking pleasure in a suggestion can thus come apart, as fantasy-consent itself can occur apart from action-consent, even though in many other cases they (the two ways of taking pleasure and the two kinds of consent) will tend to be conjoined.

Let us return to the three theses extracted from *De continentia*. It seems clear that action-consent applies to the necessity-of-consent thesis:

> The necessity-of-action-consent thesis: no specimen of bodily behavior counts as an example of sin unless it is preceded or accompanied by the soul's intention to perform the sin given the opportunity.

Fantasy-consent need never eventuate in overt action; when it does, the vehicle of translation, as the necessity-of-action-consent thesis maintains, is not fantasy-consent but rather action-consent or intention.

In contrast, the sufficiency-of-consent thesis and the guilt thesis appear to accommodate both notions of consent:

> The sufficiency-of-action-consent thesis: to intend to commit a sin given the opportunity is itself to commit a sin, even though the intention may never result in any outward, bodily behavior.
>
> The sufficiency-of-fantasy-consent thesis: to take continued pleasure from the contemplation of sinning is itself to commit a sin, even though the contemplation may never result in any outward, bodily behavior.
>
> The intentional-guilt thesis: according to the laws of God, intention is sufficient to establish moral guilt for the very sin intended.
>
> The fantasy-guilt thesis: according to the laws of God, continued pleasure taken from the contemplation of sinning is sufficient to establish moral guilt for the very sin contemplated.

Note that the sufficiency-of-fantasy-consent thesis contradicts point (2) extracted from the *New Jerome* interpretation; there can indeed be something wrong with mere wishful thinking. We will discuss these theses more fully below.

Taking Stock

Augustine's inner-life ethics occupies a territory distinctive in normative ethical theory. To get some sense of its uniqueness, we should see how it contrasts with other, perhaps more familiar, positions.

One feature that is not unfamiliar is the foundation in love of God and one's neighbor. Because he holds that every created thing is good, Augustine cannot consistently say that it is wrong per se to desire or love any particular created thing. A desire for a created thing could be wrong only if the desire is inconsistent with one's loving God or one's loving one's neighbor as oneself. At this point it is natural to confront Augustine with a version of the problem of weakness of will: if a desire for a finite good conflicts with love for the infinite goodness that is God, how is it possible to come to have such a desire? How can what is worse come to be as attractive or more attractive than what is better, especially when what is better is infinitely better? Once the question is put that way, one might expect Augustine to avail himself of the Platonic reply that such a desire is due to some sort of cognitive shortcoming. It could be that we desire something in a way that is inconsistent with loving God because there is something we do not know. We might not yet know that God is the supreme good. Or we might know that God is the supreme good and fail to realize that a particular desire we have for some created good is inconsistent with love for God, just as I might desire bodily health and fail to realize that my craving to smoke is detrimental to it. Perhaps all wrongful desires, then, are the result of ignorance?

Augustine does not deny that there are such cases. It is rather that they do not interest him when he discusses wrongful desires. The cases that do capture his attention are ones in which a person desires something, knowing that to have the desire is wrong. The latter cases more than the former dramatize for him the sheer willfulness of evil. If rationalism is the thesis that knowledge of the good is sufficient to gain mastery over the promptings of the will, and if voluntarism is the denial of that thesis, then Augustine is a voluntarist, not a rationalist.[19]

---

[19] I believe that his voluntarism on this score fits hand-in-glove with Augustine's views about the calamitousness of the Fall; see, e.g., his discussion of the nature and effects of original sin in *City of God* 14.11–15. His voluntarism is also bolstered by a plausible reading of Romans 7:22–23.

Because Augustine lays so much moral emphasis on the state of the soul and so little on bodily execution, it may be tempting to infer that he is an anticonsequentialist. But in fact no such inference follows. It is important to distinguish between two anticonsequentialistic theses. One maintains that the consequences of an action or a state of affairs are not always relevant to the moral appraisal of the action or state of affairs: the other maintains that they are never relevant. Augustine has reason to accept the first thesis but reject the second. Even though bodily states can never affect the soul, and even if, by some sort of soul-in-a-vat thought experiment, the soul were never to bring about any bodily states, the fact would remain that one state of the soul can bring about another state of the soul. If the second soul-state is morally significant, then it is open to Augustine to appraise the first soul-state in terms not only of its intrinsic value or disvalue but of its instrumental value or disvalue. For example, unrepressed musings about adultery are evil in themselves, by the sufficiency-of-fantasy-consent thesis, but also evil insofar as they are just the sorts of states that tend to lead to the formation of intentions to commit adultery (by the sufficiency-of-action-consent thesis).

There is a long tale about the influence of Stoic thought on Augustine, a tale that I am not able to tell.[20] Any adequate telling of it, however, must include the following points of divergence. Stoicism provides an ethical theory that is perfectionistic yet that also claims that its practitioners are naturally self-sufficient. It is Stoicism's contention that each of us innately has the wherewithal to lead the ideal life, a life in conformity with the rational necessity exhibited by nature, given only our natural endowment, including the capacity to reason. Augustine must reject the Stoic conception for at least two reasons. First, it fails to recognize that, as a consequence of the Fall, humans are no longer naturally capable of living the life they should live: from Augustine's point of view, Stoicism commits the same kind of error that would soon be committed by the Pelagians. The second reason lies behind the first. Natural reason, unaided by divine revelation, cannot give us the central content of Augustinian ethics, that we should love God and love our neighbors as we love ourselves.

Applications

Lying

Augustine wrote two works devoted to moral issues raised by lying, the early *De mendacio* and the late *Contra mendacium*. In both of them he argues that

---

[20] See, e.g., James Wetzel, *Augustine and the Limits of Virtue* (Cambridge: Cambridge University Press, 1992), and the references cited therein.

one must never lie, not even in an attempt to secure someone else's salvation (*De mendacio* 8.11), nor in order to disguise one's religious convictions in a hostile society (*Contra mendacium* 2.2), nor in order to trap heretics (*Contra mendacium* 3.4). I shall concentrate on the early work, connecting it to inner-life ethics.

Augustine recognizes that uttering a falsehood, even with the intention of uttering a falsehood, does not count as lying, lest jokes be labeled lies (*De mendacio* 2.2). Nor does uttering a falsehood count as lying when one believes that what one is uttering is true (although one might be culpable for being misinformed; *De mendacio* 3.3). Consider the following non-Augustinian defense of this Augustinian claim. It may be that Jones mendaciously tells a falsehood to Smith but that Smith has good reason to trust Jones's veracity. If Smith then passes on the falsehood to you, then whatever Smith has done, Smith has not thereby lied to you. It is more surprising to see Augustine claim that one can be lying while saying what is true. In an attempt to get you to fail your geography examination, I tell you that the capital of North Dakota is Bismarck, believing that the capital is Fargo. In fact, North Dakota's capital is Bismarck. Then I have lied to you while telling you the truth (*De mendacio* 3.3). Thus it is Augustine's opinion that uttering a falsehood is neither sufficient nor necessary for telling a lie.[21]

Whether one has succeeded in uttering a truth or a falsehood depends in part on the way the world is.[22] It should come as little surprise to find out that, according to Augustine, whether one has lied or not depends not on the way the world is but on the desires and motives one has. Here are two cases, modeled closely on Augustinian examples (*De mendacio* 4.4). You must choose between two paths. Fiends await you on path A; path B leads to warmth and safety. You do not know which path is which, and time is of the essence. Both Jones and Smith know which path is which, but they also know that you distrust them deeply. Unbeknownst to you, Jones wants you to avoid the fiends, while Smith wants the fiends to fasten upon you.[23] Jones tells you that there are no fiends on path A,

---

[21] In *Contra mendacium* 12.26, a lie is characterized as a false signification with the desire to deceive. The characterization appears in the context of a discussion of figurative biblical language. It looks as though a false signification need not be anything more than a misleading interpretation and that I could provide a false signification by uttering nothing but true propositions.

[22] "The world" includes the states of my soul, for I can dissemble about them as well as I can about the capital of North Dakota.

[23] Augustine points out that Jones's wanting you to avoid the fiends is compatible with Jones's not wishing well for you; Jones may want himself to be the agent of your destruction. Although the example Augustine gives spoils the point, he also thinks that Smith's wanting the fiends to fasten upon you is compatible with Smith's wishing well for you: it may be that your fate is so dismal otherwise that encountering the fiends is the best that can happen to you (*De mendacio* 4.4).

hoping that your distrust of him will lead you to believe that there are fiends on path A and thus to choose the safe path B. Smith tells you that there are fiends on path A, counting on your distrust in her to lead you to believe that path A is fiend-free. Augustine makes the following claims about these cases:

(1) If lying entails saying something with the desire to say something false, then Jones lies and Smith does not lie.

(2) If lying entails saying something with the desire to deceive, then Smith lies and Jones does not lie.[24]

(3) If lying entails saying something with a desire for some element of falsity ("cum voluntate alicujus falsitatis"), then both Jones and Smith lie; Jones because he desires that what he says be false, Smith because she desires that you believe something false based on her true statement.

(4) If lying entails saying something with the desire to say something false in order to deceive, then neither Jones nor Smith lies; not Jones, because he desires to convince you of the truth by saying what is false, not Smith, because she desires to speak the truth in order to convince you of something false.

Augustine concludes that a person who willingly makes a false statement from a desire to deceive is clearly one kind of liar (*De mendacio* 4.5). Given his claim that one can lie by telling the truth, he must believe that there are other kinds.

It will help to set this fourfold inventory in its proper perspective if one distinguishes three questions. What is lying? What makes lying wrong? When has one lied? In Augustine's hands the questions receive different sorts of answers. Lying is wrong, for example, because it contravenes the commandment against bearing false witness, a commandment justified in turn by the commandment to love God and one's neighbor. The sufficiency-of-action-consent thesis and the intentional-guilt thesis give a distinctive answer to the question about when one has lied—perhaps earlier than one might otherwise have thought. (Thus the "when" in "When has one lied?" is at least partly a request for temporal conditions.) In the early chapters of *De mendacio* Augustine is engaged in examining the first question by searching for a definition of lying. The options offered in the fourfold inventory are significant both for what they contain and what they

---

[24] One may certainly dissent from Augustine's assessment of Jones's case. Although Jones may wish you well, it does not follow that he does not try to deceive you. The success of Jones's strategy depends on your correctly taking his action to be deceptive: Jones counts on his deception, coupled with your mistrust, being the vehicle that will deliver you safely from the fiends. Note that Jones has not deceived you about what path the fiends are on; he has deceived you instead about what his beliefs are about the two paths.

do not contain. Inasmuch as he presents the inventory immediately after he has severed (to his satisfaction) any necessary connection between lying and saying what is false, the inventory seems to present what he takes to be the serious remaining candidates available for defining the notion of lying. Notice, however, that the options offered in the inventory are couched solely in terms of desires— that is, states wholly internal to the agent's soul. It appears that when he wrote *De mendacio,* Augustine thought that one could come closest to answering the question what lying is not just by knowing only what goes on in a person's soul but even more narrowly, by knowing only what goes on in a person's will.

To appreciate the radical nature of Augustine's view about what lying is, contrast it with the following attempt to specify the notion:

> A person lies if and only if the person (a) says what is in fact false, (b) believing that it is false, (c) in a communication context governed by a convention requiring truth-telling.[25]

Condition (c) makes explicit why jokes, lines uttered in plays, the use of rhetorical figures, and the like should not count as lies. Condition (b) rules out the case of the sincere but misinformed person and makes explicit something to which Augustine assented in *De mendacio* 3.3; moreover, Augustine's "clear" case of a liar, a person who willingly makes a false statement from a desire to deceive, is not a clear case unless we suppose additionally that the person believes of the false statement that it is false. Condition (a) classifies my attempt to mislead you about the capital of North Dakota and Smith's attempt to get you to choose the path frequented by fiends as non-lies, whatever else might be said by way of moral criticism of our performances. Recall that Augustine rejects condition (a). Note also that in contrast to the emphasis that Augustine places on them, desires play no role in the characterization.

While Augustine flirted with the idea of giving a purely internalistic answer to the question of what a lie is—an answer framed, that is, entirely in terms of a person's desires—it may not be obvious what role inner-life ethics plays in *De mendacio.* Augustine thinks that some lies are less serious than others. In *De mendacio* 14.25 and 21.42 he gives the following list of types of lies, graded from most to least sinful:

> Lie 1: A person lies in the teaching of religious doctrine.
> Lie 2: A person lies, causing harm to someone without helping anyone.
> Lie 3: A person lies, causing harm to someone while helping someone else.

---

[25] This characterization was suggested by David Christensen.

Lie 4: A person lies solely for the pleasure of lying.

Lie 5: A person lies solely from the desire to please his comrades.

Lie 6: A person lies, causing harm to no one while saving someone's possessions.

Lie 7: A person lies, causing harm to no one while saving someone's life.

Lie 8: A person lies, causing harm to no one while saving someone from bodily defilement.[26]

Even if one waives questions about whether Augustine has got the order right, one cannot help but note that external consequences seem to contribute in large measure to the construction of the order. It would take only a slightly quirky utilitarianism to produce the same order.

To see how Augustine's list squares with his inner-life ethics, let us begin by distinguishing an act's being wrong from its being harmful, allowing the latter to include harms done to the body and harms done to the soul. Consider now an unsophisticated variety of consequentialism that maintains that no action is wrong unless it produces harm. On this version of consequentialism harm is necessary for wrongfulness but not sufficient: an agent may be insulated from a charge of wrongdoing if the agent's harmful act results in the avoidance of greater harm or in the production of greater good, or if the act is unavoidable. A defender of our imagined consequentialism will have no quarrel with the concept of wrongfulness but will claim nevertheless that it can be assimilated to the notion of unjustifiable, avoidable harm. When the consequentialist compares lie 2, for example, with lie 6, he will protest that the cases are insufficiently specified. If it is made explicit that both lies are avoidable and have no further relevant long-range consequences, then the reason lie 2 is worse than lie 6 is simply that it is more harmful.

Without denying the existence of harm, inner-life ethics denies it the dispositive moral role that it plays for consequentialism. In particular, even though lie 2 is more harmful than lie 6, the inner-life ethicist must maintain that that fact

---

[26] By "bodily defilement" Augustine has heterosexual and homosexual rape in mind. Since lie 8 is less evil than lie 7, it seems to follow that bodily defilement is worse than death. In *De mendacio* 7.10 Augustine maintains, in effect, that, if one is sexually assaulted, one retains bodily chastity if and only if one retains spiritual integrity (by not consenting). Left-to-right, because if one consents, one ipso facto loses bodily chastity (even if the assailant then never carries out the deed). Right-to-left, because one's retaining spiritual integrity is sufficient for one's retaining bodily chastity. Augustine thus thinks that it is possible for a sexual assault to be physically committed without its affecting the victim's bodily chastity.

The eightfold classification of lies exerted great influence. See, e.g, St. Thomas Aquinas, *Summa Theologiae* 2a2ae.110.2.

does not explain why lie 2 is more sinful than lie 6. Like the consequentialist, the inner-life ethicist will insist that the two lies are insufficiently specified. But further specification should proceed, not outward, in the direction of consequences and avoidability, but inward, to the state of the liar's soul. Consider variations of lies 2 and 6:

> Intentional lie 2: A person lies, intentionally causing harm to someone without helping anyone.
> Inadvertent lie 2: A person lies, inadvertently causing harm to someone without helping anyone.
> Intentional lie 6: A person lies, intentionally causing harm to no one while saving someone's possessions.
> Inadvertent lie 6: A person lies, inadvertently causing harm to no one while saving someone's possessions.

Augustine can agree that inadvertent lie 2 is more harmful than inadvertent lie 6 while regarding them as morally equal; ceteris paribus, neither is more sinful than the other. I suggest that when Augustine wrote *De mendacio* he had in mind a comparison between intentional lie 2 and intentional lie 6. Intentional lie 2 is more sinful than intentional lie 6, not for the reason that it is more harmful but rather for the reason that to harm someone intentionally is to be further removed from fulfilling God's commandment to love him and one's neighbors. When one considers similar variations on all but one of the other kinds of lies on Augustine's list, one can easily see how the order fits in with inner-life ethics. The problem case is lie 4. I shall defer discussing it until the next section.

The Theft of the Pears

Augustine's well-known account, in *Confessions*, Book 2, of his teenage theft of pears is calculated, I submit, to dramatize his inner-life ethics. Immediately after proclaiming the sexual lust attendant upon his attaining puberty, and telling of his striding the streets of Thagaste as if he were wallowing in the mire of Babylon (*Confessions* 2.3.6–8), Augustine devotes the remaining seven chapters to a meditation upon the theft. The following points emerge from the meditation. Appearances to the contrary notwithstanding, the theft is a case of an especially serious misdeed. And appearances are to the contrary. Augustine makes no claim to the effect that the theft brought financial hardship to the tree's owner: it is compatible with everything he says about the case that the owner never even noticed the loss. Augustine suggests that he would not have stolen the pears had he not had companions (*Confessions* 2.8.16–9.17), but the necessity of confederates does nothing to explain why the theft is so seriously wrong. The core of his explanation is contained in chapters 4–6, which comprise a sequence of observations alternating between rejections, as inapplicable to his case, of various hypotheses typically used to explain many sinful deeds, and the repeated assertion of what must be the correct account of the theft, an account that underscores its sinfulness from the point of view of inner-life ethics.

Let us consider the rejected explanatory hypotheses. First, there are cases in which people steal out of need. Augustine, however, did not need the pears he stole; he in fact had plenty of better pears of his own (*Confessions* 2.4.9). Second, there are cases in general in which people sin because they are unduly attracted by worldly goods, such as gold and silver, honor, political power, and friendship (*Confessions* 2.5.10). The cases recall the third and lowest class of created goods from *De libero arbitrio* 2. In the terminology of *De doctrina Christiana*, Book 1, they are cases of seeking to enjoy what should only be used. But Augustine did not seek to enjoy the pears he stole: he threw them to the pigs. Third, there are cases in which a person sins simply as a means to attain some desired good. Although Catiline sometimes committed crimes just to keep in practice, Augustine points out that even those crimes at least had instrumental value for Catiline (*Confessions* 2.5.11). In contrast, Augustine's theft was not undertaken as a means to any extrinsic end. Fourth, there are cases in which sinful acts are best explained as the expressions of vicious habits or culpable mental conditions. Much evildoing flows from such character flaws as pride, the craving for honor and glory, cruelty, lasciviousness, idle curiosity, culpable ignorance, folly, sloth, licentiousness, prodigality, avarice, envy, anger, timorousness, and moroseness (*Confessions* 2.6.13). As Augustine's account of his sin makes clear, it might have been that he had some of these vicious character traits, but if so, they were not salient factors in his commission of the theft.

Augustine maintains that he stole the pears solely for the sake of doing something that was sinful (*Confessions* 2.4.9, 6.12, 6.14). It is worth the effort to dwell on the case a bit more than Augustine does. The necessity-of-action-consent thesis entails that no episode of bodily behavior counts as an instance of theft unless it is accompanied by the intention to steal. Every theft is thus intentional. The sufficiency-of-action-consent thesis and the intentional-guilt thesis yield the result that it is the intention to steal that makes the theft wrong. (If pressed further, Augustine would have to ground the wrongness of the intention to steal ultimately in its contravention of love of God and of one's neighbors.) So far, however, we have not uncovered any reason that would set apart his theft of the pears from his other sinful deeds or, for that matter—given the two versions of the sufficiency-of-consent thesis—that would set apart his theft from other unperformed but intended or contemplated deeds. To take but one example, why did he not choose to expatiate in *Confessions,* Book 3, on his sexual misconduct while in Carthage?

In reporting on the notorious Stoic thesis that all sins are equal, Cicero had pointed out that the Stoics, in an effort to explain the intuition that some actions are more seriously wrongful than others, had maintained that one and the same action might instantiate several sins.[27] Perhaps, then, Augustine's theft was a number of sins wrapped up in one action. He intended to steal and he intended to do something wrong. If Augustine were to suppose that the second intention is logically independent of the first—that is, that one could intend to steal without thereby intending to do something wrong—he could eke out two sins in this case by dint of the sufficiency-of-action-consent thesis. Still, the census is not very impressive, certainly not enough to justify the space that Augustine devotes to considering the theft. More important, to proceed in this quantitative fashion is to concede too much to the Stoics. As the hierarchy of lies demonstrates, not all sins are equal: some single sins are worse than others.

The purpose of the theft of the pears was not to acquire any created good but rather simply to perform some action, an action not taken as means to some further end but an action done for its own sake. Now an action done solely for its own sake seems already to be morally suspect by virtue of the use-enjoyment distinction. Suppose, for example, that I while away a portion of my time solving crossword puzzles, not for any purpose extrinsic to the activity—such as a desire to win a prize or even just to refresh my soul—but simply because I enjoy doing them. Recall that for Augustine, time itself is a part of God's creation (more accurately put, it is the mode of created existence; *Confessions* 11.13.15–14.17). As such, time is a good that can be misused. It is possible to deploy the use-enjoyment distinction to subject my activity to the following criticism: in dedicating a portion of my time to mere enjoyment, when the object of enjoyment is not what should be merely enjoyed, I am using my time badly. Now even if time-wasting action done solely for its own sake does not pass over the threshold into the realm of moral disapprobation, surely action done solely for the sake of the intrinsic wrongness of the action itself does. If God is the only being whom one ought to desire to enjoy, then to desire to enjoy the sheer activity of theft, when theft is known even by unbelievers to be intrinsically bad (*Confessions* 2.4.9), is a desire to enjoy something virtually as far removed from God's goodness as is possible.[28] It is that desire that Augustine comes to recognize later in life as morally monstrous.

---

[27] Cicero, *Paradoxa Stoicorum* 3.2.25.

[28] Virtually; the desire to enjoy blasphemy would be further removed. Augustine's anti-Manichaeanism entails that the further a thing is removed from God's goodness, the closer it is to being nonexistent (*Confessions* 7.12.18; *De natura boni contra Manichaeos* 6). Thus at one point Augustine asks rhetorically whether his theft can be a thing that exists at all (*Confessions* 2.6.12). Note that Augustine's retrospective assessment does not maintain that he knew at the time of his theft how monstrous it was.

Let us imagine the youthful Augustine in different sorts of circumstances—in different possible worlds, if you will—in Thagaste. In each circumstance the theft occurs and appears exactly as it actually appeared: hidden-camera recordings of the individual thefts would all be visually and acoustically indistinguishable. The first circumstance is the actual one; seven others track lies 2–8:

Theft 1: Augustine steals from the desire to enjoy doing something wrong.

Theft 2: Augustine steals, causing harm to someone without helping anyone.

Theft 3: Augustine steals, causing harm to someone while helping someone else.

Theft 4: Augustine steals solely for the pleasure of stealing.

Theft 5: Augustine steals solely from the desire to please his comrades.

Theft 6: Augustine steals, causing harm to no one while saving someone's possessions.

Theft 7: Augustine steals, causing harm to no one while saving someone's life.

Theft 8: Augustine steals, causing harm to no one while saving someone from bodily defilement.

What is the difference between theft 1 and theft 4? Is theft 1 like lie 1 in being more sinful than all its confreres?

Let us take on the first question while revisiting lie 4. The type-4 liar or thief is, I suggest, a person whose relevant behavior is the expression of a sinful habit, according to the account given in *De sermone Domini in monte* 1.12.34–35. That is, such a person derives augmented pleasure from repeated acts of lying or theft.[29] The person's behavior is thus vicious, in the original sense of the term but—unlike the intentional behavior of type-2 and type-3 sinners—not necessarily malicious: the habitual sinner need not intend harm to anyone. In contrast, if we assume that lies 5–8 and thefts 5–8 are not themselves expressions of habitual behavior, we are entitled to say that they are less sinful than lie 4 and theft 4, respectively.

If Augustine's theft had been theft 4, he would have acted under the influence of a habit but not necessarily with malice. It is clear that he does not take his behavior to be explicable as habitual. If theft 1, Augustine's actual theft, is more sinful than thefts 2 and 3, then it is reasonable to suppose that theft 1 is malicious. Yet the target of the malice is not explicitly identified. I suggest that Augustine's retrospective opinion is that the target was God, even though the youthful Augustine had no clear conception of God's nature. Had the youthful Augustine had a clearer conception, he would have realized that his malice could

---

[29] Aquinas understands Augustine's type-4 liar in this way. See *Summa Theologiae* 2a2ae.110.2.

not be realized by harming God. Nonetheless, the older Augustine can recognize that, whether his younger persona realized it or not, the theft, motivated as it was, constituted an attempt to offend God by flouting God's commandment against theft. At one point Augustine characterizes his theft as an effort to arrogate omnipotence to himself by doing something that is but a shadowy imitation of God's omnipotence (*Confessions* 2.6.14).

There are differences between lie 1 and theft 1, but I believe that Augustine thinks they are both affronts to God, attempts to subvert God's sovereignty either by intentionally misrepresenting the nature of that sovereignty or by defying it sheerly for the sake of defying it. It is this feature of theft 1 that makes it more sinful than the other types of theft and thus explains Augustine's choice of it to illustrate his youthful perversity.

Sinful Dreams

If inner-life ethics bases its moral appraisal of an agent upon what goes on in the agent's soul, what difference does it make whether what goes on occurs while the agent is awake or asleep? Is there any moral difference between one's consenting to the suggestion that one commit adultery and one's dreaming of committing adultery? Writing about the issue twice (*Confessions* 10.30.41–42 and *De Genesi ad litteram* 12.15.31), Augustine finds it hard to locate a significant difference.[30] It would never have occurred to him to deny that dreams involve mental activity, nor to deny that the same kinds of mental activity occur in dreams and waking experiences: to dream of consenting to the pleasure taken in an adulterous suggestion is to consent to the suggestion. He considers the possibility that he is not the agent acting in his dreams but rejects it, claiming that God's grace is necessary to cleanse his soul so that it will not continue to do in dreams what it would not do while awake (*Confessions* 10.30.42). That God's grace is necessary underscores Augustine's belief that it is not an excuse merely to plead lack of control over our dreams. The *Confessions'* discussion of sinful dreams follows immediately after the famous plea, "You command continence: give what you command and command what you will" (*Confessions* 10.29.40). The core of Augustine's anti-Pelagianism is that not all sinful action can be avoided without God's grace. So even if we cannot avoid sinful dreams without God's grace, Augustine worries that that fact by itself does not provide sufficient grounds for claiming that the dreams are not really sinful.

---

[30] These passages have been discussed recently in Gareth B. Matthews, *Thought's Ego in Augustine and Descartes* (Ithaca, NY: Cornell University Press, 1992), chap. 8, "The Moral Dream Problem." See also Gareth B. Matthews, "On Being Immoral in a Dream," *Philosophy* 56 (1981): 47–54; and William E. Mann, "Dreams of Immorality," *Philosophy* 58 (1983): 378–385.

When Augustine returns to the issue of sinful dreams in *De Genesi ad litteram,* he has in mind dreams culminating in nocturnal emissions. He appeals to the following exculpatory analogy. Just as there is nothing sinful in the thoughts of a person awake discussing the phenomena of nocturnal emissions, so there is nothing sinful in the dreamt thoughts leading to an emission. The analogy is reminiscent of point (2) of the *New Jerome* commentary on Matthew 5:27–28. But the analogy is faulty and inconsistent with Augustine's inner-life ethics. Faulty, because the person awake may be discussing nocturnal emissions not for clinical but for lecherous purposes. Inconsistent with inner-life ethics, because, as Matthews puts it, "what Augustine exonerates—the nocturnal emission following a lewd dream image—is different from what, in his own terms, would incriminate him, namely, a suggestion within the dream of the possibility of having intercourse."[31] The locus of sin is not in the bodily behavior. Nor does it lie in the possession of the concepts necessary for dreaming the relevant dream or carrying on the relevant discussion. Augustine confounds the issue by picking a type of dream that has overt physiological consequences. Think instead of a dream with no relevant external consequences. You dream of strangling the mindless lout who abruptly cut into your lane as you drove along the freeway earlier in the day, only to wake up to find your hands resting at your sides. If the same sorts of activities go on in your soul when asleep as when awake, are you guilty of homicide, according to the sufficiency-of-action-consent and the intentional-guilt theses?

Here is the inner-life ethicist attorney for your defense. "I agree with Augustine and against the Pelagians that unavoidability is in general no excuse. But I assert that it is an excuse in the special case of dreamt misdeeds. Consider the cases in which we discount unavoidability. Some behavior, such as behavior while intoxicated, may be unavoidable because of the agent's now-impaired faculties, but we hold the agent culpable because the agent got into that impaired state voluntarily and avoidably. Other behavior, such as behavior that results from beliefs and attitudes instilled in a person while very young, may have been unavoidably instilled; they are culpable nonetheless if the agent can avoid the circumstances that elicit the behavior and take steps to extinguish the offensive beliefs and attitudes. Dreaming, however, is not like either of these situations. We cannot voluntarily avoid sleep. As Augustine himself points out, our dreams have us do what we would never do when awake. Why not then think of our dream episodes as entertaining, for an instant, what we firmly reject when we awaken? Where is the sin in that? Surely it cannot be a sin to overcome the momentary temptation to sin."

---

[31] Matthews, *Thought's Ego in Augustine and Descartes,* 102. Strictly speaking, it would be consent to a suggestion that would incriminate him.

And here is the inner-life ethicist attorney for the prosecution. "I can agree with much of what my opponent has just said, because he defends where I do not choose to attack. He has not succeeded in exculpating his client, for reasons that Augustine would have appreciated. Dreams are like plays, in which the dreamer is sometimes a member of the cast, sometimes a member of the audience, but of which the dreamer is always the author. The *De Genesi ad litteram* discussion of sinful dreams falls fast on the heels of a discussion of diabolical deception (*De Genesi ad litteram* 12.14.30; see also *De Genesi ad litteram* 12.18.39–21.44), yet Augustine never even hints that dreams are produced in the dreamer by any agency other than the dreamer. Authors bear the onus of moral responsibility for the works they produce. If we think that there is something morally reprehensible about the very depiction of scenes of unjustified and unpunished violence or wanton depravity, then we should worry about our depiction of such scenes in our dreams. Our sinful dreams indicate that we are closer to the portrayer of sadism or the pornographer than we would like to admit. Augustine is aware of this fact. In *Confessions* 10.30.42 he says that God's grace will enable him not only not to commit sinful deeds in dreams but also not even to consent to them. The notion of consent in this context cannot be action-consent, because action-consent is what is involved in committing the deeds in dreams. To pursue the play analogy a bit further, we can say that one indulges in action-consent in those dreams in which one is a member of the cast. But in those dreams in which one is merely a member of the audience, one still engages in fantasy-consent. Not only is one the dream's author, but one fails to storm out of the theater when confronted with the depravity that one concocts. What God's grace can enable one ultimately to do is to cease having both sorts of dreams altogether, to cleanse one's soul so thoroughly that one will not even entertain sinful dreams. Augustine claims that Solomon's soul was in this state (*De Genesi ad litteram,* 12.15.31; see 1 Kings 3:5–15). But until our souls are in this state, we are responsible for our sinful dreams."

What verdict should the jury deliver?

Conclusion

Think of our plight as an exercise in moral progress. Our first task is to gain control over our external behavior. But that is not enough. We must also put our internal house in order; our behavior must issue from the right motives and intentions. But that is still not enough. The Sermon on the Mount enjoins us to be perfect. We must strive to purge the wrong motives and desires from our souls, even were they never to gain the upper hand. There is nothing wrong with overcoming temptation, but, pace the attorney for the defense, there is something wrong with being tempted. Sinful dreams bear the unwelcome tidings that we have not yet succeeded in the third task: dreams provide the stage on which desires we are able to overcome while awake can still strut their stuff. It takes a Solomon to walk—and dream—in the ways of the Lord. It is Augustine's belief that no one can do that without divine assistance. It may be fortunate that other humans cannot eavesdrop on our dreams. For that reason, I believe that Augustine would tell us that the present case can only be adequately tried before a judge who is both supremely just and supremely merciful.

7

To Catch a Heretic

Augustine on Lying

"Tell me, then: what do you believe?"

"My lord, I believe everything a good Christian should. . . ."

"A holy reply! And what does a good Christian believe?"

"What the holy church teaches."

"And which holy church? The church that is so considered by those believers who call themselves perfect, the Pseudo Apostles, the heretical Fraticelli, or the church they compare to the whore of Babylon, in which all of us devoutly believe?"

"My lord," the cellarer said, bewildered, "tell me which you believe is the true church. . . ."

"I believe it is the Roman church, one, holy, and apostolic, governed by the Pope and his bishops."

"So I believe," the cellarer said.

"Admirable shrewdness!" the inquisitor cried. "Admirable cleverness de dicto. You all heard him: he means to say he believes that I believe in this church, and he evades the requirement of what he believes in!"
—Umberto Eco, *The Name of the Rose*

The implacable Bernard Gui knows the wiles of heretics. Remigio the cellarer, the heretic Gui seeks to expose, will do almost anything to avoid telling a lie. Remigio attempts to exploit an ambiguity. One implication of "So I believe" is "I believe the same thing." Remigio indeed intends his audience to interpret his utterance in that way. But what the utterance really conveys, by Remigio's lights, is his endorsement, not of the content of Gui's belief, but of the sincerity of Gui's expression of it.

The dialogue is fictional; Bernard Gui is not. Gui really was a Dominican inquisitor, pressed into fictional service in Eco's tale of fourteenth-century intrigue. And although the dialogue is fictional, it is not a pure flight of fancy.

It captures what could have transpired between a wily heretic and a shrewd inquisitor. Remigio's tactic is a specimen of what was called, naturally enough, "equivocation."[1] The tactic is in service of a strategy, which might be expressed as follows: Do not lie in order to conceal the truth if you can mislead your adversary by other, evasive means. The strategy in turn is sanctioned by the principle that lying is always, without exception, morally wrong, whereas certain kinds of evasive techniques can be right, wrong, or morally neutral, depending on the circumstances. (One such technique, for example, is to answer a question with a question or request, as when Remigio says, "Tell me which you believe is the true church.")

Eco's dialogue does not happen to illustrate this constraint as it applies to Gui. But no inquisitor of Gui's stature could have failed to be aware of and obedient to the doctrine against lying laid out in Augustine's *Contra Mendacium ad Consentium* (hereinafter referred to as *CM*). The work was written in 422 to address the issue whether it was permissible to use entrapment techniques to identify Priscillianists, a heretical sect with Manichaean leanings. Augustine's opinion is a resoundingly clear endorsement of the principle that lying is always wrong, even when—especially when—employed to smoke out heretics.

Although Augustine makes it abundantly clear in *CM* and in his earlier *De Mendacio* (hereinafter, *DM*)[2] that he subscribes to the principle that lying is always wrong, he is less forthcoming about *why* lying is wrong. Nor, I shall argue, does he supply a clear account of what lying *is*, in distinction from other kinds of deceptive practices. These two projects, justification of the principle and definition of the concept, are not unrelated. It might be, for instance, that if one delimits the notion of a lie narrowly enough, one will thereby make defense of the principle easier. I shall begin by surveying Augustine's remarks on definition.

What Are Lies?

Here is a trio of passages, two from *DM* and one from *CM*. The translations are subject to modification as we proceed.

---

[1] See Bernard Williams, *Truth and Truthfulness: An Essay in Genealogy* (Princeton, NJ: Princeton University Press, 2002), 102–105. For useful discussion of other approaches to the moral problem of lying, see Alasdair MacIntyre, "Truthfulness, Lies, and Moral Philosophers: What Can We Learn from Mill and Kant?," in *The Tanner Lectures on Human Values*, vol. 16, ed. Grethe B. Peterson (Salt Lake City: University of Utah Press, 1995), 309–361.

[2] Written in 396. Augustine seems to have regarded *CM* as superseding *DM*. See *Retractationes* 1.27. But he also seems to regard the supersession as due to an improvement in writing clarity, not a change in philosophical position.

(A) In *DM* 3.3 Augustine allows that just as a person who says what is false may not be lying, so long as she believes that what she says is true, so a person who tells the truth may nonetheless be lying if he believes that what he is saying is false. As if in anticipation of our incredulous stares regarding the second claim, Augustine hastens to add, "For he is to be judged as lying or not lying by the intention (*sententia*) of his own soul, not by the truth or falsity of the things themselves."

(B) In *DM* 4.5 Augustine says that "[n]o one doubts that he lies who willingly states what is false for the purpose of deceiving (*causa fallendi*)," and that therefore it is obvious that a lie is a "false statement put forward with a will to deceive (*enuntiatem falsam cum voluntate ad fallendum prolatum*)." He then immediately adds, "But whether this alone is a lie, is another question."

(C) In *CM* 12.26 Augustine says that a lie is a "false signification with a will to deceive" (*falsa significatio cum voluntate fallendi*).

The first thing that may strike the reader of these passages is that they appear to be inconsistent. (B) and (C) comport with each other well enough. Their separation in composition by twenty-six years makes a strong case for saying that they represent Augustine's settled opinion on the matter. The odd one out is (A). We could try to admit (B) and (C) as part of the Augustinian canon and dismiss (A) as an aberration, were it not for the fact that (A) is located in such close proximity to (B), separated from it by approximately four standard-size pages. To dismiss (A) we would have to suppose not merely that Augustine nodded but that he fell asleep at the wheel. The last sentence of (B) throws out a bit of an interpretative lifeline. It encourages us to think that although a false statement put forward with a will to deceive is the paradigm or most salient case of a lie, there may be other cases of lying that do not fit that mold. Perhaps, then, the kind of case described in (A) can be tolerated. However, (A) does not just nibble at the periphery of the opinion put forward in (B) and (C). The case described in (A) flouts one-half of what (B) and (C) maintain, namely, that a lie involves a false statement or signification.

There is a way of harmonizing the three passages. The way I am going to suggest will also help us to see the rationale behind Augustine's position that lying is always wrong.

The first thing to do is to examine more closely the translations in (B) and (C). Both of them make crucial use of the term *voluntas*. I have translated it as "will," a term that descends etymologically from the Latin *volo*. The problem is that *voluntas* is as ambiguous in Latin as "will" is in English. A will to deceive can simply be a desire to deceive, and that is how the translators of *DM* and *CM* in the Fathers of the Church series have chosen to translate *voluntas* in (B) and (C).[3] On this translation, then, Augustine's definition of a lie is this:

(D1) A lie is a false statement put forward with a desire to deceive.

(D1) is a definition whose deficiency can be demonstrated by means of examples that Augustine himself provides. Suppose that I were to tell you that Burlington is the capital of Vermont under the following circumstances. (1) What I say is false: Vermont's capital is Montpelier. (2) I sincerely believe that Burlington is the capital. (3) I indeed have a desire to deceive you, but, ashamed by the baseness of that desire, I came to have a stronger desire not to deceive you, and it was the stronger desire that triggered my utterance. Now if just conditions (1) and (2) applied in this case, I think we would agree that although I misinformed you, I did not lie. (I may still be guilty of other lapses in this case, such as speaking too confidently on the basis of insufficient research.) The addition of condition (3) does not alter the verdict. The operative desire was the desire not to deceive, even though, seething cauldron of conflicting passions that I am, the desire to deceive persisted. The desire to deceive accompanied my false statement, yet I did not lie. So the definition of a lie as a false statement put forward with a desire to deceive is inadequate.

Nor is there an obvious patch that repairs the definition. The one most likely to suggest itself is this:

(D2) A lie is a false statement *effectively motivated* by a desire to deceive.

What (D2) maintains is that for an utterance to count as a lie, the desire to deceive must be in the driver's seat, so to speak; it must be the desire one would correctly cite in answer to the question, "What prompted her to say that?" Now the problem with (D2) is that many lies are not so motivated. Augustine knows this very well. He supplies us with a rich variety of counterexamples to the thesis that lies must be effectively motivated by a desire to deceive. A person can lie in circumstances in which the effective desire is a desire to seek someone else's salvation (*DM* 8.11 and *CM* passim); or to conceal one's religious, moral, or political convictions in a hostile society (*CM* 2.2); or to prevent someone else from committing greater sins (*CM* 9.20); or to protect the innocent (*CM* 10.23 and 15.32); or to keep a shocking truth from someone who will not be able to bear it (*CM* 18.36).

---

[3] Saint Augustine, *Treatises on Various Subjects*, ed. Roy J. Deferrari (New York: Fathers of the Church, Inc., 1952).

We can press this line of thought further. In *DM* 11.18 Augustine distinguishes the *mentiens* from the *mendax*. Call them, respectively, the "raconteur" and the "mythomaniac." The raconteur lies reluctantly, that is, she has no desire to lie, and would prefer to tell the truth, but she also prefers pleasing her listeners with harmless lies over remaining silent. In contrast, the mythomaniac "truly loves to lie and frequently indulges his soul in the pleasure of lying." There are two points worthy of note here. First, the raconteur's lying conflicts with what she most wants to do, namely, please her listeners by telling them truths. Since she cannot please them by telling them truths, pleasing them by lying is, by her lights, the next best thing. Augustine's claim about reluctance generalizes: we can say on his behalf that an agent acts reluctantly whenever she does what she does not most want to do. This conception of reluctance is at odds, to be sure, with a maneuver in a priori psychology that maintains that in general, whatever people do is what they most want to do; otherwise they would not do it. Thus because the raconteur did tell lies, telling lies must be what she most wanted to do. I see nothing to commend this maneuver. Centuries after Augustine's time but in the spirit of Augustine's moral psychology, Peter Abelard pointed out that inferences like "She wanted to lie from a desire to please her audience; therefore she wanted to lie" are invalid. She need have *no* desire to lie, a fortiori no effective desire to lie. She may very well regard her lying as something she must endure in order to achieve what she really does want, namely, the attention and admiration of her audience.[4]

Many cases of lying will thus be cases of reluctant lying; many of them will be tinged with regret that some other course of action was unavailable or even more unacceptable. But perhaps not all. For—this is the second point—the mythomaniac lies wholeheartedly: if anybody fills the bill of lying effectively motivated by a desire to deceive, it will be the mythomaniac. Surely, however, the genuine mythomaniac is or is close to being a psychopath. Till Eulenspiegel and Don Juan are literary approximations. But if we have to scour the resources of legend to find our best examples, that suggests that the phenomenon of lying effectively motivated by a desire to deceive may not be all that common, certainly not as common as lying reluctantly.

I suggest, then, that we do Augustine a disservice by translating *voluntas* as "desire." That translation requires us to suppose not only that Augustine's attempt at definition fails but that Augustine himself obligingly supplies us with

---

[4] For details see my "Abelard's Ethics: The Inside Story," in *The Cambridge Companion to Abelard*, ed. Jeffrey Brower and Kevin Guilfoy (Cambridge: Cambridge University Press, 2004), 279–304. Reprinted as Chapter 9 of this volume.

the materials necessary to chart its failure. We search in the wrong place if we rummage through the closet of desires in an attempt to locate a definition of lying. I want to argue for an alternative translation of *voluntas,* one that makes a stronger case for Augustine. *Voluntas* can also mean "intention." Under that translation Augustine's definition is this:

(D3) A lie is a false statement put forward with an intention to deceive.

How does this help? It can help only if there is some significant philosophical difference between desires and intentions. And there is. Our desires come to us unbidden (but not necessarily unwelcome). We generally have no more direct voluntary control over them than we do over our ordinary beliefs. Just as my beliefs can be inconsistent, my desires can conflict with each other: the satisfaction of one can logically preclude the satisfaction of others. In contrast, many intentions are arrived at voluntarily. And although desire-conflict betokens merely a less than optimal psychic order, a conflict of intentions would be a symptom of a breakdown of rationality. You can understand someone who says "I want to φ and I want not to φ" ("I want to have the crème brûlée and I want not to have the crème brûlée"). That is the stuff of which human frailty is made. Now try to fathom what could be going on internally with someone who said, in all seriousness, "I intend to φ and I intend not to φ." One might be able to interpret this diachronically, as "I intend to φ and *then* I intend not to φ" ("I intend to live the life of a wastrel until 30; I intend after that to put aside my prodigal ways"). But if the avowal is interpreted synchronically, its speaker beggars comprehension.

The reason for the lack of parallel between conflicting desires and conflicting intentions is not far afield. Our garden-variety desires, like our garden-variety perceptual beliefs, are more or less just *there,* taking up residence in our psyches. We do not fabricate them so much as we find them. (Of course, some desires are not garden-variety but rather the product of cultivation, such as a preference for Cabernet Sauvignon over Merlot. But then so are some perceptual beliefs, like the belief that the painting before me is an early Monet.) Our intentions, however, are more the product of fabrication. Our desires are an essential building material: it is hard to see how a being who had no desires whatsoever could have any intentions. Intentions are not merely fancy (or fancier) desires. They are more like plans of action whose function is to satisfy some desires (or, in the unhappy dispensation, to thwart some desires), plans that the agent will act on if the circumstances are right.

Augustine saw this clearly by the time he came to write *DM.* In *De Sermone Domini in Monte,* written two years before *DM,* he introduced a trio of concepts, suggestion, pleasure, and consent, that he regarded as critical to the analysis of sin.[5] A suggestion is a representation in a person's mind, quite often brought about by some external set of circumstances. The representation is of some possible state of affairs whose actualization would typically involve the person's agency. The person may or may not take pleasure in the suggestion. It is at this point that desires will arise. To consent to the suggestion is to intend to bring about its associated state of affairs should the opportunity arise (*De Sermone Domini in Monte* 1.12.34).

This conceptual apparatus provides good reason for accepting the intentional translation of *voluntas*, thereby imputing to Augustine definition (D3). But there is more work to be done if we are to determine whether the definition is acceptable to us and to Augustine.

It is useful to compare Augustine's fifth-century (D3) with a twenty-first-century definition:

> (D4) A lie is "an assertion, the content of which the speaker believes to be false, which is made with the intention to deceive the hearer with regard to that content."[6]

Augustine's (D3) and Williams's (D4) converge on the importance of an intention to deceive. They diverge on two other points. First, (D3) specifies that the statement must be false and is silent on the question whether the speaker must believe the statement to be false. (D4) focuses on the speaker's belief to the exclusion of the truth-value of the statement. Second, (D3) simply refers to an intention to deceive that accompanies the false statement. (D4) explicitly ties the intention to the content of the statement.

Consider the first difference first. For all that (D3) says, it might seem that the speaker could believe of the false statement that it is true. Or is this not even a possibility, given that the speaker is bent on deception? In analogous fashion, for all that (D4) says, the assertion that the speaker believes to be false might be true. Has the speaker then failed to lie, contrary to his intention? We can and perhaps should ring the changes here on the truth-value of the statement and

---

[5] See William E. Mann, "Inner-Life Ethics," in *The Augustinian Tradition*, ed. Gareth B. Matthews (Berkeley: University of California Press, 1999), pp. 140–165 [Chapter 6 of this volume], for details.

[6] Williams, *Truth and Truthfulness*, 96. Williams adds, "I . . . believe that this is what most people understand by the word 'lie'; despite a very promiscuous use of it by some theoretical writers, it seems to me that in everyday use this is clearly its definition." Everyday users may be surprised to find out that by this account they take as a lie a *true* assertion believed to be false by its speaker; see the discussion below. In fact, it is a consequence of Williams's definition that whether a person has lied does not depend on the way the world is; it depends solely on what is in the speaker's head. For reasons I hope to make clear below, Williams's (D4) is more Augustinian than Augustine's (D3).

the speaker's belief about the statement in order to test (D3) and (D4). Let us set aside cases in which the speaker has no doxastic attitude vis-à-vis the statement,[7] and consider just those cases in which the speaker either believes that the statement is true or believes that the statement is false. And let us hold fixed the assumption that the speaker intends to deceive the hearer, allowing for the intention, however, to be articulated further in light of the cases. Finally, let us press into service the hapless Remigio. There are, then, four possibilities open to Remigio:

(1) The statement is true and Remigio believes that the statement is true.
(2) The statement is true and Remigio believes that the statement is false.
(3) The statement is false and Remigio believes that the statement is true.
(4) The statement is false and Remigio believes that the statement is false.

For the sake of convenience, I shall refer to (1)–(4) almost always as cases, though they are, more strictly speaking, *types* of cases. Case (4), about which little needs to be said, is the standard case of a lie. Let us turn our attention to cases (1) and (3). They are startling in that they suppose that Remigio, who has set out on a path of deception, believes that the statement being used, the vehicle of that deception, is true. A non-startling hypothesis that shows the possibility of a type-(1) case is case (1′): Remigio utters a true statement, say, "Montpellier is the capital of Hérault," to a hearer who Remigio believes distrusts him. Remigio counts on the distrust leading the hearer to come to believe that Montpellier is not the capital of Hérault.[8] Another non-startling hypothesis that would exemplify cases (1) and (3) is that Remigio is employing a relatively long-range strategy to overcome the present suspicions that the hearer harbors toward Remigio, to gain the hearer's trust thereby, in order that Remigio might succeed in deceiving the hearer about some more significant item at a future date. These instantiations of cases (1) and (3) can be labeled (1*) and (3*), respectively. Remigio's

---

[7] Such cases would include the student who, having no idea what the correct answer is on a multiple choice question, picks one at random, hoping that it is correct. I suppose that in an attenuated sense of "deceive," the student is trying to deceive the teacher into thinking that the student knows the answer. The irony here is that if the student is lucky and picks what happens to be the correct answer, the analogue in this setting to telling the truth, that will go further toward deceiving the teacher than if the student picks an incorrect answer, the analogue to lying. In any event it seems a mistake to describe the case as a case of lying.

[8] This kind of case is suggested by some of the ingenious examples that Augustine raises in *DM* 4.4. Case (1) also subsumes instances like Remigio's equivocation, with the proviso that the speaker assigns to the statement a different proposition from the proposition the speaker hopes will be assigned to it by the audience.

present attempt at spreading the truth might thus be construed as a "loss leader." Under this interpretation of Remigio's actions, case (3*) shows Remigio to be somewhat inept. But should any of these cases, (1'), (1*), and (3*), be counted as cases of lying?

In case (3*) Remigio puts forward a false statement and Remigio has an intention to deceive. One may be disinclined, however, to call this a lie, and not simply because Remigio believes the statement to be true. It is rather that the intention to deceive is not connected in the right way to Remigio's present utterance. We might distinguish here between remote and proximate intentions. A remote intention is an intention presently held by an agent, whose realization is at some time in the future, requiring a chain of events to bring it about. We are to suppose that some of the links on the chain are the products of other intentions of the agent, functioning as means in service of the remote intention. These other intentions are proximate intentions, although nothing prevents some of them from being remote themselves, relative to other, more proximate intentions on the chain. It can happen that some proximate intentions involve outcomes quite different in kind from the outcome envisioned in the remote intention. But the proximate outcomes are no less genuinely intended for all that. Wanda's ultimate goal is to live a life of ease by the time she turns fifty. She may nevertheless embark, at the age of thirty, on a career that she knows will be fraught with hardships because she believes that the career is an effective means to her goal. The proximate hardships are really intended (but probably not really desired!) for the sake of the remote goal. In similar fashion, Remigio's present proximate intention can be not to deceive even though Remigio's present remote intention is to deceive and even though the proximate intention is in service of the remote intention.

Thus if we think it is correct to clear Remigio of charges of lying in case (3*), we should also think that Augustine's definition (D3) leaves the notion of an intention to deceive too indeterminate. Although Williams does not tarry to offer a rationale for incorporating into (D4) the constraint that the intention to deceive must be directed at the content of the assertion, the incorporation explains how type-(3) cases can involve a false statement, be tainted with deception, yet not be cases of lying. And if case (3*) is judged not to be a lie, it seems that case (1*) should also not be so judged. That leaves case (1'). In (1') Remigio is counting on his hearer's distrust to lead the hearer to believe of a true statement that it is false. A case of intentional deception, to be sure. But can one lie by telling the truth? While there is nothing in Williams's (D4) that precludes the possibility, one might think, reasonably enough, that Augustine's (D3) does rule it out. Yet it is Augustine who tells us in passage (A) that a person can lie by telling the truth. The case Augustine explicitly cited in (A) was a type-(2) case, in which the speaker believes that what he says is false. But the rationale

Augustine offers for classifying case (2) as a lie makes it tempting also to number case (1′) among the lies: "For he is to be judged as lying or not lying by the intention of his own soul, not by the truth or falsity of the things themselves." Has Augustine embraced principles that result in inconsistency? On the one hand, (D3) requires a false statement, which (1′) lacks; on the other, passage (A) does not merely waive (D3)'s requirement, it *rejects* the requirement.

One might try to reconcile Augustine's views by maintaining that although case (2) is a lie by the light of passage (A), (1′) is not. Before we see an argument for discriminating between case (2) and case (1′) in this way, we should keep in mind that even if the argument is successful, we have not thereby addressed the issue of how to square Augustine's verdict in passage (A) on case (2) with his (D3) definition, which requires a false statement, not merely a (true) statement believed to be false.

By hypothesis, in both cases (1′) and (2) Remigio is out to get his hearer to believe a falsehood. That may or may not be behavior for which we have sympathy on Remigio's part: it depends on why Remigio wants to deceive the hearer and, in case (1′), why the hearer is distrustful.[9] Setting those issues aside, we have to acknowledge in case (2) that Remigio believes that he is telling a falsehood and that he intends to deceive his hearer about the content of his assertion. By any reasonable account, everything *internally* required for lying has been met. It is just that in case (2) the world did not cooperate with Remigio; what he succeeded in doing outwardly was to tell the truth, unbeknownst to himself and no doubt contrary to his wishes. That Remigio is not numbered among the liars *externally* is thus a matter of moral luck. Let us say, then, that case (2) is a case of an *internal lie*. And let us say that a *necessary* condition for an assertion's counting as an *external lie* is that the assertion be false. This way of treating case (2) comports with the sentiment expressed in passage (A). However, the internal conditions present in case (2) are only partly met in case (1′). In particular, Remigio does not believe that his statement is false. If we insist that for something to count as an internal lie, the speaker must both believe that what he says is false and intend to deceive the hearer about the content of the assertion, then case (1′) qualifies as neither an internal nor an external lie.

It may have occurred to you that the notion of an internal lie recapitulates Williams's (D4) and that the notion of an external lie picks up the feature of Augustine's (D3) not already explicit in (D4). That suggests putting forward the following hybrid definition of a *full-blown lie,* a lie that is both an internal and external lie:

____

[9] Having sympathy for an agent's behavior does not entail regarding the behavior as right. Augustine saw this clearly; see below.

> (D5) A full-blown lie is (a) a false statement, (b) the content of which the speaker believes to be false, (c) which is made with the intention to deceive the hearer with regard to that content.

Recall the tantalizing remark Augustine makes immediately after the presentation of his (D3) definition from *DM* 4.5, cited in passage (B): "But whether this [(D3)] alone is a lie is another question." Augustine has special reason to regard internal lies as genuine lies even though they are not full-blown lies or lies picked up by (D3). In *De continentia,* a work written shortly before *DM,* Augustine amplified his conception of intention as consent to produce an audacious account of sin. The amplification has three components. The first component is that consent to something that is forbidden by God is necessary for a sin to have been committed. That is, no sin is unintentional. The second component is that to consent to something forbidden by God *is* to commit a sin, even if external circumstances should prevent the consent from being translated into action. That is, to intend to do what is forbidden by God is sufficient for having already committed a sin. The third component maintains that one's consent to φ, when φ is forbidden by God, convicts one, in the eyes of God, of the sin of φing. That is, if one intends to murder, for example, then one is guilty of the sin of murder, by God's accounting, not just attempted murder, even if the killing is never carried out! (*De continentia* 2.3–5.)[10] We can now see why Augustine calls case (2) a lie in passage (A). Even had Remigio uttered nothing, his belief and intention in case (2) are sufficient to qualify him as a liar. The fact that he actually uttered a truth does not alter the verdict, any more than the fact that Jones unwittingly used a toy weapon would clear Jones of a charge of assault.

Why, then, the emphasis on the official-looking definition, (D3), when (D3) does not acknowledge the existence of internal lies? The context in which *DM* passage (B) is embedded makes it clear that (D3) is intended to pick out only the most salient, public lies. And the practical and pressing concern that dominates the discussion in *CM,* namely, the use of full-blown lies to trap heretics, makes a discussion of internal lies something of a luxury.

I think the most sympathetic interpretation of Augustine's views on defining the notion of a lie is that lies divide into two sorts. There are internal lies and there are full-blown lies. Full-blown lies are defined by (D5), and I suppose on Augustine's behalf that clause (b) and the more precise clause (c) of (D5) are clauses that Augustine would be happy to add to his (D3). Internal lies satisfy clauses (b) and (c) of (D5) but not clause (a). They can fail to satisfy clause (a) in either of two ways. The speaker can say nothing or the speaker can say

---

[10] See Mann, "Inner-Life Ethics."

something that is true, not false. Described in this way, internal lies can seem to be truncated, lies that never make the big time in the external world. They are, nevertheless, in Augustine's view, morally serious.

Why Are Lies Always Wrong?

It is one thing to maintain that lying used to uncover heretics is wrong, another to argue that *all* lying is wrong. Augustine espouses both theses, sometimes relying on the second thesis to argue for the first. I shall begin by looking at his strategy for arguing for the first thesis, then turn my attention to the second.

One way of seeing what Augustine is up to in *CM* is to imagine his correspondent, Consentius, putting forward or at least wondering about the following *Permissibility Thesis*:

(PT) If x's doing φ for the sake of ψ will have better consequences than x's not doing φ, then it is permissible for x to do φ for the sake of ψ.

When the contemplated activity is lying for the sake of uncovering heretics, Consentius might suppose that the betterment to be achieved is twofold. Orthodox Christians will be insulated from the potentially baneful influence of heretics feigning orthodoxy while insinuating blasphemous doctrines. And the heretics themselves, once exposed, will have the opportunity of recanting the heresy that stymies their prospects for salvation.

(PT) is not to be confused with cruder versions of act-utilitarianism that maintain that if x's doing φ will have better consequences than x's not doing φ, then x's doing φ is obligatory. It is not (PT)'s ambition to tell us what our duties are. (PT) simply alleges a sufficient condition for an action's not being forbidden. Even so, Augustine rejects (PT) and, for good measure, argues against the likelihood of the two supposed benefits being delivered by a policy of lying.

Augustine's brief against (PT) takes the following form. There are some types of action whose goodness or badness depends on the reasons for which the agent performs them. Call these types of action "intrinsically neutral." Volunteering to work in a soup kitchen is laudable if the intention is to aid the unfortunate; an act of cynical manipulation if undertaken as a publicity stunt. There are other types of action that remain sins no matter what reason might be given for committing them. Let us call these types of action "intrinsically sinful." Augustine's examples are theft, debauchery, and blasphemy: the purpose of *CM* is to demonstrate that lying is also on the list (*CM* 7.18).[11]

---

[11] Both claims run contrary to versions of act-utilitarianism that maintain that the sole dimension upon which an action is to be evaluated morally is its consequences and that (as a consequence) no type of action is intrinsically sinful.

Before proceeding further, we should note that Augustine does not do what we might have expected him to do—complete his taxonomy of actions by specifying types of actions that are intrinsically good, good no matter for what reason they are performed. It could be that, because *CM* is out to consign lies to the category of intrinsically sinful acts, Augustine saw no need to introduce the intrinsically good ones. But I suspect that there is a deeper reason. Augustine may have thought there *are* no intrinsically good actions. Suppose that we try to name one. Surely working for someone else's salvation would be a likely candidate. But if I work for your salvation because I think it will confer earthly power on me, then my action is tainted by my (no doubt confused and foolish) reason for acting. If this conjecture is correct, then there is a kind of asymmetry between the good and the bad as these notions apply to actions. Some actions are intrinsically bad (or intrinsically wrong) but no action is intrinsically good (or intrinsically right).[12]

Augustine need have no quarrel with (PT) when "φ" and "ψ" range over intrinsically neutral actions, but he will deny (PT) in cases in which either or both of the variables range over actions that are intrinsically sinful. The case against both φ and ψ being intrinsically sinful is obvious. A person's stealing in order to sustain his debauchery is doubly wrong and two wrongs do not make a right. Consider now the case in which "φ" picks out an intrinsically neutral act-type while "ψ" picks out an intrinsically sinful act-type. Working in the soup kitchen in order to poison one of the customers might pass muster by the lights of (PT) if the customer is a fiend, but will not be endorsed by Augustine.

Consider finally a case in which "φ" picks out an intrinsically sinful type of action, and suppose that "ψ" picks out an intrinsically neutral act-type. Stealing from Peter to pay Paul is still theft, no matter how rich and base Peter is or how poor and noble Paul is; circumstances and motives cannot make a theft not to be a theft. This latter kind of pattern—φ intrinsically sinful, ψ intrinsically neutral— matches lying for the sake of unmasking heretics. Even if doing φ for the sake of ψ were to have better consequences than not doing φ, doing φ would remain impermissible, thus falsifying (PT). Or so Augustine wants to claim. But there are two gaps in this procedure. He has justified neither the thesis that some types of action are intrinsically sinful nor the dependent thesis that lies are included among the intrinsically sinful types of action. What we get instead are arguments denying the alleged beneficial effects of heretic entrapment by mendacious means. Those arguments at first appear to be independent of the argument

---

[12] If this conjecture about Augustine's views is correct, then Augustine is committed to holding that Jesus's redemption of humankind was good but not intrinsically good. Some of the sting of that judgment can be removed by claiming that on some appropriate interpretation of "could not have done otherwise," Jesus could not have acted for any other reason than love of humankind.

against (PT). In fact, they, too, depend on the thesis that some types of action are intrinsically sinful. In what follows I shall highlight in boldface the turns in the arguments that depend on the thesis.

Let us first examine the defense of lying that maintains that by exposing heretics by deceitful means, we prevent them from spreading their heresy and provide the occasion for their reform. Augustine's attack on this defense takes the form of a cost-benefit analysis. When heretics lie to orthodox Christians, feigning orthodoxy, orthodox Christians are not harmed because what they hear is the truth. Orthodox Christians who lie to heretics, falsely endorsing heretical beliefs, risk entrenching the heretics in their heresy and winning new converts to that heresy, in direct proportion to their effectiveness at deceit. **Moreover, when orthodox Christians reveal their true beliefs at the conclusion of a campaign of deceit, their pattern of duplicity tends to confirm in heretics the erroneous opinion that lying is sometimes permissible** (*CM* 3.4–5), along with distrust about whether the orthodox are telling the truth *now* (*CM* 4.7). A comparison between the sincere heretic and the dissembling orthodox believer actually tells in favor of the heretic. The former merely (though perhaps dangerously) *believes* mistakenly; the latter *knowingly* broadcasts falsehoods about a religion that confesses the Truth (*CM* 5.8–9 and 6.12)

The tally does not end there. Further difficulties emerge when we examine the heretic-hunter who knowingly lies. The content of his lies will be sufficient to qualify them as blasphemy. It is no defense for him to say that he was only pretending to blaspheme; that the words on his tongue were not the words in his heart. As Augustine points out, it was not open to Peter, when he denied Christ, to claim that he was only pretending to deny Christ (*CM* 6.13). Augustine's point is worth amplifying a bit. There are communication contexts in which the norm of truth-telling is suspended. Augustine mentions jokes as an example (*DM* 2.2), to which we can add novels and plays. Pretending is also one such context, at least partly so. There is a kind of pretending in which all parties affected are "in on" the pretense. Children's play, in which every child pretends to be a space alien, or a student at Hogwarts School of Witchcraft and Wizardry, is a prime example. Another kind of pretending, however, is unilateral. In an effort to impress someone I have just met I might pretend to be a Nobel laureate in philosophy. If the person is not in on my pretense, the pretense is unilateral. Because not all parties in unilateral pretending are on the same cognitive footing, unilateral pretending is more open to abuse and therefore to moral criticism. Its consequences to the factually ignorant victims can range from minor annoyance through humiliation up to loss of life. As the consequences grow more severe, the perpetrator's "I was only pretending" defense rings more hollow. But apart from consideration of consequences, the "I was only pretending" defense can be false, even when the speaker really was seeking only to pretend. Sometimes to pretend to φ *is* to φ.

J. L. Austin pointed out that the only convincing way to pretend to be washing windows while casing a joint is to be actually washing the joint's windows. And in some social settings merely to pretend a show of vulgarity is, alas, to be vulgar.[13] The moral appraisal of the perpetrator can thus vary with the severity of the consequences to the victims, but it need not vary only along that dimension. In particular, one might justifiably regard the perpetrator's pretense as censurable even if no harm or embarrassment were to befall the victim.

We can now put Augustine's point this way. It does no good to try to assimilate the practice of lying to heretics to a case of unilateral pretending, because to pretend to blaspheme *is* to blaspheme, and **there are no circumstances in which blasphemy is permissible.** Thus the lying heretic-hunter places his soul in terrible jeopardy.

Augustine has more in store for the prospective undercover heretic-deceiver. Recall (PT). Hold "ψ" fixed to the act-type *uncovering heretics*. Hitherto we have coupled "ψ" with "φ" when "φ" was held fixed to the act-type *lying*. One of Augustine's strategies is to allow "φ" to vary over other act-types, such as *committing adultery*. If (PT) allows lying to capture heretics on grounds of better consequences, then it also allows committing adultery to capture heretics on the same grounds (*CM* 7.17). **For that matter (PT) allows the commission of any intrinsically sinful action as long as it has better consequences than not committing it would have.** If we now let "ψ" vary in tandem with "φ," and **assume that some intrinsically sinful action types are worse than others,** we will get the results, according to Augustine, that in typical circumstances it is permissible to commit theft to prevent someone else from committing debauchery, to commit debauchery to prevent someone else from committing incest, and to commit incest to prevent someone else from doing whatever is worse than incest. These are examples of what Augustine calls "compensatory sins" (*compensativa peccata*), sins a person undertakes to thwart some other person from committing more grievous sins (*CM* 9.20). **The seductive power of their aura of self-sacrifice is such that one can come to hold the erroneous opinion, not merely that they are permissible under (PT), but that they are praiseworthy and justified in themselves** (*CM* 9.20, 10.23). As a consequence, a zealous Christian may come to believe that undertaking the sin of lying in order to prevent the sins that flow from heresy is either obligatory or supererogatory.

But this way lies madness. If compensatory sins are justified, then a conscientious person will find herself vulnerable to the tyrant who incessantly threatens to commit greater sins unless she commits lesser sins (*DM* 6.9 and *CM* 9.20).

---

[13] "Pretending," in J. L. Austin, *Philosophical Papers,* ed. J. O. Urmson and G. J. Warnock (Oxford: Clarendon Press, 1961), 207.

If she acquiesces in the sin, it is still a sin even though it prevents a greater sin from occurring (*CM* 9.20, 9.22). And *she* has sinned, not the tyrant, although the tyrant may be guilty of a separate sin of coercion. But if she does nothing and the tyrant carries out his threat, his sin is not imputable to her. Even if it is true that he would not have done ψ if she had done φ, that does not entail that she is a partner to his doing ψ. As Augustine points out, it might be true that the burglars would not have broken down my door if I had left it unlocked, but when they do break the door down because it was locked, I am not a party to their destruction (*DM* 9.14).

Augustine thus believes that he has shown that there is no obligation to commit compensatory sins. He also argues for the stronger thesis that we are obligated not to sin, even compensatorily. The Second Great Commandment, that we should love our neighbors as ourselves, does not require that we love our neighbors *more* than ourselves; the person who interprets it that way "exceeds the rule of sound doctrine" (*DM* 6.9). Augustine's point is that to sacrifice one's own eternal life by sinning, even if that were the *only* way to secure someone else's eternal life—a circumstance Augustine is inclined to regard as impossible—is to treat oneself as less than a child of God.[14]

This completes Augustine's case against the so-called benefits of lying to expose heretics. As I have tried to indicate, the case is shot through with steps that presuppose the existence of a class of intrinsically sinful actions, a class that includes all acts of lying. You will search in vain, however, in *DM* and *CM* for justification for the claim that some types of action are intrinsically sinful or for the claim that lying is such a type. Why is that? I suggest that for Augustine, the answer is too obvious for words. Both works were composed for Christian audiences, who could be expected to be guided by the commandments of love, to be sure, but also by the Ten Commandments. I suggest, then, that Augustine's opinion would be that the types of action explicitly forbidden by the Ten Commandments are intrinsically sinful, that what makes them intrinsically sinful is their being contrary to the commandments of love, and that what validates the commandments of love is that they issue from a perfectly good and loving God.[15]

[14] Secular analogues of this style of argument surface in Kant's second formulation of the Categorical Imperative and in Williams's "A Critique of Utilitarianism," in J. J. C. Smart and Bernard Williams, *Utilitarianism: For and Against* (Cambridge: Cambridge University Press, 1973).

[15] For recent variations of this sort of view, see Robert Merrihew Adams, *Finite and Infinite Goods: A Framework for Ethics* (New York: Oxford University Press, 1999); Philip L. Quinn, "Divine Command Theory," in *The Blackwell Guide to Ethical Theory*, ed. Hugh LaFollette (Malden, MA: Blackwell Publishers, 2000), 53–73; and William E. Mann, "Theism and the Foundations of Ethics," in *The Blackwell Guide to the Philosophy of Religion*, ed. William E. Mann (Malden, MA: Blackwell Publishers, 2005), 283.

If this is the sort of opinion that Augustine would enunciate, then there is an obvious challenge to it coming from within the ranks of conscientious Christians. "On some occasions," some will say, "the commandments of love dictate that we should lie. Even though we might concede that lying should never be used to trap heretics, there are cases in which it would be needlessly cruel not to lie. We adherents to the commandments of love thus should view the commandment not to bear false witness to be compatible with the telling of some lies."

As if in anticipation of this challenge, Augustine raises the following case. You are asked by a patient whose life is threatened by a serious illness whether her only child is alive or not. You know that the child has died. You also believe that if you tell her the truth, it will kill her, but, we may suppose, if you do not tell her the truth, she will survive. You can choose among three answers, "He is dead," "He is alive," and "I do not know." Any other verbal maneuver will be interpreted by the patient as an attempt to deflect the question and thus as an admission that the child has died. (Unlike the case in which an officer of an invading army of oppression asks you whether you know the whereabouts of any freedom fighters, you cannot take the heroic high road and say "Yes, I do, but I refuse to tell you." If it were given to the patient, that answer would inform her that her son is dead.) So, you can either tell her truth, ensuring her demise, or you can lie, aiding her recovery.

Augustine says of the arguments for lying in a case like this that he is moved by them "more powerfully than wisely" (*CM* 18.36). The temptation to lie in such a case is so great that Augustine himself seems uncertain about whether he could resist it. One thing he is certain about, however, is that if he were to succumb to temptation even here, he would be committing a sin. Our imperfect human condition inclines us to identify the irresistible with the permissible; to go so far as to identify failing to lie in this case with homicide. These tactics are desperate exercises in special pleading. Counterpoised to them and to the intimate awareness of our psychological infirmity is our image of Jesus, from whose mouth nothing false proceeded (*CM* 18.36). To those who maintain that lying to the patient is not sinful, Augustine's reply is sympathetic but firm disagreement. Still, some types of sinful action are better or worse than others, and of instances of the same type of sin, some are performed for better or worse reasons (*CM* 8.19). Although all lies are sinful, some may be forgivable. So we should hope.

Coda

In a remarkable passage in *DM*, Augustine offers three possible glosses on Sirach (Ecclesiasticus) 7:13, "Refuse to utter any lie, for the habit of lying serves no good" (*DM* 16–17.34). The Latin text that Augustine uses for the first part of

the verse is *Nolite velle mentiri omne mendacium*. According to Augustine, on one
interpretation, we have:

> (I1) Do not utter any lie, and do not will to utter any lie.

A second interpretation maintains:

> (I2) Do not utter any lie except a lie that (a) does not pertain to religious doctrine
> and (b) is such that a greater evil can be avoided by telling it than by telling
> the truth.

Finally, we have:

> (I3) Do not utter any lies that are forbidden but only those lies that are permitted.

Augustine dismisses (I3) on grounds that its defenders simply misconstrue
the *omne* in the Sirach passage as "every" instead of "any," thus supposing that
the passage says "Refuse to utter every lie" instead of "Refuse to utter any lie."
Augustine could subscribe to (I3); it is, after all, compatible with his view that
every lie is forbidden. But that very compatibility testifies to the emptiness and
indeterminateness of (I3). (I2) is certainly more determinate. (I2) would allow
for lying in the case of the ailing patient's dead child but would disallow blasphemous lying. We know already that Augustine rejects (I2). His attitude toward
(I2) vis-à-vis (I1) is revealing. The Hebrew midwives who lied to the king of
Egypt (Exodus 1:15–21) found favor with God because their lie was motivated
by mercy and concern for the welfare of others. Their behavior was evidence
of progress towards spiritual perfection. But it would be a mistake to think that
their spiritual perfection would be aided by their cultivating a disposition to lie
whenever they find themselves in a position fitting the pattern of conditions
(a) and (b) in (I2). Quite the contrary. For, as the second part of the Sirach passage emphasizes, "the habit of lying serves no good." (I2) specifies a standard of
truth-telling performance that many humans would find hard enough to meet.
Even so, its demands are not as stringent as those of (I1). For those who take
seriously the injunction to be perfect, as their heavenly father is perfect, (I1) sets
the correct standard. The first part of (I1) forbids all full-blown, (D5)-type lies,
including but not restricted to lies uttered to trap heretics, compensatory lies,
and lies of mercy. In the second part of (I1), I have let *velle* stand as "will," despite
my earlier fussiness about desires versus intentions. We can, if we wish, split the
second part of (I1) into two claims, depending on how we translate *velle*:

> (I1′) Do not utter any lie, and do not intend to utter any lie.
> (I1*) Do not utter any lie, and do not desire to utter any lie.

The second half of (I1′) forbids internal, (D4)-type lies, the lies that never register in the public forum but are nonetheless known by omniscient God.[16] The person who hews his behavior to the line of (I1′) will be charged with no lies, full-blown or internal. But if, as Augustine thinks, desire is the psychological antecedent of intention, the person who satisfies (I1*), who no longer has desires to lie—not even desires, too weak to be effective movers to action—will have perfected herself even further.

Suppose that Remigio and Bernard Gui complete their pas de deux without a false step: neither of them resorts to telling a lie. Should we then conclude that nothing morally objectionable occurred in the interrogation? Remigio availed himself of some deceptive tactics. Is deception always morally wrong? Consider St. Athanasius, who was asked by his persecutors, who did not recognize him, "Is Athanasius close at hand?" His reply, "He is not far from here,"[17] gets high marks from the point of view of truth, low marks from the point of view of candor. But to assess the moral status of deception would require another paper, or book.

---

[16] Thus I take Augustine's treatment of the Sirach passage to vindicate the taxonomy of lies developed in the first section of this paper.

[17] MacIntyre, "Truthfulness, Lies, and Moral Philosophers," 336.

8

Perplexity and Mystery

The *agent provocateur* behind this session is Meno. Not Plato's *Meno*—although without Plato's *Meno* we would not have Meno before us—but the character Meno himself. For it is Meno who, after liberal exposure to Socrates's elenctic technique, in what Gareth B. Matthews calls "perhaps the most famous expression of philosophical perplexity in all literature,"[1] attributes his state of aporia to Socrates, likening Socrates to a torpedo fish. And it is Meno who, on the same Stephanus page, balks at the prospect of continuing the process of Socratic inquiry, endorsing the position that if we do not already know what we are looking for—an account of virtue, for example—then we will not know it even should we come across it, and if we do already know what we are looking for, then we have no need to look for it. The first Menonian observation serves as a springboard for Matthews's reflections on perplexity in Augustine's *Confessions*. The second provides a backdrop for Peter King's discussion of the "Paradox of Teaching," Augustine's argument in *De Magistro* that it is impossible for anyone to teach anyone else anything. I shall comment on these two papers in the order in which Meno's observations appeared.

According to Matthews, it is a "paradox" that "Augustine, one of the great dogmatic thinkers in our Western tradition, is also one of the most Socratic." How can this be? "How can it be that Augustine, the supremely dogmatic thinker, is also Augustine, the wonderfully Socratic one?" Let me begin by asking why we should regard these dual Augustinian roles as paradoxical. Suppose I were to ask, "How can it be that Augustine, the bishop of Hippo, is also Augustine, the father of Adeodatus?" You might hasten to assure me that there is no paradox here. Although bishops are supposed to have no children, or no children to speak of, Augustine's son was born years before Augustine's conversion to Christianity. Paradox evaporates when we come to see that I have picked out two different segments of Augustine's life.

---

[1] All quotations from Matthews are from "The Socratic Augustine," *Metaphilosophy* 29 (1998): 196–208.

Is it the same with Augustine the dogmatist and Augustine the Socratist? That is, at that time in his career when Augustine was exercising his winsome Socratic ways, was the dogmatist in him slumbering its dogmatic slumbers? Well, you can make that strategy work approximately two-thirds of the way. His anti-Pelagian and anti-Donatist writings were written substantially later in his life than the *Confessions,* the one work from which Matthews draws all the Augustinian aporetic examples. Still, by the time Augustine came to write the *Confessions* he had already established himself as Augustine the polemicist against the Manichaeans. Moreover, Augustine the anti-Manichaean cannot be separated from Augustine the author of the *Confessions.* The *Confessions* would never have been written had Augustine not seen his way clear of Manichaeanism. So although the author of the *Confessions* cannot say what time is, he can say with thundering assurance what evil is—sheer non-being, unadulterated by any tincture of being.

Matthews's solution to the paradox found in the *Confessions* is this. Instances of the question-form "How is it possible that *p*?" can be asked in one or the other of three different modes, either the Assumption, Rejection, or Neutral Mode. To ask in the Assumption Mode how it is possible that *p* is to ask how *p* is possible while not harboring any doubt that *p* is actual. The expected characterizations are then given of the Rejection and Neutral Modes. Now, according to Matthews, "The point is that, although he keeps on asking, Socratically, questions of the form 'How is it possible that *p*?' *most* of the time he does not ask these questions in the Rejection Mode, or even in the Neutral Mode; rather he asks them in the Assumption Mode. Typically, his firm belief that *p* is not made hostage to his ability to say how it is possible that *p*. This is faith, often rock-solid faith, in search of understanding."

I worry about this solution. If I understand it correctly, it appears to me that it has the effect of allowing Augustine the dogmatist to overrun Augustine the Socratist. It seems to represent Augustine's attitude as something like this: "I've racked my brains trying to figure out how I can be in a certain specific mental state (calling on God to find out who he is, knowing pain or sadness without being in pain or being sad, remembering what forgetfulness is, successfully measuring time) and I can't give you an account. But I'm going to continue to trust that I really *can* be in the relevant state, even though for all I know, it's not possible that I can be in that state." The solution thus appears to endorse a version of the principle of doxastic conservatism, namely, the thesis that there is a presumption in favor of the beliefs I have, even in cases in which I do not know how they could possibly be true, simply because they are beliefs I already have. Principles of this sort are controversial, and have been controverted with great forcefulness, to my mind, by my colleague David Christensen (1994). If we can have it, I would prefer a solution to Matthews's paradox that did not commit Augustine wholesale to the Assumption Mode.

You may think, however, that doxastic conservatism is precisely the saddle we should place on this warhorse. For Augustine is the one who famously rides to battle under the banner *Nisi credideritis, non intelligetis* (Unless you believe, you will not understand). In defending the phenomenon of accepting the contents of revelation "on faith," Augustine points out that the practice of believing on the basis of less-than-conclusive reasons is a doxastic practice that we have been engaged in all along. Our default setting is to trust our friends and the authority of our parents and teachers. There would be something monstrous, Augustine says, about a person who withheld love from his parents for fear that, in some scenario envisionable only from Cartesian ramparts of certainty, they might not *really* be his parents (*De Utilitate Credendi* 10.23–12.26).

All well and good. But we should distinguish between a cautious principle of credulity and a rash principle of credulity. When it comes to belief retention, I suggest that "Continue to believe what you already believe even when you don't see how what you believe is possible" is rash. Let us baptize this doxastic policy Tertullian's Principle, in honor of the second-century church father who adopted an aggressive version of it, saying, so it is claimed, *credo quia absurdum,* "I believe *because* it is absurd." You may "luck out" by following Tertullian's Principle; it may be that what you steadfastly believe turns out true. There are cases, outside of the domain of religious belief, where what *appears* to be Tertullian's Principle has been vindicated. Confronted with Lord Kelvin's seemingly impeccable 1865 demonstration that the world cannot be more than thirty million years old, Charles Darwin stuck by his guns in his belief in descent with modification. But as a result, Darwin sadly came to rely more heavily on Lamarckism, or the doctrine of the inheritance of acquired characteristics, simply because Lamarckian mechanisms, if they existed in nature, would work much more quickly than natural selection in furthering the process of modification through species generations. As it turned out, of course, Kelvin was mistaken and Lamarckism was false, thus paving the way for evolution through natural selection. What shall we say of Darwin's post-1865 attempts to save his theory? Noble perseverance or unjustified but fortuitous fixation of belief? More needs to be said about the details of the case before we should rush to judgment or even accept the terms of the dichotomy. But those who at the end of the day opt for the latter diagnosis will wish to point out that although the case is a vindication of Tertullian's Principle, it is not a justification for relying on the principle.

Augustine does not endorse Tertullian's Principle, certainly not in religious matters. As Matthews points out, Augustine's religious faith is a faith *seeking* understanding. Now surely no doctrine of Christian faith taxes one's understanding more than the doctrine of the Trinity, the doctrine that, as Augustine is inclined to put it, God is one substance and three persons. Augustine's *De Trinitate* is a five-hundred-plus-page attempt to provide understanding for this central item of Christian faith. I imagine that if Tertullian had bothered to write a work with the same title, it would have consisted entirely of a diatribe directed against all atheists and heretics.

You might insist that Tertullian's Principle is one thing; the Assumption Mode is another. So you might point out that Augustine is justified in adopting the Assumption Mode with respect to the perplexities he unveils in the *Confessions* without lapsing into Tertullianism. He takes himself not to be believing (or practicing) what he does not understand to be possible, because he *actually* does measure time, recall sadness without feeling sad, and so on. *Ab esse ad posse valet.* But this is precisely what we need not concede to Augustine and what he should not grant to himself. To be sure, it seems to him as if he can measure time, recall sadness without feeling sad, and so on. But it might be that he is mistaken nevertheless. It seemed to Girolamo Saccheri that he was freeing Euclid from every flaw by deducing absurdities from the denial of Euclid's fifth postulate (the "parallel postulate"). Had he had a taste for writing in the confessional mode, Saccheri might even have framed his enterprise by asking, in the Assumption Mode, "How is it possible that I know that Euclidean geometry is the one true geometry?" But what Saccheri succeeded in doing was to undermine the very enterprise he took himself to be engaged in. Denial of the fifth postulate leads not to absurdities but to non-Euclidean geometries.

Or, to adapt a case mentioned by Richard Sorabji (1971), let us suppose that there is someone, call her Rosa, who sincerely believes of herself that she is capable of feeling colors. That is, even when placed under experimental conditions tightly controlled to prevent peeking, conscious and unconscious signaling, and the like, Rosa can unerringly identify the colors of all sorts of objects simply by running her fingers across them. Rosa describes the experience as one that is exactly as immediate and non-inferential as when she sees objects. We can imagine that, realizing that she is unusual in this respect, but emboldened by her perceptual success, Rosa asks, in the Assumption Mode, "How is it possible that I feel colors?"

Now it might be that when the day is done, the best neurophysiological theory will answer Rosa's question by explaining how it is that she feels colors, thus vindicating her assumption that she is a genuine synesthetic. But it might also be that the best neurophysiological theory delivers the verdict that Rosa does not feel colors. The theory might maintain, for example, that Rosa is actually seeing colors, but that in her case, visual input can occur at bodily locations elsewhere from her eyes. (That would help explain the phenomenological immediacy Rosa claims for her experience.) Or it might be that Rosa has an ultra-sensitive neurophysiological mechanism in place that enables her to *infer* the presence of colors from subtle environmental cues, such as wavelength. If either of the latter two accounts is correct, then Rosa's question, posed in the Assumption Mode, rests on a false assumption; she is simply not feeling colors.

What should we make of these examples? I suggest on Augustine's behalf that we pay attention to two points. First, the world is a strange and wonderful place, not given to divulging its secrets at first inspection. Augustine took himself to be realizing part of this strangeness and wonder when he arrived at the conclusion that time is as much a part of creation as matter is, not an everlasting receptacle existing independently of the rest of creation (*Confessions* 11.13.15–14.17). Second, we humans do not have the cognitive prowess to decode nature effortlessly, let alone penetrate the realm that must be given to us by revelation. Augustine took ignorance to be one of the consequences of the Fall (see, for example, *De Libero Arbitrio* 3.18.52). I suggest that if we keep these points in mind, then, when confronted with what we take to be an ordinary phenomenon for which we can give no satisfactory explanation, it is not irrational for us to assume that we are mistaken about the phenomenon. Perhaps, for example, we really are in pain whenever we call pain to mind, and really sad whenever we attend to sadness. Why assume that we have Cartesian lucidity about our own mental states, that we are the final arbiters of what states we are and are not in? Why preclude out of hand a theory that maintains that we *do* feel pain and sadness on the relevant occasions? Why not leave that issue to experimental psychology?

But neither is it irrational for us to assume that we are correct: absence of explanation is not the same as presence of disconfirming evidence. For these reasons I would prefer to nudge some of Augustine's questions over into the realm of questions asked in the Neutral Mode. In taking this approach, however, I lose an advantage enjoyed by Matthews's interpretation, namely, uniformity of treatment between Augustine the dogmatist and Augustine the Socratist. So now I must explain why I think we can afford to sacrifice this uniformity. My explanation will consist of a sketch—only a sketch—of an alternative account of Augustine's methodology.

The juxtaposition of two examples found in the *Confessions,* uncertainty about the nature of time and certainty about the nature of evil, may suggest another strategy—compartmentalize. A person might suppose, that is, that there are some subjects of inquiry about which there is no harm done by giving free rein to intellectual speculation, while there are other subjects of inquiry too important and too potentially harmful to sustain an attitude of sanguine toleration. Perhaps Augustine's dogmatism asserts itself with most saliency in matters of religious faith, and perhaps his Socraticism surfaces only in areas far removed from the tenets of faith. Your very salvation may depend on having the correct beliefs about God and his relation to the world, but no one of sound mind would claim that the gates of heaven will be barricaded against those unable to answer the question "How is it possible that I know what sadness is without being sad?" And if your salvation does not depend on knowing the answer to that question, then I should think that you can be allowed to challenge the presupposition behind that question, namely, the presupposition that it is possible that I know what sadness is without being sad. But then you have entered the Neutral Mode Zone.

It would count in favor of my interpretation if we could find Augustine taking a latitudinarian stance on some nondoctrinal issue, coupled, preferably, with an overt avowal that such permissiveness cannot be tolerated at the core of religious belief. Here I commend to you the truly remarkable discussion of the origin and embodiment of souls in *De Libero Arbitrio* 3.20–21. According to Augustine there are four different views one might take on this subject: (1) God may have created only one ancestral soul, from which all other souls would then be descended by propagation; (2) God may create new souls individually for each person who is born; (3) souls may have preexisted elsewhere and may be assigned by God to the bodies of those who are born; and (4) souls may have preexisted elsewhere and may choose to animate the bodies of those who are born.

Which view is correct? Let me string together a series of passages from Book 3, Chapter 21, of Thomas Williams's (1993) recent translation of *De Libero Arbitrio*:

> It would be rash to affirm any of these [views]. For the Catholic commentators on Scripture have not solved or shed light on this obscure and perplexing question; or if they have, I have not yet come across any such writing. What matters is that we have the faith to believe nothing false or unworthy about the nature of the Creator, for in our journey of piety we are aiming at him. . . . By contrast, if we have a false belief about a creature, we are in no danger, as long as we do not regard that belief as knowledge.

Since souls count as creatures in Augustine's census, it follows that in the doxastic circumstances as described, Augustine holds that (a) it would be rash to *affirm* (as knowledge?) any one of the four views, but (b) we are not at risk if we merely believe one of the four.

But the doxastic circumstances could change:

> [I]f by divine authority we are told anything about such creatures, whether past or future, we ought to believe it without hesitation.

How do we know when divine authority has spoken? There is at least this check on false prophets:

> [I]f any error arrogates to itself the role of divine authority, it is most forcefully refuted if it requires one to believe or affirm that there is any changeable form other than God's creation, or that there is any changeable form in the nature of God, or that the divine nature is anything more or less than the Trinity.

More positively, Augustine suggests the following pragmatic test:

> With respect to created things, we ought to believe without hesitation whatever we are told about the past or future that serves pure religion by arousing our sincerest love for God or our neighbor. When it comes to defending these beliefs against the attacks of unbelievers, either we should defend them in such a way that their unbelief is crushed under the weight of divine authority, or else we should first show that it is not foolish to believe such things, and then show that it is foolish not to believe such things.

Even so, having correct beliefs about the pasts of creatures is less important than having correct beliefs about their futures:

> So what does it matter to me if I do not know when I began to exist, since I know that I exist now, and I do not despair of existing in the future? There is no great harm done if I have false beliefs about the past, since the past is of no concern to me; I direct my course toward what I am going to be, guided by the mercy of my Creator.

(This passage is underscored by two analogies in quick succession. It doesn't matter whether I remember last winter, but it does matter if I don't believe that there is cold weather ahead this winter. And there is no harm done to someone sailing for Rome if he can't remember his port of origin, so long as he has accurate beliefs about his port of destination.) Partly because Augustine is willing to discount the value of knowledge about the pasts of creatures, he concludes that

> [i]t is permissible to consider and discuss these matters [e.g., the four views in question] if they bear on some necessary question, or if there is time to spare from more pressing matters. Rather, I said these things to keep anyone from becoming petulant when others hesitate to accept his own, perhaps better-informed, opinion on such a matter; and so

that, if anyone does have a clear and certain understanding of this issue, he will not think that others have lost all hope for the future because they have no concern for the past.

I have omitted some of Augustine's other observations from Chapter 21. But I think we have enough before us now to see that if we try to extract doxastic principles here, none of them will be as ham-fisted as Tertullian's Principle.

Let us now return to the five questions that Matthews extracts from the *Confessions*:

(1) How is it possible that I try to find out who God is by calling on him?
(2) How is it possible that I know what a pain is without being in pain?
(3) How is it possible that I remember what forgetfulness is?
(4) How is it possible that I know what sadness is without being sad?
(5) How is it possible that I measure a time and find that it is long or short?

By now you may expect that I am going to regiment all of them into the Neutral Mode. I am not. I think that the crew is more motley than that.

Question (1) pertains to an important part of the practice of Augustine's Christian faith, namely, prayer. It should not be surprising, then, that Augustine asks (1) in the Assumption Mode. Even so, I am inclined to think that for Augustine, (1) is rhetorical, not aporetic. Augustine is not worried that his prayer might get intercepted by Moloch or Baal or some other impostor. Nor is he worried that God might somehow misinterpret the prayer. Nor is he worried that God will stint in responding to him. If so, then (1) produces no more philosophical suspense or puzzlement than, say, "How is it possible that I try to find out who Joe Shlabotnik is by telephoning him?"

Questions (2), (3), and (4) seem to me to be instances of a more general question—"How is it possible that I can know what an experience of kind *E* is without presently having an experience of kind *E*?" For reasons I've already given, I would prefer to think of Augustine asking these questions in the Neutral Mode. Here I will just add a remark about question (3). Remembering forgetfulness had better not entail the impossible task of remembering and forgetting the same thing simultaneously. Remembering forgetfulness, however, does not rule out the possibility that whenever I remember what forgetfulness is, I relive an episode in which I had forgotten something. Of course it may not seem to me that that is what is going on. But once again, why should my phenomenological impressions be dispositive?

I believe that there is too much evidence internal to the *Confessions* to deny that Augustine asked question (5) in the Assumption Mode. But, speaking for myself, I would have to say that if the adoption of the Assumption Mode is what leads Augustine to his resolution of the question, then it would have been better had Augustine adopted the Neutral Mode. But the Assumption Mode is not the only mischief-maker. Augustine's discussion yields the disjunction "Either time is something mental or I do not measure time." The Assumption Mode contributes "I do measure time." And so we get "Time is something mental." Now of course one can be an idealist about time. But idealism about time should not be *that* easy to establish!

Imagine Darwin saying to himself in 1870, "Either there are Lamarckian mechanisms in nature or there is no evolution of species." The Assumption Mode contributes "There is species evolution." And so we get "There are Lamarckian mechanisms in nature." Whatever we may think of the doxastic propriety of Darwin's sticking by evolutionary theory, we can surely acknowledge that one culprit in this case is the Hobson's choice offered by the disjunction. With the luxury of hindsight, we can see that it is a choice we can decline to make.

So it is with Augustine's disjunction. It is easy enough to insist both that time is not something mental and that we do measure time.

I turn now to King's discussion of Augustine's Paradox of Teaching. As a prologue, let me read into the record some remarks of Jonathan Lear's (1988) on Aristotle's notion of efficient causation:

> If we think of a teacher teaching and a student learning we should not, according to Aristotle, think of two activities which are related to each other: "teacher teaching" and "student learning" are two different ways of characterizing the very same happening. One description captures the perspective of the agent, the other captures the perspective of the patient. Although there may be various ways to characterize this activity, Aristotle argues that there is nevertheless only one activity and it is occurring in the student. It may sound odd at first to think of the teacher's teaching as occurring in the student, but for Aristotle if it is happening anywhere at all, this is where it would have to be. And, on second thought, the idea is not so odd: where else could *teaching* be occurring? We can imagine a teacher going through the motions in an empty classroom, or lecturing to a flock of geese, but Aristotle would deny that he was teaching. Unless a student is learning a teacher cannot be teaching. (32; italics in original)

Lear's Aristotle—let us call this character "Learistotle" in order to set aside questions about the accuracy of Lear's portrayal of Aristotelian doctrine—espouses three theses about teaching. The first thesis is a robust version of what King calls the "information-transference account" of teaching (or the ITA for short). Teaching for Learistotle consists of an agent's actualizing a potentiality in a patient's soul by means of the transference of *form* from teacher to student, a process describable literally as *information*. The second thesis is that the verb "to teach" is a success verb, not a mere task verb. Whatever I am doing, I am not teaching you if you are not learning from me. (Shades of "outcomes assessment"!) And the third thesis is that the doxastic or epistemic change that is brought about by teaching occurs nowhere else than in the student's soul. Lear goes on to claim on behalf of Learistotle that the relation between teacher and student is like the relation between artificer and artifact: the teacher's activity *shapes* the student, *making* the student become what he or she becomes.

It thus seems that Learistotle's account of what goes on in education is at odds with both Plato's *Meno* thesis that all learning is recollection and Augustine's *De Magistro* thesis that no one (except Christ) teaches anyone else anything. But if *A* is incompatible with both *B* and *C*, it does not follow that *B* and *C* are equivalent. I would like to point out four ways in which the *Meno* and *De Magistro* diverge.

First, Meno's Paradox does not have the consequence that *all* learning is impossible. Meno's Paradox is a challenge to *inquiry,* especially inquiry undertaken when all parties are ignorant about the answers. It thus seems to be aimed exclusively at the acquisition of *propositional* learning, leaving untouched "learning how," that is, the learning of a skill, an art, or a craft. In contrast, Augustine seems to have created an engine of destruction that mows down learning how in addition to learning that, even if learning how should happen to involve only showing rather than telling. Here's a crucial example from *De Magistro* 10.32:

> Suppose that someone unfamiliar with how to trick birds (which is done with reeds and birdlime) should run into a birdcatcher outfitted with his tools, not birdcatching but on his way to do so. On seeing this birdcatcher, he follows closely in his footsteps, and, as it happens, he reflects and asks himself in his astonishment what exactly the man's equipment means. Now the birdcatcher, wanting to show off after seeing the attention focused on him, prepares his reeds and with his birdcall and his hawk intercepts, subdues, and captures some little bird he has noticed nearby. I ask you: wouldn't he then teach the man watching him what he wanted to know by the thing itself rather than anything that signifies?[2]

---

[2] St. Augustine, *Against the Academicians and The Teacher*, translated by Peter King (Indianapolis, IN: Hackett Publishing Company, 1995), 134.

But of course if no one transmits knowledge to anyone else, then Papageno does not teach birdcatching: showing is no better off in this respect than telling (Burnyeat 1987).

Second, the *Meno* Theory of Recollection strongly suggests that the kind of knowledge for which Plato is seeking an account is knowledge of necessary truths, knowledge of propositions that, in virtue of their necessity, are so stable in their truth that they are not subject to revision through successive reincarnations of the soul. "A square constructed on the diagonal of a given square has twice the area of the given square" passes muster, but not, say, "Juneau is the capital of Alaska." In contrast, Augustine's Illuminationism appears fit to apply to any truth, necessary or contingent. If Christ is the inner teacher, the *only* teacher, then to come to know the reasons why Juneau is Alaska's capital (and not, say, Nome) is due as much to Christ's activity as is one's coming to know about squares and diagonals.

Third, primarily because of its restriction to necessary truths, Recollection plays a role for Plato different from the role that Illumination plays for Augustine. Matthews alludes to Plato's assumption of the "Kinship of All Nature." Plato uses the Kinship of All Nature assumption to maintain that one's Recollection of the square-on-the-diagonal theorem, for example, will be perfected only when one *understands* the theorem. Understanding the theorem involves seeing how it fits into a coherent deductive network—how it depends on axioms and simpler theorems, how it leads, in turn, to further, more complex theorems, and so on. Until one has achieved this kind of holistic appreciation, the theorem will be like one of those marvelous statues of Daedalus that run away if they are not tied down (*Meno* 97d–98a). In the case of the theorem, the tether is Recollection. Better to say, perhaps, that the *chain* is Recollection and its links the deductive connections exhibited by geometry, thereby illustrating the Kinship of All Nature assumption.

Augustine's Illuminationism does not imply that understanding is holistic. For all I can tell, Christ the Teacher might choose to illuminate, and thus lead one to understand fully, some individual truth without shedding light on any of its affiliated truths.

Finally, an obvious difference between Plato's Recollection Theory and Augustine's Illuminationism is that the latter but not the former depends essentially on divine action for its operation.

King claims that Augustine's argumentation in *De Magistro* shows that the process of learning is internal to the student, thus seeming to comport with Learistotle's third thesis. At the same time, however, King's interpretation of *De Magistro* has Augustine rejecting any kind of causal transaction, including, I presume, an account like that described in Learistotle's first thesis. King claims that this leaves things "in the end, mysterious. . . . For if the teacher doesn't cause the student to understand—and it's clear that the teacher cannot literally *cause* the student to understand, since otherwise everyone in the classroom would get it, or nobody would—then what is it that takes place? What *is* learning, if not a mysterious inner episode of awareness?"[3]

Now I like a mystery as much as the next person, but in this case I must confess that I am a bit mystified by what the mystery is supposed to be. Let me begin to expose my mystification—or is it my ineducability, a specimen of the very phenomenon under scrutiny?—in this way. Surely it can't be a condition on causation that a cause must produce the *same* effect on each member of a class of disparate entities. Confronted with a classroom of students, some of whom "get" the subject matter, some of whom do not, I do not conclude that I am not causing *any* student to understand. I am more apt to conclude that some students are natively brighter, or more attentive, or more industrious, or more familiar with the subject matter than others. As the Stoics pointed out, given the same impetus, a cylinder will roll down a hill more easily than a cube will. Clearly there are similar sorts of internal differences among students, but none of the ones I have just listed is sufficient to motivate doctrines as distinctive as Plato's Recollection Theory or Augustine's Illuminationism.

There is a special constraint imposed by Augustine's soul-body metaphysics on learning by means of any process involving physical transmission. Augustine maintains that the body cannot affect the soul. He regards this doctrine as a straightforward consequence of another doctrine, namely, the doctrine of the soul's superiority over the body. He thus is led to maintain, for example, that with regard to sense perception, physical modifications to the body's sense receptors do not cause the soul to have sensory experiences. If the body could affect the soul in these ways, then in that respect the soul would be passive to and dependent upon the body, and in that respect the soul would not be superior to the body. It is rather that the soul, in the process of monitoring the body, is able actively to take notice of the physical modifications and produce in itself the appropriate sensations. It is then also capable of making judgments about the sensations that have thereby been produced (*De immortalitate animae* 16.25, *De musica* 6.5.9–15, *De Genesi ad litteram* 12.16.32–33).[4]

The passage from Augustine's *Homilies on John the Evangelist* cited by King to illustrate the ITA makes it clear that Augustine regards speaking as a physical process whose end stages include "the sound of the syllables convey[ing] your

---

[3] All quotations from King are from "Augustine on the Impossibility of Teaching" in *Metaphilosophy* 29, no. 3 (1998): 179–195.

[4] See also my "Inner-Life Ethics," in *The Augustinian Tradition*, ed. Gareth B. Matthews (Berkeley: University of California Press, 1999), 140–165. Reprinted as Chapter 6 of this volume, from which most of the material in the previous paragraph is taken.

thought to my ear" and "through my ear your thought . . . descend[ing] into my heart." After that, one presumes, the soul takes over. This particular twist in Augustine's metaphysics does entail that any learning that involves input by physical means requires the active, attentive acceptance and interpretation of the soul. But I do not see that this is mysterious. It seems to me to amount to saying no more than that someone has to be home when educational opportunities come knocking. The Illuminationism of *De Magistro* adds something critical to this view, however. When educational opportunities do come knocking, I will not be able to answer the door if I am totally in the dark, and whether I am in the dark or will remain in the dark is not up to me.

I think it helps to sort out two theses here, one metaphysical, the other epistemological. The metaphysical thesis is a thesis distinctive to (but not obligatory for) theism. According to it, every creature depends on God, its creator, not just for its coming into being but for its continuing to exist and to function. Now many Christian theists would agree that their ability to do anything, including their ability to understand anything, depends on God's sustaining them and their faculties.

The thesis that is distinctive to *De Magistro,* however, according to King, is epistemological. It is the thesis that human learning is interior, conscious, and, it would seem, *occurrent,* occurring when and only when Christ chooses to illuminate a soul. To repeat the last sentence of King's paper, "What *is* learning, if not a mysterious inner episode of awareness?"

I have distinguished the two theses because I believe that they are relatively independent of each other; in particular, that it is possible to accept the first and reject the second. I can imagine a theist, that is, who offers the following answer to King's question: "We have neglected to consider the role played by the soul being illuminated. It has to be the sort of thing *capable* of understanding. Not even God can produce understanding in an igneous rock. I grant that the soul has been created by God and is sustained by God; these beliefs are metaphysical givens for me. But I don't see any compelling reason to believe that when the soul comes to understand something, the coming to understand must be an episode of awareness. Perhaps it is sometimes. It seems to me, however, that a person can come to understand something without being aware of it at the time. The proof of the understanding is then subsequently revealed by the person's ability to perform in certain ways. But the public exercise of the understanding is not to be confused with the understanding itself. The proof surely does not lie in some special character attaching to one's consciousness, an awareness of certainty. Remember Saccheri, who felt absolutely certain that Euclid was right. If coming to understand is the not-necessarily-conscious exercise of a dispositional capacity, where is the mystery? Or if this is a mystery, is it any more of a mystery than the fact that birds have the capacity to build nests, or that cylinders have the capacity to roll downhill easily?"

I think that I have just begun to broach issues that would take us far afield from Augustine. So I will stop here.

References

Augustine. (1993). *On Free Choice of the Will.* Translated by Thomas Williams. Indianapolis, IN: Hackett Publishing Company.

Burnyeat, Myles F. (1987). "Wittgenstein and Augustine *De Magistro.*" *Proceedings of the Aristotelian Society*, supplementary volume, 1–24.

Christensen, David. (1994). "Conservatism in Epistemology." *Noûs*, 28, 69–89.

Lear, Jonathan. (1988). *Aristotle: The Desire to Understand.* Cambridge: Cambridge University Press.

Sorabji, Richard. (1971). "Aristotle on Demarcating the Five Senses." *The Philosophical Review*, 80, 55–84.

SECTION II

ABELARD

9

Abelard's Ethics

The Inside Story

Peter Abelard's contributions to ethics are concentrated in two works, his *Ethics* (or *Scito te Ipsum* [cited herein as *Sc.*]) and his *Dialogue between a Philosopher, a Jew, and a Christian* (or *Collationes* [cited herein as *Coll.*]).[1] There are ethical insights to be found scattered elsewhere in his works, but for the sustained presentation of an ethical theory, one can only turn to these two works. The *Dialogue* is actually two dialogues, one between a philosopher and a Jew, the other between the philosopher and a Christian, debating the relative merits of pagan philosophy, Judaism, and Christianity. The *Ethics* concentrates on the development of a distinctively Christian ethical theory. It was to have consisted of two books.

The unfinished second book of the *Ethics* begins with a description of what Abelard takes himself to have accomplished in the first book, namely, the provision of an understanding of what sins are, how they are rectified, and how they differ from vices (*Sc.* 128.1–4, Spade 1995, 226). The second book was supposed to have taken up the topic of what it is to do good, or, as he prefers to put it in his more careful moments, what it is to do well (*Coll.* 163.3229–3230, Spade 1995, 404). The text was abandoned after one page. The *Ethics,* then, consists of a rather elaborate and zestful account of wrongdoing along with the merest of gestures toward an account of right-doing. It is as if Dante had neglected to write *Paradiso* after finishing *Inferno.* But as the newspapers attest daily, accounts

---

[1] I provide references to the standard Latin editions of both works, as well as to numbered paragraphs of the translations in Spade 1995. Peter Abelard, *Ethical Writings: His Ethics or "Know Yourself" and his Dialogue between a Philosopher, a Jew, and a Christian,* trans., Paul Vincent Spade (Indianapolis, IN: Hackett Publishing Company, 1995). For *Coll.* see Petrus Abaelardus, *Dialogus inter Philosophum, Iudaeum et Christianum,* ed. Rudolf Thomas (Stuttgart-Bad Cannstatt: Frommann Verlag, 1970). For *Sc.* see Peter Abelard's *Ethics,* ed. and trans., by D. E. Luscombe (Oxford: Clarendon Press, 1971). All translations, however, are my own.

of wrongdoing fascinate us more than accounts of right-doing: how many more people have read *Inferno* than *Paradiso*?

We can speculate, however, about what the general contours of Abelard's account would have been by deploying these strategies. First, if a thing's functioning badly gives us clues about how it should function well, then an examination of Abelard's account of sin should repay our efforts. Second, we can hope to exploit other writings of Abelard. Third, as the focus on sin indicates, Abelard seeks to provide an account of ethics that is theistic—more specifically, Christian—in its essential features. Although Abelard is a maverick on many philosophical matters, his project would misfire fundamentally were it to present an ethical theory that is unrecognizable or indefensible from the point of view of scripture and the Christian tradition. We can appeal to the constraints thereby provided to impart some direction to our speculation.

I shall begin by examining Abelard's presentation and defense of his account of sin in the *Ethics,* organizing the examination in the hopes of shedding light on what it is to act well.

I The Big Idea

Early in the first book, Abelard puts forward three theses about what sin is *not* and one thesis about what sin *is.* A sin is not a mental vice, like irascibility or wantonness, that disposes us to do bad deeds. Nor is a sin the bad deed itself (*Sc.* 2.21–22, Spade 1995, 4). A bit later, Abelard claims that the *will* to perform a bad deed is also not a sin (*Sc.* 6.11 ff, Spade 1995, 9ff.). What sin is, according to Abelard, is contempt of God (*Sc.* 4.31–32, Spade 1995, 7). What are Abelard's arguments for the three negative theses? And what is contempt of God, such that it is not any mental vice, or deed, or act of will? I shall begin by examining the negative theses, and defer discussion of the contempt-of-God thesis until Section II.

A sin is not a mental vice, according to Abelard, because one can have a vice and yet, by resisting it, not sin. A person with a tendency toward irascibility, for example, who successfully resists it is not to be charged with a sin just for having the tendency. Vices dispose us to sin but they are not the sins to which we are thereby disposed.[2]

---

[2] Abelard appears to regard irascibility and wantonness as vices due to our bodily constitution, natural liabilities that we should learn how to control. They are distinct from vices, like greed and gluttony, that are acquired, typically by sinful choices. The distinction plays no role here, but is relevant to the issue of vicious motivation; see section III.

There is no concise, straightforward argument for the remarkable thesis that no sin is a deed. Instead there are reiterations of that thesis interspersed in the argument for the positive thesis that sin is contempt of God. (And this comes after Abelard's defense of his third negative thesis.) But an argument for the positive thesis does not by itself establish the thesis that no deed is a sin. Abelard must exclude the possibility that one way to scorn God is to *act* in ways contemptuous of God.

We get some help when Abelard says, as if summing up results established previously, that "outward deeds," which are "equally common to reprobates and the elect, are in themselves all indifferent" (*Sc.* 44.30–31, Spade 1995, 90). In fact, he had hitherto neither explicitly characterized deeds as outward (*exterior*), nor made the (sociological?) observation about their distribution among saints and sinners, nor described them as indifferent. Nevertheless, the quasi-summary is helpful, enabling us to construct the following edifice on its foundation.

Here is an example that Abelard uses at least twice (*Sc.* 28.11–17, Spade 1995, 58; and *Coll.* 164.3237–3241, Spade 1995, 404): two people participate in the legal execution of a criminal. One acts out of a desire to see justice served, the other out of personal hatred of the criminal arising from a long-standing feud. No matter how intense our scrutiny of their behavior, we might not be able to discern who is acting justly and who is acting unjustly. We can have a complete specification of the "outward deeds"—the overt, publicly observable bodily motions of a person—and still not know about the person's *inner* life—the beliefs, desires, motives, intentions, and the like—that result in the outward deeds.

Outward deeds can thus be epistemologically inconclusive regarding an agent's mental states. Although this phenomenon is related to the conception of indifference mentioned above, it does not explain the claim that outward deeds are indifferent. In the *Dialogue* Abelard says that a thing is indifferent if it is neither good nor evil (*Coll.* 160.3158, Spade 1995, 397). Abelard's claim, then, is that no outward deed is good or evil in itself: all bodily motions are morally neutral.

Perhaps what Abelard has in mind is this. One and the same bodily motion can, depending on circumstances, be embedded in a conductor's downbeat, a minister's blessing, and an executioner's coup de grace. To the extent to which bodily motions are interpreted as having moral significance, it is because of the inferences people make about the mental states and activities behind them. But, as we shall see, it is Abelard's view that, even when the inferences are correct, it is a mistake to call the bodily motions good or bad, righteous or sinful. Predicates of moral appraisal attach properly to internal items, the states and activities residing in the agent's soul. Thus, no deed is a sin.

The inward-outward dichotomy is a time-honored one in the history of philosophy. It is frequently associated with some sort of soul-body dualism. If Abelard had a philosophical theory about the relation between soul and body, it is certainly not prominent in his writings. At one point in the *Ethics,* in order to emphasize the point that the commission of an outward deed does not augment the soul's sin, Abelard concludes, "As if that which occurred outwardly in the body could contaminate the soul!" (*Sc.* 22.30–32, Spade 1995, 47). It is tempting to read into this remark Augustine's dualism, which entails, among other things, that because the soul is superior to the body, it cannot be affected by what happens to the body. As we will see below, Abelard was influenced, directly or indirectly, by Augustine's thought. But this one passage is too isolated to serve as a basis for an imputation of Augustine's extreme dualism to Abelard.[3] It will suffice for our purposes to suppose that whatever Abelard's theory might have been, it would legitimize his use of inward-outward imagery.

Abelard's third negative thesis, that to sin is not to will to perform a bad deed, eliminates one more likely suspect—recall that vices have already been dismissed—from the interior rogue's gallery. In the process of defending the thesis, Abelard considers an example that had first appeared in Book 1 of Augustine's *De libero arbitrio.* Abelard reworks the example to present an analysis of it at odds with Augustine's own analysis. But Abelard's reworking of the example relies on conceptual apparatus that Augustine had developed after having written *De libero arbitrio.* Examination of the example and its reworking will help us to see not only the rationale for the negative thesis but also for Abelard's positive thesis.

Here is the example. A servant flees his sadistic master, who is bent on torturing and killing the servant. Cornered finally by the master and fearing for his own life, the servant kills the master. Augustine and Abelard agree that the servant has done something wrong. They offer differing diagnoses of what the wrongness consists in. In *De libero arbitrio* Augustine tries out the hypothesis that all wrongdoing is motivated by inordinate desire,[4] desire that is disproportionate to the value of the object desired. The example of the servant killing his master seems at first blush to be a counterexample to the hypothesis, for we are

---

[3] For further discussion of Augustine's dualism, especially in relation to his ethics, see Mann "Inner-Life Ethics," in *The Augustinian Tradition,* ed. Gareth B. Matthews (Berkeley: University of California Press, 1999). Reprinted as Chapter 6 of this volume.

[4] Augustine, *De libero arbitrio* 1.3.8–1.4.10. "Inordinate desire" is Thomas Williams's translation of *libido* in Augustine, *On Free Choice of the Will,* trans. Thomas Williams (Indianapolis, IN: Hackett Publishing Company, 1993). Although somewhat tendentious in the context, the translation has the virtues of not confining Augustine's use of *libido* to sexual passion and emphasizing that the desire in question is somehow out of order.

to suppose that the servant's desire is to live a life without fear, and no one can be faulted for having that desire. Augustine's resolution of the case is to claim, in effect, that the servant's desire is inordinate nevertheless, because it leads the servant to overvalue his own life. His life is a good thing, to be sure, as is, Augustine might have added, his master's life. But the servant's life is not the sort of thing that can be possessed without the fear of losing it. Thus to desire to possess one's life without fear of losing it, no matter what the cost, is to fail to appreciate that sometimes the cost is too high.[5]

Augustine's hypothesis pins wrongdoing on a set of unruly desires. Abelard does not accept the maneuver. Let us look first at what he says about Augustine's example. There is nothing wrong with the servant's wanting to preserve his life; no hint from Abelard that this desire is inordinate. If there is nothing wrong with the will for self-preservation, what about the servant's will to kill his master? Abelard's reply is that the servant has no such will; in the case as described, he kills his master unwillingly (*Sc.* 6.32–8.4, Spade 1995, 14). A critic might protest that Abelard is surely mistaken: Because the servant's action of slaying the master was not a matter of inadvertence or accident, it seems obvious that the servant wanted to kill the master and that that very desire was what brought about the action. The servant, after all, could have acquiesced in his own death rather than kill his master. Abelard acknowledges that that would have been the right thing to do. That the servant chose to kill his master shows that even if he had a desire not to kill, that desire was outmatched by the desire to kill. It is disingenuous, then, for Abelard to claim that the servant killed unwillingly. Since Abelard agrees that the homicide was unjust, what else could its evil consist in for him if not the evil desire?

It is crucial to see that Abelard's strategy in reply is to assert that the servant has no evil desire. Abelard does not help himself to a more radical claim that might have been suggested by the moral neutrality of bodily behavior, that no desire is bad. Some desires are bad. It would be better for a person not to have them. Even so, one's harboring bad desires does not make one a sinner. Bad desires are something to be fought against and overcome. Indeed, Abelard suggests that if we had no bad desires with which to contend, if our desires always naturally conformed to God's will, then we would be deprived of the opportunity to achieve anything great for God's sake (*Sc.* 12.3–17, Spade 1995, 22–23).

The key to understanding why the critic's protest misfires is to see that, for Abelard, one and the same action can be done unwillingly yet intentionally. An intentional action need not be whatever action happens to have the strongest

---

[5] Augustine is referring to one's earthly, embodied life. His resolution foreshadows the hierarchy of values that he develops in Book 2 of *De libero arbitrio*; see this volume, 94–95 for citations.

desires behind it. When Abelard uses the verbs *volo* (I want) and *nolo* (I do not want), they apply exclusively to desires. Correspondingly, when he speaks of an agent's *voluntas* (will) he is simply referring to what the agent would most want to do, assuming that the agent is not subject to any kind of coercion.[6] In happy circumstances what the agent does intentionally just is what the agent most wants to do. But not all circumstances are happy. Abelard submits the master-killing servant to illustrate the possibility of an agent acting intentionally but unwillingly.[7] It might be useful to consider a simpler example, one in which the issue of the agent's sinning does not arise. The mugger's menu, "Your money or your life," most likely will induce you to surrender your money intentionally but unwillingly. There is some element of choice even in this harrowing circumstance, a choice whose potential for gallows humor was exploited by the radio comedian Jack Benny ("I'm thinking, I'm thinking . . ."). Abelard allows that your surrendering your money can be voluntary even when performed unwillingly. But "voluntary" here can only mean that your action was not committed with the necessity of inevitability or that the action corresponds to *some* desire of yours, for example, a desire to escape or defer death (*Sc.* 16.24–32, Spade 1995, 34). Abelard does not take the fact that you have a desire to avoid death to tell against the claim that you act unwillingly. To adapt a point of his, "I wanted to give him the money from a desire to save my life" does not entail "I wanted to give him the money." There is no will or desire to surrender the money; it is rather that surrendering the money is something you suffer in order to achieve something you *do* want (*Sc.* 8.21–10.6, Spade 1995, 17–18). The cases of the homicidal servant and the mugger's victim have this in common: they are specimens of intentional, unwilling, but voluntary action. They differ in that one is sinful, the other not.

The distinction between desire and intention matters to Abelard because he wants to locate an action's sinfulness not in the agent's desires but in the agent's intention. Although Abelard relies on the distinction, he does not provide much explicit help in seeing how he arrived at it or how its two central concepts differ.

---

[6] Thus Abelard does not use *voluntas* to refer primarily to anything as substantive as a mental faculty, something apart from but in communication, say, with another faculty called "intellect." See, e.g., St. Thomas Aquinas, *Summa theologiae* 1.79, 82.

[7] John Marenbon, *The Philosophy of Peter Abelard* (Cambridge: Cambridge University Press, 1997), 259, pairs this case with another one mentioned by Abelard: "Often too it happens that, attracted by her appearance, we want to lie with a woman whom we know to be married, yet by no means would we want to commit adultery with her as much as we would want her not to be married" (*Sc.* 16:16–18, Spade 1995, 32). As the context of Abelard's discussion clearly implies, we have not sinned merely in having those desires. So if the case is to parallel the master-killing servant case, we must suppose, as Marenbon does, that we actually commit adultery while wishing that our partner were not married.

In the next few paragraphs I shall comment on the provenance and the contours of the distinction. I warn the reader that the comments stray increasingly beyond the confines of the text.

I.1 Intention as Consent

Abelard suggests that to form an intention to do something is to *consent* to that thing. The terminology of consent traces back to Augustine, who, in *De sermone Domini in monte,* a work written approximately six years after Book 1 of *De libero arbitrio,* develops an account of sin that supplements or supplants the earlier account of sin as inordinate desire. On this later account, a sin is the culmination of three stages, suggestion, pleasure, and consent. Suggestions, Augustine says, come about typically through the workings of memory or the bodily senses, and can range from a momentary thought about having sex with someone to a vivid fantasy about ramming one's car into the vehicle that just cut into one's traffic lane. In Abelard's hands, suggestion is linked more closely to conscious instigators, including demons (*Sc.* 34.3–38.4, Spade 1995, 69–76). One may or may not take pleasure in such suggestions. Abelard has no brief to file against pleasure, any more than he did against desires. Perhaps, like desires, some pleasures are bad, for instance, taking pleasure in another person's suffering. But Abelard asserts that no natural *bodily* pleasure is a sin. If fiends were to force some helpless monk to lie amid amorous women, he says, and if that helpless monk were to be thus led into pleasure, but not consent, who would dare call the pleasure a sin? (*Sc.* 20.15–19, Spade 1995, 42.) If bodily pleasures were sins, then God would be at fault for having created us in such a way that we cannot help but enjoy the taste of some foods (*Sc.* 18.13–16, Spade 1995, 37). Finally, Abelard follows Augustine in giving a subjunctive analysis of consent: to consent to a pleasurable suggestion to φ is to set oneself to φ should opportunity arise (*Sc.* 14.17–19, Spade 1995, 29).[8]

"There are those," Abelard observes, "who completely regret being drawn into consent to lust or to a bad will, and are compelled out of the weakness of the flesh to want what they by no means want to want" (*Sc.* 16.22–24, Spade 1995, 33). (This passage immediately precedes the observation that some intentional actions are voluntary only in the attenuated sense that is compatible with their not being done willingly.) It is tempting to see in this passage a prefiguration of

---

[8] Augustine, *De sermone Domini in monte,* 1.12.33–34. Abelard refers to the trio of suggestion, pleasure, and consent at *Sc.* 32:23–25 (Spade 1995, 68), even though he had not hitherto mentioned suggestion.

Harry Frankfurt's distinction between freedom of action and freedom of will.[9] Roughly, one has freedom of action if one is free to do what one wants to do. One has freedom of will if one is free to want what one wants to want; if, that is, there is harmony between one's first-order desires and one's second-order desires. A narcotics addict who takes drugs because he wants to has freedom of action. Nonetheless he lacks freedom of will if his second-order desire not to have a first-order desire for narcotics is powerless over the first-order desire. Conversely, a person who does not realize that she is locked in her room may have freedom of will, the freedom to pick and choose among her first-order desires, even though she would lack the freedom to act on a desire to leave her room, were she to adopt that desire. Abelard does not examine further the phenomena of first- and second-order desires and the harmonies and dissonances that are possible among them. His focus is on intention, since that is where sin finds it home. But an examination of the philosophical contours of intentions and desires may help us to understand why Abelard endorses the change in the account of sin given by Augustine.

I.2 Intentions and Second-Order Desires

Like intentions, second-order desires presuppose the capacity for self-awareness. An intention is a setting *of oneself* to do something. The object of a second-order desire is not just any first-order desire but a first-order desire *of one's own*. There is thus some cognitive capacity required of any creature capable of entertaining intentions and second-order desires. There may be a further similarity between them. A second-order desire can be directed favorably or unfavorably at a first-order desire already in place. ("I am glad I want to have a large family." "I wish I did not have a craving for tobacco.") A second-order desire can also be directed at a nonexistent first-order desire. ("I want to become more willing to help others.") One might think that some second-order desires are thus synchronous with their first-order, object desires while others are future-directed. Plato put forward the thesis in the *Symposium,* however, that the desire to have x, when one already has x, is really the desire to retain x.[10] It would seem to be a trivial extension to add that the desire not to have x, when one in fact has x, is really the desire to lose x. If Plato is correct, then all desires are future-directed. And even if Plato is mistaken in general, one might be able to make a case for the

---

[9] Harry Frankfurt, "Freedom of the Will and the Concept of a Person," *The Journal of Philosophy,* 68 (1971): 5–20.

[10] Plato, *Symposium* 200c–d.

more circumscribed claim that all second-order desires are future-directed. If such a Platonic case could be made, then second-order desires would share an important feature with intentions, which seem to be essentially future-oriented.

Still, there would be these differences, differences that suggest that intentions are further up the cognitive stream. Second-order desires have first-order desires as their objects. Can there be second-order intentions, that is, intentions that take other, garden-variety intentions as their objects? The schema, "I intend to intend to φ," if not a typographical error, induces a kind of mental vertigo. It is hard to imagine a circumstance in which it does not boil down to "I intend to φ." In contrast, "I intend to have only charitable intentions" and "I intend not to have vicious intentions," however rare, pompous, and foolhardy they may appear, are intelligible. If wanting to want always points to a future, intending to have intentions points to a future in the future. For if we intend to acquire or retain certain intentions, then we must intend that those future intentions will lead to action, if opportunity arises, at a time subsequent to their acquisition or retention. Whereas second-order desires, given the Platonic thesis, require that we cognize ourselves as continuing subjects in the future, second-order intentions require that we envision ourselves not merely as continuing in the future, but as having intentions in the future that we may or may not have now, and as being prepared to act on those intentions at a still further future time.

I.3 Conflicting Desires and Conflicting Intentions

We humans are no strangers to the phenomenon of one person having conflicting desires, that is, two or more desires such that the satisfaction of one or more of them precludes the satisfaction of others. The phenomenon is as familiar as wanting to have your cake and eat it too. On first thoughts we might regard cases of intrapersonal desire conflict as a kind of volitional immaturity. On second thoughts it might occur to us that there are some occasions when *not* to be pulled in opposite directions would be a symptom of less than full humanity. Sophie can save one of her children but not both; which will it be? A reply of "Oh, well, flip a coin," might pass muster from a decision-theoretic point of view. But were Sophie not to persist in wanting to save both children even when she knew she could not, then Sophie would have become as brutalized as those who forced the choice upon her.

The situation is quite different with conflicting intentions. We understand Hamlet's wanting and not wanting to slay Claudius and appreciate the dramatic tension that his ambivalence contributes to the play and to the psychological complexity of its protagonist. We are gripped by the pivotal scene in which Hamlet, fully intent on killing Claudius, forswears his intention at the last moment because to kill Claudius while Claudius is praying would be to allow Claudius to go to heaven.[11] The logic of decisions is nonmonotonic: one's intentions can and should change sometimes with the addition of a new consideration. Suppose now that I tell you that Shakespeare contemplated inserting material into *Hamlet* that has Hamlet announcing in the same breath, without benefit of intervening considerations and without equivocation, that he intends to kill Claudius and that he intends not to kill Claudius. I ask you to speculate on how the scene would have fit into the play. Two hypotheses might occur to you. One is that Shakespeare was thinking of portraying Hamlet as not merely burning to avenge his father's death yet frozen by inconclusive evidence: Shakespeare had contemplated having Hamlet become completely unhinged. The other is that Shakespeare was planning to have Hamlet feign being unhinged by putting the unused material into the scene with the barmy but pointed banter with Polonius. Either hypothesis rightly regards the simultaneous holding of both intentions as a sign of massive irrationality.

To depict intention as a kind of consent following on the heels of suggestion and desire enables us to see why this regard is appropriate. Consent, as employed by Augustine and Abelard, suggests an executive decision that has taken into account various suggestions received from the executive's constituents, weighted by the strengths of the constituents' desires, but mindful of the executive's own desires concerning the desirability or undesirability of the constituents' desires. The palate favors going out for a pizza. The conscience reports unreadiness for tomorrow's examination. The person has a pizza delivered and spends the saved time studying. An executive who promulgates inconsistent policies provides no coherent guidance for her constituents or herself. We may not be surprised to find different components of a corporate body in competition with each other. But we should think that the corporate head is derelict or inept if her decisions and policies take no steps toward diminishing the internal competition by restructuring the desires. Inconsistent policies have the effect of sanctioning all actions and legitimating all desires in a *bellum omnium contra omnes*. A cynical corporate head, whose personal interests diverged from the interests of the corporation, might find an occasion to hamstring the latter for the sake of the former. But, to return the analogy to the individual case, when the interests of one's constituents are literally one's own interests, to pit the one against the other is to court schizophrenia.

---

[11] Act III, scene iii.

I.4 Ends and Means

We have seen that Abelard rejects the following inference pattern about desires: if *A* wants *y* and *x* is the only means to *y*, then *A* wants *x*. This inference pattern seems to rest on a false descriptive generalization. Desire for an end may or may not confer desire on the means necessary to achieving the end. Consider now an analogous inference pattern for intentions: if *A* intends *y* and *x* is the only means to *y*, then *A* intends *x*. In the history of philosophy after Abelard's time, the analogous pattern for intentions (and patterns bearing a strong family resemblance to it) has often been put forward as a normative principle, imputing responsibility to *A* for intending the necessary means in the very process of intending an end. Here, for a recent example, is Allen Wood's introduction to his discussion of Kant's notion of a hypothetical imperative:

> To set an end is to undertake a self-given normative commitment to carry out some plan for achieving the end. Sometimes when I have set an end, I subsequently feel an impulse or desire either to perform some action that precludes achieving the end or else to refrain from an action that is necessary for achieving the end. In such cases, I must (on pain of a failure of rationality) make up my mind whether to abandon the end or to abstain from acting on the impulse.[12]

Abelard does not discuss this feature allegedly attaching to intentions. If intentions do impose a standard of instrumental rationality on agents who have them, this is yet another respect in which intentions carry with them more cognitive baggage than do desires. Perhaps because Abelard neglects the topic of means–end rationality, he also does not seem to be aware of a vexing distinction that would become crucial to the principle of double effect, namely, the distinction between what one intends and what one merely foresees as consequences of one's actions.[13]

In sum, I have speculated, I hope on Abelard's behalf, that to locate sin in the realm of intentions rather than the domain of desires is to imply that sins require for their commission beings whose level of rational, cognitive sophistication is higher than that of beings who are merely capable of desires, even second-order desires. Infants and animals have desires. But, "as blessed Jerome has remarked, and as plain reason maintains, as long as the soul remains in the stage of infancy, it lacks sin" (*Sc.* 22.1–3, Spade 1995, 44).

---

[12] Allen Wood, *Kant's Ethical Thought* (Cambridge: Cambridge University Press, 1999), 61.

[13] See, e.g., Audi, *The Cambridge Dictionary of Philosophy*, second edition, edited by Robert Audi (Cambridge: Cambridge University Press, 1999), s.v. "principle of double effect."

II Details

So far we have been following the ramifications of Abelard's three negative theses. His positive thesis is that all sins are acts of intention, whether they be translated into physical action or not. But not all acts of intention are sins. What makes an intention, or an act of consent, a sin? Abelard's answer is that sinful consent is "contempt of God and an offense against him" (*Sc.* 4:32, Spade 1995, 7). The terms are carefully chosen: as Abelard points out immediately, no one can literally damage God, but contempt and offense are not the same as damage.[14] More formally, Abelard says that contempt of God is "not to do for his sake what we believe should be done by us for his sake, or not to omit doing for his sake what we believe should be omitted" (*Sc.* 6.3–6, Spade 1995, 8; reaffirmed at *Sc.* 54.30–32, Spade 1995, 110).[15] The definition specifies two kinds of failures, failing to do what one believes should be done and failing to refrain from that which one believes one should refrain. Abelard discusses both kinds of failures. The principal case offered in illustration of failing to do is a case involving non-culpable ignorance. The case illustrating a failure to refrain is a case of mistaken belief. As it turns out, the distinction between acting in ignorance and acting on a mistaken belief tends to occupy Abelard's attention more than the distinction between failing to do and failing to refrain.

II.1 Sinning through Ignorance

The star example of the first sort of failure appears in Abelard's discussion of the persecution of Christ. It is not just that Christ's persecutors were not sinning if they believed that they were pleasing God by punishing a dangerous heretic. Even more strongly, Abelard claims that had they *failed* to punish Christ when they believed that he was a dangerous heretic, they *would* have been sinning (*Sc.* 54.27–56.8, 66.31–34, Spade 1995, 110–111, 131). Abelard spends more time defending the former claim than the latter, a reasonable strategy if he thought that the former claim is a consequence of the latter.[16] If Christ's persecutors were

---

[14] For more on this distinction in another context, see William E. Mann, "Piety: Lending a Hand to Euthyphro," *Philosophy and Phenomenological Research*, 58 (1998): 123–142.

[15] Abelard defines contempt negatively, as *not* doing or *not* omitting, in order to conform to the Augustinian thesis that evil is non-being. See "Augustine on Evil and Original Sin," in *The Cambridge Companion to Augustine*, ed. Eleonore Stump and Norman Kretzmann (Cambridge: Cambridge University Press, 2001). Reprinted as Chapter 5 of this volume.

[16] One can make a case that "They would have sinned by not punishing" entails "They did not sin by punishing," especially if one is inclined to deny the possibility of moral dilemmas. For more on the topic of moral dilemmas, see the discussion of the case of the judge punishing a person the judge knows to be innocent, in the next section, "Natural Law."

not sinful, why did Christ say "Father, forgive them, for they know not what they do" (Luke 23:34)? Why is forgiveness necessary if they were free of sin?

Abelard's reply is to distinguish four senses of the term "sin," only two of which need concern us here. The *proper* sense of the term is the sense Abelard has advocated—consent that is contempt of God. There is in addition what I shall call on Abelard's behalf a *public* sense of "sin," which applies to external deeds, in particular to those deeds which have not been "performed or willed correctly" (*Sc.* 56.32–58.1, Spade 1995, 130). Christ's persecutors have committed a public sin but not a sin proper. The commission of a public sin exposes its agents to divine punishment even though they might be without sin proper. Christ's petition, then, amounts to asking that God remit punishment on the persecutors that is otherwise justified by their deed. "Thus to sin through ignorance is this sort of thing: not to have a fault in this [act], but to do what is not fitting for us" (*Sc.* 66.27–28, Spade 1995, 116). To put the point in more contemporary terms, Abelard has just claimed that at least from the divine point of view, some offenses are *strict liability offenses,* that is, cases of culpable wrongdoing in which the offender has no mens rea. We shall see that Abelard countenances a similar class of offenses from the point of view of secular authority. When the point is put this way, however, it becomes obvious that Abelard needs to provide an account of what it is that makes a deed a public sin, something not performed or willed correctly. Contempt of God cannot be the only dimension of moral wrongness. We need an account of what it is that makes an act "not fitting for us."

II.2 Natural Law

As a prelude to his definition of sinning through ignorance, Abelard discusses the case of Cornelius the centurion, "a devout man who feared God with all his household" (Acts 10.2). As Abelard interprets the case, Cornelius had come to recognize and love God "by the natural law" (*Sc.* 64.17, Spade 1995, 126), but did not believe in Christ until Peter informed him. Abelard says that had Cornelius passed away believing in God before his acceptance of Christ, he would have been numbered not among the faithful but among those without faith. The reference to natural law is seemingly offhand and certainly isolated. Even so, I suggest that it may be the key to understanding why Abelard thinks some actions are fitting or unfitting for us independently of whether they express contempt of God.

In the *Dialogue,* the Philosopher claims that the natural law is "the science of morals we call 'ethics'" (*Coll.* 44.85, Spade 1995, 11). It is "first" both in time and in nature to the "Old Law" given to the Jews—the precepts contained in the Pentateuch—and to the "New Law" given to Christians and contained in the Gospels and the apostles' teaching. Its temporal primacy explains how the ancient pagans were able to achieve moral sophistication without knowledge of the Old or New Law. Its natural primacy involves its being simpler than the Old or New Law. The Old and New Law are less simple in that they contain everything contained in natural law, but add to natural law's content. The Old Law, for example, includes precepts concerning circumcision and forbidden food. Among the New Law's edicts is a precept concerning baptism. The challenge the Philosopher sets the Jew and the Christian is to convince him, by rational argument alone, that these sorts of additions make the Old Law or the New Law superior to natural law. The presupposition behind the challenge, a presupposition made explicit in the Philosopher's discussion of Job (*Coll.* 59.489–492, Spade 1995, 63), is that the content of natural law is discoverable by natural reason, that is, reason unaided by supernatural revelation. In contrast, insofar as the Old and New Law are less simple than natural law, their complexity is attributable to content that appears not to be backed by reason but by faith based on revelation alone. We should note that the Philosopher takes the content of natural law—and thus the power of natural reason—to be fairly extensive. We know by it that God exists and that we must love God, neighbor (*Coll.* 53.332–334, Spade 1995, 48), parents, punish the depraved, and in general observe whatever practices are so necessary for all people that without them individual human merits would be insufficient (*Coll.* 125.2223–2225, Spade 1995, 283). Like Cornelius, then, the Philosopher is no atheist. Yet, also like Cornelius, there is no assurance that the Philosopher will be saved, no matter how fervent his piety, if he lacks faith in Christ (*Sc.* 64.17–23, Spade 1995, 126). Abelard is careful *not* to say that Cornelius, and by implication, the Philosopher, would definitely be damned. To say that would be to presume to know too much about God's plans.

One of the examples Abelard uses to illustrate the notion of sinning through ignorance is a hunting accident (*Sc.* 66.19–21, Spade 1995, 129). Overeager Nimrod may mistake a companion for a deer, death resulting. Not intentional homicide, but a substandard performance nonetheless. If one of the precepts of natural law enjoins us to exercise due diligence when engaging in dangerous activities, then Nimrod has disregarded natural law. Note here two different pleas of ignorance. "I didn't know that my companion had moved behind that bush," an acknowledgment of ignorance of factual circumstance, helps to explain how the homicide occurred, may exonerate Nimrod from a charge of murder, but still betokens negligence. "I didn't know that I was supposed to be careful while engaged in dangerous pastimes," a confession of ignorance of a relevant part of natural law, would betray not only Nimrod's behavior but Nimrod himself as substandard.

Let us return to the case of Christ's persecutors. Perhaps what Abelard has in mind is the thought that the persecutors have violated a precept of natural law.

A likely candidate for such a precept might be that one should not punish the innocent. That Christ's persecutors violated this precept unwittingly exculpates them from a charge of sin but not from a charge of acting in a way not fitting for them. As appealing as this solution may be, we shall see that it is at tension with other things Abelard has to say.

II.3 Sinning through Mistaken Belief

Recall that the second part of Abelard's definition of contempt of God is failing to refrain from that which one believes one should refrain. Abelard does not discuss such a case in the *Ethics* or the *Dialogue*. We get some help from his *Commentary on Paul's Letter to the Romans* [*Comm. Rom*]. Paul says of types of foodstuff that none is unclean in itself (Romans 14:14, 14:20). Yet, Paul continues, "He who has doubts is condemned, if he eats, because he does not act from faith; for whatever does not proceed from faith is sin" (Romans 14:23). Abelard interprets the passage as maintaining that "he sins who uses even lawful things against his conscience" (*Comm. Rom.* 306.313–314).

It appears that Abelard is speaking in his own voice and intends his remark to apply universally. The Old Law contains a prohibition against eating pork. The New Law does not (see *Sc.* 18.19–23, Spade 1995, 38). Abelard believes that the New Law supersedes the Old Law. Does the New Law's supersession rescind all parts of the Old Law that are not also part of natural law? Or does the Old Law still remain in effect on the Jews? In either case consider a Jew who believes that it is illicit for him to eat pork, but who consents to eating pork nonetheless. If the Old Law is in effect, he is expressing contempt of God by consenting to something that actually transgresses God's law. If the Old Law is no longer in effect, then although he is not actually transgressing God's law, it would seem that as long as he mistakenly believes that he is, he actually is expressing contempt of God.

Abelard's definition of contempt of God sows the seed of what the agent believes into it essentially. What we are seeing, I suggest, is the harvest. Is the crop welcome? John Marenbon observes:

> But if Abelard had thought about the more general application of the principle he appears to admit, he could hardly have remained complacent. . . . Applying the principle generally: I sin if I contravene what I believe, wrongly, is a revealed precept that applies to me. But I might believe wrongly that any precept is a revealed precept which applies to me, including ones which contradict precepts of natural law (for instance, supposedly revealed precepts commanding human sacrifice).

I may even believe that my revealed precept includes the command to follow it, not natural law . . . Abelard does not see the difficulty which wrongly believed revealed precepts (whether general or particular) present for his theory.[17]

One might think that Abelard's complacency would be shaken upon seeing that, according to his theory, an agent, *A*, has sinned by intentionally refraining from human sacrifice when *A* believes that human sacrifice is commanded. How can *A* sin by doing the right thing? A related question: because refraining from human sacrifice is not otherwise sinful, how can *A*'s merely believing that it is sinful make it sinful? An unflappable Abelard should reply by reminding us that his theory countenances two dimensions of wrongdoing, acting in a way unfitting for us to act and sinning proper. If there is anything that is picked out by the phrase, "*A*'s doing the right thing," it can only be *A*'s act of eating pork or refraining from human sacrifice, which, we may suppose, *A* does fittingly. *A*'s sin is not this, however, nor is *A*'s sin established by *A*'s belief. *A*'s sin is in *consenting* to the sinful suggestion to which the belief gives rise.

If Abelard needs two dimensions of wrongdoing, sin proper and unfit action, parity of reason leads us to expect two dimensions of good conduct, namely, having the right intention and action that is fit for us to perform. Abelard takes pains to argue that when we call an intention and its ensuing action good, we correctly distinguish two things, the intention and the deed. We are mistaken, however, if we think that the *goodness of the intention* and the *goodness of the action* are two commensurable instances of goodness. Abelard's position on this point is not entirely stable. His first pronouncement, consonant with his thesis that all deeds are indifferent, is that when "good" is predicated of an action, the predication is akin to synecdoche. That is, the predication extends to a whole, the complex of intention plus action, what properly applies only to a part, the intention (*Sc.* 46.4–16, Spade 1995, 91). A bit later he seems willing to settle for a weaker view. Even if deeds can be good in some sense, the sense in which they can be good is different from the sense in which intentions can be good. This difference in sense is sufficient to preclude addition of the one good to the other to produce a complex whose goodness is greater than the goodness of the intention alone (*Sc.* 52.4–15, Spade 1995, 105).

In either case it is clear why Abelard insists on the claim that deeds do not amplify an agent's goodness. Suppose that two people have the same charitable intentions, but that one of them is robbed of his money through no fault of his own while the other brings her plans to fruition. It cannot be that the second

---

[17] Marenbon 1997, 272.

person earns more divine credit or that the first person's credit diminishes in the eyes of God because of the robber's malice. For if merit could be enhanced by external deeds, then the rich could become more meritorious than the poor simply by plowing their wealth into external projects. To think that wealth can by itself contribute to true happiness or the worth of the soul, says Abelard, is the height of madness (*Sc.* 48.25–30, Spade 1995, 99).

The performance of deeds does not add to an agent's sinfulness or merit. What is the point, then, of secular institutions of justice, especially punishment? If the real sin in murder lies in the murderer's consent, which will be duly assessed by a supremely knowledgeable and just judge, and if performance does not aggravate the felony, the imposition of punishment on a murderer by secular authorities might seem to be akin to double jeopardy. It is true that natural law is supposed to warrant punishing the depraved. Abelard does not rest content with a bare appeal to natural law; moreover, the cases he presents involve punishing those without relevant fault, not the depraved. His discussion unfolds in two stages. First Abelard argues for the permissibility of secular punishment. Then he argues for its practical value. The discussion would warm the hearts of many consequentialists.

The permissibility argument takes this form. If there are cases of legitimate secular punishment where there is no sin on the part of the defendant—cases where secular authorities may punish even if God remits punishment—then a fortiori there should be cases of legitimate secular punishment where the defendant has sinned. But there are cases of sinless deeds meriting secular punishment. Abelard cites two, one involving negligence, the other the knowing punishment of an innocent person. Therefore there are cases of legitimate secular punishment of sinners.

I do not propose to defend the first premise. It may appear to beg the question against those who worry about the justice of double jeopardy. Its defense would seem to depend, then, on the distinction between two kinds of wrongdoing, prosecuted in two different jurisdictions. I do want to look at Abelard's two cases more closely. In the first one, a destitute mother, in an attempt to keep her baby warm, takes him into bed with her and, while asleep, smothers him. Abelard maintains that a legal authority[18] is justified in exacting a heavy penalty on the woman, even though she lacks sinful consent, in order to deter her and others from similar future behavior (*Sc.* 38:13–22, Spade 1995, 79–80). Divine justice scrutinizes the inner workings of the mind, where human justice cannot penetrate. Human justice attends to the outer behavior (*Sc.* 40.7–19, Spade 1995,

---

[18] A bishop, in Abelard's example, but the case is not materially changed if we suppose the authority not to be ecclesiastical.

82–83), attempting to modify it, not so much with an eye to serving justice as to ensuring the common utility by preventing public injuries and the corruption of others (*Sc.* 44.3–5, Spade 1995, 88). This is the practical value of secular punishment. In pursuit of this value it may happen that a lesser offense should be punished more severely than a greater one, if the lesser offense, left unchecked, would tend to erode the common good more than the greater one. Thus arson is punished more severely than fornication even though fornication is the more serious sin from God's point of view (*Sc.* 42.5–44.2, Spade 1995, 86–87).

Abelard's second case is more troublesome. We are to imagine a judge before whom a defendant has been brought by unscrupulous plaintiffs. The plaintiffs impute something to the defendant. The judge realizes from the imputation that the defendant cannot be guilty. Yet at trial, the plaintiffs, using perjurious witnesses, make an unrebuttable case for the defendant's guilt. In discharging his judicial duties, the judge justly imposes punishment on someone he knows to be innocent (*Sc.* 38.22–40.5, Spade 1995, 81).

Let us suppose, on Abelard's behalf, that whatever it is by means of which the judge realizes the defendant's innocence, it cannot be admitted into the legal proceedings. Let us also suppose that there is no legal mechanism in place for the judge's recusing himself. These are very large suppositions indeed, but without them the judge's behavior cannot plausibly be described as the just fulfillment of his secular official duties. Even with them, however, Abelard's case is still vexing. Recall that in the case of Christ's persecutors, Abelard says that they did not sin, because they unwittingly failed to live up to a precept of Natural Law that one should not punish the innocent. What should we say of Abelard's judge, who *wittingly* consents to a violation of that precept? How can this fail to be a case of sin? It can be maintained that there is another Natural Law precept that dictates that one ought to discharge those legitimate duties entailed by one's voluntary acceptance of a particular vocation. Without further elucidation, however, we now must conclude that Abelard's judge is ensnared in a moral dilemma. One precept says he must punish, the other says he must not. No matter what he does, he sins.[19]

One might try to dissolve the dilemma by claiming that one of the judge's two conflicting duties is weightier and takes precedence over the other. There are two problems. First, it is not clear that the duty to discharge one's office trumps the duty not to punish the innocent, as is required by Abelard's verdict. Second,

---

[19] Aquinas would later distinguish between simpliciter and *secundum quid* moral dilemmas. A *secundum quid* dilemma is one that arises because of previous wrongdoing on the agent's part. A *simpliciter* dilemma is one in which the agent has done no relevant previous wrong that leads to it. The judge's plight seems to be a simpliciter dilemma. For references and discussion, see William E. Mann, "Jephthah's Plight: Moral Dilemmas and Theism," *Philosophical Perspectives*, 5 (1991): 617–647.

even if one could make out a case to that effect, one would not thereby have shown that Abelard's judge is free from sin. All one would have shown is that Abelard's judge sins less grievously in punishing the innocent defendant than in failing to meet the obligations of his office.

It is possible to maintain that given the assumption that the judge has sinned, it does not follow that the sinless defendant's punishment is illegitimate. Abelard may be prepared to embrace a purely formalistic conception of secular judicial conduct, one that would maintain that as long as all public procedure is duly followed, the result is legitimate. This attitude would be consistent with the importance Abelard lays on the inward-outward distinction.

Fornication is a worse sin than arson, says Abelard, but one may wonder how Abelard's theory can accommodate degrees of sin. Contempt is contempt. It cannot be that the psychological intensity of the contempt is an accurate index of the gravity of sin, lest the guiltridden fornicator become less of a sinner than the swaggering arsonist. Psychological intensity would seem at most to provide a gauge to the distance the sinner has to travel to make repentance. Abelard scoffs at the Stoic doctrine that all sins are equal, calling it "plain foolishness" (*Sc.* 74.9, Spade 1995, 145) and the kind of insanity that consists in believing the most patent falsehood (*Coll.* 109.1795–1796, Spade 1995, 230). Yet his own theory raises the question of how it is that not all sins are equal.

Although Abelard presents a taxonomy of sins according to their gravity, the taxonomy is disappointing in its conventionality. According to Abelard, some sins are venial, others damnable; of damnable sins, some are criminal, some are not (*Sc.* 68.27–29, Spade 1995, 134). "Sins are venial or light when we consent to what we know should not be consented to; nevertheless at the time what we know does not occur in memory" (*Sc.* 68.31–70.1, Spade 1995, 135). Examples are boasting and overindulgence: there are occasions when, caught up in the spirit of the moment, we brag or eat or drink too much and only in retrospect come to recall what we knew all along–the excessive nature of our behavior. It is distinctive of damnable sins that no one can have forgotten, even momentarily, that perjury, homicide, or adultery are sinful.[20] Finally, damnable sins that are criminal are those that have been carried out and made known publicly.

Set aside the fact that the taxonomy is a mixed bag: by Abelard's strictest lights, criminal sins are not a third class of sin proper. Set aside the fact that the taxonomy is too coarse-grained to help us see why, for instance, fornication is a

---

[20] Compare Abelard's observation with the 1843 M'Naghten rule defining criminal insanity. A person is criminally insane if "at the time of committing the act, the party accused was laboring under such a defect of reason, from disease of the mind, as not to know the nature and quality of the act he was doing; or if he did know it, that he did not know he was doing what was wrong" (A. S. Goldstein, *The Insanity Defense* (New Haven: Yale University Press, 1967), 45).

more serious sin than arson. Abelard would still face the complaint that appealing to the phenomenon of forgettability does nothing to explain why damnable sins are worse than venial ones.

Let us raise a related problem for Abelard's theory. It bears some resemblance to his case of the two differently motivated executioners. Consider two cases of homicide, alike as they can be in their external manifestations and consequences. Suppose further that in both cases, the agent acts intentionally, consenting to the suggestion to kill the victim. In the first case, Grimesby stands to inherit a fortune upon the victim's death, and is motivated entirely by greed. In the second, Philemon has witnessed Amanda, Philemon's sister, suffer from a slow, painful, degenerative disease for which there is no cure. In her lucid moments, Amanda has urged Philemon to kill her. Philemon understands that he will gain nothing from Amanda's death and risks being charged with murder. He kills Amanda nevertheless; he can no longer bear seeing Amanda suffering. A natural reaction to the two cases is to say that motive should make a difference, a difference to which Abelard's theory seems insensitive. Grimesby intended to kill out of greed, Philemon out of compassion. As far as Abelard's theory is concerned, however, the only relevant moral dimension to sin is the intention. Would Abelard have us believe that Philemon's act is exactly as contemptuous of God as Grimesby's is? That God, "the examiner of the heart and reins," can see no significant moral difference between the two?

III Conjectures

At one point Abelard says that adultery is more displeasing to God than overeating because adultery does more injury to love of neighbor (*Sc.* 74.12–19, Spade 1995, 146). Abelard alludes to what lies at the core of New Testament ethics. Love of God and love of neighbor are enjoined on Christians as the two great commandments, on which depend all the law and the prophets (Matthew 22:37–40). The more we come to love God, the more eager we are to avoid what offends him, and our eagerness will wax or wane in proportion to the magnitude of the offense (*Sc.* 72.24–26, Spade 1995, 142). To be sure, much the same could be said of fear of God, except that anxiety replaces eagerness. Fear motivates us to avoid incurring God's wrath. But fear can only produce painful and grudging compliance with God's will, while love involves endorsing God's will and taking on God's projects as the lover's own. Abelard depicts fear as standing to the Old Law as charity stands to the Gospel (*Sc.* 72.2–14, Spade 1995, 139–140). Fear of divine punishment is the source of what Abelard calls unfruitful penitence; love is the source of genuine and fruitful penitence (*Sc.* 76–92 passim, Spade 1995, 151–171 passim).

To say only this much, however, is to leave crucial questions unanswered. Why should we want to love God? Why should we want to love our neighbor? Abelard says precious little in answer. To provide a detailed response on his behalf would risk the charge of invention masquerading as exposition. I offer the following remarks as the least daring answer I can think of. They are anchored in a claim made by Abelard's Christian in the *Dialogue,* that the ultimate good for humans is to love the ultimate good itself, which is God (*Coll.* 132–133.2437–2440, Spade 1995, 315). We can presume that Abelard would regard it as axiomatic that we desire to be happy. If greater goods contribute to greater happiness and if God is the greatest of all goods, then Abelard has the ingredients of an answer to the first question. Themes that are prominent in the thought of Augustine would help to answer the second. Suppose that created goods exhibit different degrees of goodness to the extent to which they reflect God's goodness. Humans, who are (feebly) like God in possessing the capacity for judgment, are superior to animals, who lack the capacity. Animals, who are like God in being alive, are in turn superior to inanimate objects. In our ordinary, literally mundane affairs, then, the other people we encounter are the most God-like creatures around, thus deserving to be loved as much for their goodness as we love ourselves.[21]

Skating on even thinner ice, we are led to speculate about how to connect an ethics of love to Abelard's views about sin. This much seems clear: the Augustinian account sketched in the previous paragraph tolerates, indeed, rests on, the thought that love should vary in intensity depending on the worthiness of the object of love. Abelard's Christian argues for this thesis (*Coll.* 110–113.1826–1924, Spade 1995, 235–243). Lovers may thus err in two ways, either by investing too much love in an object not meriting it or by failing to love strongly enough something they should.[22] Now while degrees of mislocated love might help Abelard to explain how sins can vary in their severity, one may still wonder how this fits his analysis of sin in the cases of Grimesby and Philemon. No doubt Grimesby fastens far too much love on wealth and far too little on his victim. Philemon's love for Amanda seems harder to fault. Yet Abelard's analysis of sin brands both cases equally.

There are two components to the solution I suspect Abelard would give. The first is that what motivates Philemon's action is not genuine love but "tender-heartedness" (*misericordia*), a natural inclination—thus not a moral virtue— that tends to work against justice and God's plans (*Coll.* 122–123.2152–2176, Spade 1995, 275–277). The second is that Abelard's account of sin is not, and is

---

[21] This sentiment is compatible with the beliefs that (1) humans are nevertheless a fairly miserable lot and (2) there are other created beings—angels, for example—superior to us in virtue of being immaterial. Augustine held both beliefs; see especially Books 2 and 3 of *De libero arbitrio.*

[22] This is a vindication of the utility of the Augustinian notion of inordinate desire.

not intended to be, an account of human depravity. Grimesby displays a character more depraved than Philemon's because Grimesby's greed is not just another natural inclination like tender-heartedness. Greed is a moral vice, voluntarily acquired, disposing its possessor to sin. Ceteris paribus it would take considerably more effort to establish in Grimesby's soul the relations of love that constitute its ultimate human good. Yet for all of that, Abelard can maintain that Grimesby's and Philemon's consenting to homicide are equally sinful.

It may have occurred to you that we have already embarked on speculation about the content of the unfinished second book of the *Ethics*. Let me indulge myself for one more paragraph. In the second book Abelard would have maintained that moral virtues dispose us to do well but they are not what doing well is. Nor is doing well simply a matter of doing good deeds: first, because goodness attributed to deeds is parasitic on a more fundamental goodness; second, because the widow's mites count for more than the sums of the wealthy (see Mark 12:41–44). Finally, doing well is not simply a matter of desiring to do well; if wishes were horses, beggars might ride. To do well is to consent to do well, to take on as one's own projects, insofar as one can, projects that are pleasing to God, out of love of God. Looking back at Abelard's definition of contempt of God as a model, we can ask which of these two definitions would more closely match his conception of love of God:

> Love of God is to do for God's sake what *we believe* should be done by us for God's sake.
> Love of God is to do for God's sake what should be done by us for God's sake.

By incorporating the agent's beliefs into it, the first definition more closely parallels Abelard's definition of contempt of God. But it also entails that one could have genuine love of God while committing atrocities, based on false beliefs, in God's name. The second definition requires of genuine love of God that the lover's actions actually comport with God's will, not some misguided conception of it. The second definition sets a loftier standard. The first definition is audacious, controversial, the sort of thing that would require defense from a brilliant if pesky philosopher. Which one would Abelard have chosen?[23]

---

[23] An earlier draft of this essay benefited from comments from Jeffrey Brower, Kevin Guilfoy, Scott MacDonald, Gareth B. Matthews, Christopher Taylor, and Thomas Williams.

ANSELM

10

Definite Descriptions and the Ontological Argument[*]

Jan Berg has presented, in a painstaking and highly compressed paper, St. Anselm's Ontological Argument, dressed in the garb of a formal language, L.[1] L is the first-order predicate calculus with identity and, particularly, with Russell's theory of descriptions.[2] It is the task of Berg's paper to reconstruct Anselm's argument in L with an eye toward (1) preserving historical accuracy and (2) preventing the argument from begging the question. In this paper I will argue that he has not completely satisfied either objective, and further, that the reason he has not is that Russell's theory of descriptions is particularly unsuitable for Anselm's argument. I will then investigate the implications of reconstructing the argument in L, supplemented not with Ruussell's theory, but with some alternative theories.

I

Berg presents four major arguments as candidates, only the fourth of which he thinks is successful in not begging the question. I will discuss only the first, third, and fourth; the second falls as the first does.[3]

Let "G" be an interpreted predicate such that "Gx" means that nothing greater than x can be conceived. "E" will be interpreted as "exists *in re*"; thus, "Ex" means that x exists *in re*. Then we have the following arguments in L:

---

[*] This paper benefited greatly from the criticism and encouragement of Professor Gareth B. Matthews. [The present version is somewhat revised, incorporating new translations of the passages from Anselm's works.]

[1] Jan Berg, "An Examination of the Ontological Proof," *Theoria* 27 (1961): 99–106.

[2] The theory is presented formally in Alfred North Whitehead and Bertrand Russell, *Principia Mathematica*, 2nd ed., vol. 1 (Cambridge: Cambridge University Press, 1960), 30–31, 66–71, 173–186 (*14).

[3] See Berg, "Examination of the Ontological Proof," 104–105.

$$(A1)$$

(P1) God $=_{df} (\iota x)(Gx)$	Presupposition
(P2) $- (E(\iota x)(Gx)) \supset -(G(\iota x)(Gx))$	Presupposition
(P3) $G(\iota x)(Gx)$	Presupposition
(1) $E(\iota x)(Gx)$	(P2), (P3), Modus tollens
(2) $E(\text{God})$	(P1), (1), Substitution

We can eliminate "E" as a predicate in favor of the existential quantifier and an identity sign: "Ex" will then be expressed by "$(\exists y)(y = x)$." (A1) will then become:

$$(A1')$$

(P1) God $=_{df} (\iota x)(Gx)$	Presupposition
(P2') $- (\exists y)(y = (\iota x)(Gx)) \supset - (G(\iota x)(Gx))$	Presupposition
(P3) $G(\iota x)(Gx)$	Presupposition
(1') $(\exists y)(y = (\iota x)(Gx))$	(P2'), (P3), Modus tollens
(2') $(\exists y)(y = \text{God})$	(P1), (1'), Substitution

One problem with (A1) and (A1') lies in (P3). As an instance of (*Principia Mathematica*) *PM* *14.22, we have

(A) $E! (\iota x)(Gx) \equiv G(\iota x)(Gx)$

From (P3) and (A) we get

(B) $E! (\iota x)(Gx)$

which is equivalent by definition (*PM* *14.02) to

(C) $(\exists y)(x)(Gx \equiv x = y)$

However, (C) is equivalent (by *PM* *14.202 and substitution) to

$(\exists y)(y = (\iota x)(Gx))$

which is (1'). Of course, we need not have gone further than (B): with (P3) as a presupposition, we establish not only the existence of God, but of a monotheistic one at that. Thus (A1) and (A1') beg the question.[4]

Dropping (P3), then, Berg considers another possible argument, (A3).

$$(A3)$$

(P1) God $=_{df} (\iota x)(Gx)$	Presupposition
(P2b) $- (\exists y)(y = (\iota x)(Gx)) \supset - ((\iota x)(Gx)$ $= (\iota x)(Gx))$	Presupposition
(P3b) $(\iota x)(Gx) = (\iota x)(Gx)$	Presupposition
(1') $(\exists y)(y = (\iota x)(Gx))$	(P2b), (P3b), Modus tollens
(2') $(\exists y)(y = \text{God})$	(P1), (1'), Substitution

(A3) offers little solace for someone of Anselm's persuasion, for we have trouble with (P3b). As an instance of *PM* ˙14.28, we have

$$(D) \quad E! \, (\iota x)(Gx) \; \equiv ((\iota x)(Gx) = (\iota x)(Gx))$$

which, along with (P3b), yields (B) again, and thus, eventually, (1') again.

Berg finally offers a reformulation of the argument that he thinks is free from the circularity that plagues (A1)–(A3). There are three alternatives tendered to patch up our troublesome "(P3)" position: it will be sufficient for my purposes to consider any one of them.

---

[4] Berg shows that (P3) cannot be taken as an instance of a theorem of the form " $\vdash F(\iota x)(Fx)$," where "F" is any predicate whatsoever, for if this were a theorem, then, by *PM* ˙14.01, we could derive " $\vdash (\exists y)((x)(Fx \equiv x = y) \,\&\, Fy)$," and by distribution of the existential quantifier, obtain " $\vdash (\exists y)(x)$ $(Fx \equiv x = y)$" and " $\vdash (\exists y)(Fy)$." Of these, the former asserts that every property is exemplified by exactly one thing, while the latter says that every property is exemplified. (See "Examination of the Ontological Proof," 104–105.) Karel Lambert has shown that a contradiction can be derived from our purported theorem. If "F" can be any predicate at all, then it can be the predicate "$(\lambda x)(Fx \,\&\, - Fx)$", from which we get, by concretion, "$F(\iota x)(Fx \,\&\, - Fx) \,\&\, - F(\iota x)(Fx \,\&\, - Fx)$." See Lambert, "Notes on E! III: A Theory of Descriptions," *Philosophical Studies* 13 (1962): 51–59, esp. 54.

$$(A4)$$

(P1) God $=_{df} (\iota x)(Gx)$	Presupposition
(P2c) $-(\exists y)(y = (\iota x)(Gx)) \supset (-G(\iota x)(Gx))$	Presupposition
(P3c′) $-(-G(\iota x)(Gx))$	Presupposition
(1′) $(\exists y)(y = (\iota x)(Gx))$	(P2c), (P3c′), Modus tollens
(2′) $(\exists y)(y = \text{God})$	(P1), (1′), Substitution

II

Throughout all his reformulations of the ontological argument, there is one presupposition that Berg leaves constant and unaltered—(P1). One ought to be chary about maintaining that Anselm would hold "the unique x such that nothing greater than x can be conceived" to be a definition of God. In Anselm's *De Grammatico* it is made clear that to define a thing is to specify its essence, for ". . . the essence of any individual thing is fixed in a definition."[5] Furthermore, in Chapter X of the *Monologion* we get the picture that we know or understand a thing, if and only if we know its essence, or its definition.

> For I express *man* in one way, when I signify him by this name, that is, "man"; in another, when I think the same name silently; in another, when the mind considers the man himself, either through an image of the body or through the reason. Through an image of the body, when it [the mind] imagines his sensible form; through the reason, when it thinks of his universal essence, which is *rational mortal animal*.
>
> These three distinct varieties of speaking constitute the words of one's nation. But the words of that [kind of] speaking that I have put third and last, when they are of things not unknown, are natural and are the same among all nations. And since all other words are grounded on the basis of these, where these are, no other word is necessary for recognizing a thing, and where these cannot be, no other [word] is helpful for making a thing known.[6]

---

[5] St. Anselm, *De Grammatico*, in *S. Anselmi Cantuariensis Archiepiscopi Opera Omnia*, tome I, vol. 1, ed. Franciscus Salesius Schmitt (Stuttgart-Bad Cannstatt: Friedrich Frommann Verlag [Günther Holzboog], 1968), 152. All translations are my own. [Hereafter, all references to this work will be to "Schmitt."]

[6] St. Anselm, *Monologion* X, in Schmitt (Note 5), 25.

Is it so clear that, when we consider God as the being than whom nothing greater can be conceived, we now know all the essential properties of God? And, therefore, that "the unique x such that nothing greater than x can be conceived" is a definition of God? It seems that Anselm did not think so, for after using the notion of a being than whom nothing greater can be conceived to show *that* God is, Anselm devotes the rest of the *Proslogion* to uncovering *what* God is. In the beginning of Chapter V, he asks: "What then are you, Lord God, than whom nothing greater can be conceived?"[7] The very asking of this question would be superfluous, as indeed would most of the remainder of the *Proslogion*, if the answer were simply "the being than whom nothing greater can be conceived." Moreover, if one took "the unique x such that nothing greater than x can be conceived" as a definition of God, then it would seem that one would be hard-pressed to make much sense of the enigmatic Chapter XV of the *Proslogion*: "Therefore, Lord, not only are you that than which a greater cannot be conceived, but you are also something greater than can be conceived."[8] This amounts to saying that God is so great that he cannot be entirely conceived. I take it that this would imply that his essence cannot be fully understood. But if his essence were to be the being than which nothing greater can be conceived, then it would follow that "the being than which nothing greater can be conceived" cannot be fully understood. Yet Anselm maintained in *Proslogion* II that even the fool understands "the being than which none greater can be conceived."[9] Following through on this line of reasoning, we would be forced to conclude that Anselm has contradicted himself between Chapters II and XV. To absolve Anselm of the charge of inconsistency, it is sufficient to distinguish between God's essence and God's characterization as the being than which nothing greater can be conceived.

Of course, it may be replied that the phrase "the being than which nothing greater can be conceived" plays a dual role for Anselm. There is the low-grade role where just enough of its meaning is employed early in the *Proslogion* to reduce the fool to absurdity, and there is the high-grade role which is such that if it were possible to explicate fully this phrase, we would have God's essence or definition. So the phrase can be understood sufficiently to establish with certainty that God exists, yet not even Anselm himself understands it completely.[10] However, to admit this distinction is to admit that as it stands, the phrase "the being than which nothing greater can be conceived" is not a specification of God's essence,

---

[7] *Proslogion* V, in Schmitt (Note 5), 104.

[8] *Proslogion* XV, in Schmitt (Note 5), 112.

[9] See Schmitt (Note 5), 101.

[10] "So when 'that than which nothing greater can be conceived' is said, without doubt what is heard can be conceived and understood, even if that being, than which a greater cannot be conceived, cannot be conceived or understood." St. Anselm, *Responsio Editoris* IX, in Schmitt (Note 5), 138.

simply because explication of the phrase is necessary. If so, it would be the *explicans* that gives us God's essence (and would thus be a definition of God), and not the explicated phrase.

If the relation between the term "God" and the phrase "the being than which nothing greater can be conceived" is not one of definiendum to definiens, what then is it? Whatever else might be involved in this relation, this much seems clear: "the being than which nothing greater can be conceived" is a definite description and "God" is a name, both of which purport to pick out one and the same being. On the basis of this, we might try to modify (P1) into an identity statement:

$$(\text{P1}')\quad \text{God} = (\imath x)(Gx)$$

Some unwelcome results are attendant upon (P1'), however. As an instance of *PM**14.13, we have

$$(\text{E})\quad (\text{God} = (\imath x)(Gx)) \equiv ((\imath x)(Gx) = \text{God})$$

(P1') and (E) give us

$$(\text{F})\quad (\imath x)(Gx) = \text{God}$$

From *PM**14.15 we get

$$(\text{G})\quad ((\imath x)(Gx) = \text{God}) \supset (F(\imath x)(Gx) \equiv F(\text{God}))$$

where "F" is any predicate whatsoever. Applying modus ponens to (F) and (G), we get

$$(\text{H})\quad F(\imath x)(Gx) \equiv F(\text{God})$$

By *PM**14.01, "$F(\imath x)(Gx)$" is definitionally equivalent to "$(\exists y)((x)(Gx \equiv x = y)\ \&\ Fy)$," and applying a definitional interchange to (H) yields

$$(\text{I})\quad (\exists y)((x)(Gx \equiv x = y)\ \&\ Fy) \equiv F(\text{God})$$

Inasmuch as "F" stands for any property, we can let it be Berg's property G and get

$$(\text{I}')\quad (\exists y)((x)(Gx \equiv x = y)\ \&\ Gy) \equiv G(\text{God})$$

But look what has happened now. One-half of the biconditional (I′) asserts that if God is such that nothing greater than he can be conceived, then there exists exactly one entity such that nothing greater than that entity can be conceived. We get an even more general result from (I). If God is claimed to have any property at all, then he exists. Yet there certainly are properties for which it is difficult to see how they could be denied of God. For example, let "*H*" be the predicate "is identical with God." Then, from (I), we have

$$(\text{I}'')\ \ (\exists y)((x)(Gx \equiv x = y)\ \&\ Hy)\ \equiv H(\text{God})$$

If we say, then, that God is identical with himself, then on Russell's theory of descriptions, we obtain the left-hand side of the biconditional (I″).[11] Similarly, let "*J*" be the predicate "is identical with the unique *x* such that nothing greater than *x* can be conceived." Substituting into (I) gives us

$$(\text{I}''')\ \ (\exists y)((x)(Gx \equiv x = y)\ \&\ Jy)\ \equiv J(\text{God})$$

But "*J*(God)" just is (P1′), and once again we obtain the left-hand side of our biconditional.

(I) puts Anselm's fool in quite an embarrassing position: either he cannot say anything about God at all, or he already agrees that God exists. Not only is the fool embarrassed; so is Anselm, for now the ontological argument has been trivialized, and Anselm is indeed guilty of the charge that God has been presupposed into existence.

Well and good, it might be argued, but so far it has only been shown that (P1′) has this undesirable consequence. It may be that if we reinstate (P1), even though it does not seem to be something that Anselm would have accepted, then (A4) will go through. After all, the kind of definition that (P1) is need not be taken to be what Anselm would have called a definition—something that gives the essence or nature of some being. We can just treat (P1) as a stipulation or an abbreviation, with none of the metaphysical trappings of an Aristotelian real definition.

---

[11] We might attempt to block this consequence by allowing identity ascriptions to hold only when the term in question is known to designate. Such a restriction strikes me as too ad hoc. Consider this elegant and succinct argument of LeBlanc and Hailperin: "We feel indeed that a statement of the form *W = X* is true if and only if *X* designates whatever *W* designates. But *W* designates whatever *W* designates, whether or not *W* designates anything. Hence *W = W* should be true, whether or not *W* designates anything." Hugues LeBlanc and Theodore Hailperin, "Nondesignating Singular Terms," *Philosophical Review* 68 (1959): 239–243, esp. 242.

This will not help matters either. For one of the cardinal features of a definition in a system (such as L) is that definiens and definiendum be mutually substitutable, at least in all extensional contexts, without change of truth value.[12] Consider any extensional predicate "F," and suppose it is predicated, either truly or falsely, of God. Thus we have "$F(\text{God})$." But by our principle of substitutivity, this gives us "$F(\imath x)(Gx)$." On Russell's theory, this is definitionally equivalent to "$(\exists y)((x)(Gx \equiv x = y) \,\&\, F y)$," and again the fool (and Anselm) is in a box. It was the task of Berg's paper to show that formulations (A1)–(A3) ran into difficulties at (P2) and (P3) and their variants, whereas (A4) would save Anselm. However, (A4) still contains (P1) or my variant (P1′), in which case even it presupposes the existence of God.[13]

<h1 style="text-align:center">III</h1>

All the difficulties encountered above are engendered, I suggest, by the utilization of Russell's theory of descriptions. The theory has come under attack from many quarters, for many reasons, and the reason why it is an unfortunate candidate for giving a sympathetic rendition of Anselm's argument in L can be given on an intuitive level. Consider these two sets of sentences:

<h2 style="text-align:center">(A)</h2>

(1) The winged horse ridden by Bellerophon was born, full-grown, from Medusa's slain body.

(2) The winged horse ridden by Bellerophon lives an immortal life on Olympus.

(3) The author of "On denoting" wrote *Introduction to Mathematical Philosophy* while in prison.

(4) The author of "On denoting" once thought the ontological argument was sound.

---

[12] See, e.g., Whitehead and Russell, *Principia Mathematica* (note 2), 11, where the stronger claim, "without change of meaning," is made.

[13] It is perhaps significant to note that textually, Anselm himself does not invoke the doctrine of (P1) until after he has proved the existence of the being than which nothing greater can be conceived. (See Berg's "Examination of the Ontological Proof," (Q4) and (Q5), 101.) Thus, perhaps a more historically accurate rendition of Anselm's argument would proceed only with, say, (P2c) and (P3c′) to get (1′). The transition from (1′) to (2′) might then be licensed by the following "meaning postulate": "God" means the same as "the being than which nothing greater can be conceived." It would seem that the difficulties of (P1) and (P1′) are circumvented, because the crucial terms are being mentioned, and not used.

(B)

(1) The winged horse ridden by Bellerophon was sired by Bellerophon.
(2) The winged horse ridden by Bellerophon won the Triple Crown in 1959.
(3) The author of "On denoting" has never changed his mind in philosophy.
(4) The author of "On denoting" is an arch-conservative.

We should like to say that the members of (A) have at least one thing in common—they are all true. Similarly, all the members of (B) are false. There is a difference between those members numbered (1) and (2), and those numbered (3) and (4). In the former, the subject does not exist; in the latter, the subject does. On Russell's view, (A1) and (A2) are false, and this is where his theory parts company from ordinary life. On Russell's theory, (A2), for example, will be true just in case (a) there is a winged horse ridden by Bellerophon, (b) there is only one such horse, and (c) he lives an immortal life on Olympus. (A2) is false, then, because condition (a) is not met. (B1) will be false for exactly the same reason. But in ordinary life we would like to say that (B1) is false, all right, but not simply because Pegasus does not exist—rather, that his father was Poseidon, not Bellerophon.

The trouble with Russell's theory, with respect to the ontological argument, is that ordinarily we sometimes want to affirm some properties, and deny others, to things we know not to exist, or whose existence is putative. On Russell's view, the privilege of ascribing properties is reserved only for those things we know to exist, or, to put it differently, predication presupposes the existence of the subject of predication. Russell's theory is inappropriate because Anselm's argument depends essentially upon a notion of predication more akin to what we might call the ordinary sense of predication. In order to justify this claim, I want to present a way of looking at Anselm's motivation and strategy behind the ontological argument.[14]

It is illuminating to consider Anselm as being sensitive to the problems of negative existential statements—that is, statements denying the existence of some individual or species. Traditionally, one such problem might be put as follows: The statement, "Pegasus does not exist," is apparently true, yet on closer inspection, it seems to be either false or meaningless (assuming we do not equate, as has often been done, a false statement with a meaningless one). For if Pegasus in no sense exists, then the noun of the sentence "Pegasus does not exist" has no referent, or is not about anything, and thus the sentence is meaningless. On the other hand, if "Pegasus" does have a referent, then the statement is false. There

---

[14] This way of appreciating Anselm was pointed out to me by Professor Matthews. This does not imply that he would agree with my presentation of it, or with the conclusions that I draw from it.

has been a host of solutions proposed to deal with this, and other kindred problems, and Russell's theory itself (especially as it is employed by Quine) is one of the most brilliant of them all.

Anselm has a solution to this sort of problem, although it is an implicit one: there is no explicit discussion that I know of in the Anselmian corpus. The reader is referred to the previously mentioned Chapter X of the *Monologion,* and this passage from Chapter II of Anselm's *Response*:

> For just as what is conceived is conceived by conception, and what is conceived by conception, as it is conceived so it is in conception; so what is understood is understood by the understanding, and what is understood by the understanding, as it is understood so it is in the understanding. What is clearer than that?[15]

Given this background, it would seem natural enough for Anselm to maintain that in the sentence "Pegasus does not exist," we understand the term "Pegasus" because and only because Pegasus is in our understanding. Pegasus thus has a mode of existence, *in intellectu.* What we are denying when we deny the existence of Pegasus is that he exists *in re,* in the real world outside our understanding or imagination. So the statement "Pegasus does not exist" can be counted as meaningful and true, if it is taken in the sense of "Pegasus does not exist *in re.*" The statement is false if it is uttered significantly and intended in the sense of "Pegasus does not exist *in intellectu.*"[16]

If we accept this account of what Anselm would say about negative existential statements, we can now come to grips with a negative existential statement that does interest him very much—"The being than which nothing greater can be conceived does not exist." It is Anselm's claim that when the fool says this, he certainly does not mean that the being than which nothing greater can be conceived does not exist *in intellectu.*[17] Rather, the fool means to say that no such being exists *in re.* From this assertion, Anselm proceeds to derive a contradition, thus establishing the existence of the being than which nothing greater can be conceived.

The relevant feature that emerges from this is that Anselm has a way of making sense of negative existential statements, and moreover, has a way of ascribing

---

[15] *Responsio Editoris* II, in Schmitt (Note 5), 132.

[16] Not only false but self-defeating: on the theory that I am attributing to Anselm, if a person uttered this sentence, understanding its terms, he would be making a pragmatic contradiction.

[17] "Therefore, even the fool is convinced that something than which nothing greater can be conceived is at least in the understanding, since when he hears this, he understands it, and whatever is understood is in the understanding." *Proslogion* II, in Schmitt (Note 5), 101.

properties to things that do not exist *in re,* or whose existence *in re* is being argued for. In the case of, say, "Pegasus is swift," the predicate "swift" is predicated of the Pegasus which exists *in intellectu;* the statement is about something that exists in our understanding. There is no commitment made to Pegasus' existence *in re* from the mere fact that we assign some properties to him. Similarly, there is no apparent commitment to the real existence of God if one assents to the statement "The being than which nothing greater can be conceived is greater than all other beings." As it stands, we need say no more than that this statement is about the being than which nothing greater can be conceived which exists in *intellectu.*

It is important to notice that Anselm is quite explicit in maintaining that when one understands something, that very thing exists in the understanding. We have seen one passage already from Chapter II of the *Response* bearing this out. Consider now the very next paragraph, paying attention to the occurrences of the word "it":

> Next I said that if *it* [the being than which nothing greater can be conceived] is even in the understanding alone, *it* can be conceived to exist in reality also, which is greater. Therefore if *it* is in the understanding alone, *it* itself, namely 'that than which a greater cannot be conceived', is that than which a greater can be conceived. What, I ask, is more logical? For if *it* is even in the understanding alone, can *it* not be conceived to exist also in reality? And if *it* can be, does not he who conceives of this conceive of something greater than that being, if *it* is in the understanding alone? Thus what is more logical than that if 'that than which a greater cannot be conceived' is in the understanding alone, that is the same as to be that than which a greater can be conceived?[18]

Finally, consider these passages concerning the claim that there is no commitment to a thing's existing *in re* from the simple fact that it exists *in intellectu:*

> For it is one thing for a thing to be in the understanding, and another to understand a thing to exist. For when a painter conceives beforehand that which he is to make, he certainly has it in the understanding, but he does not yet understand to exist that which he has not yet made. However, when he has painted it, he both has it in the understanding and understands that that which he has now made exists.[19]

---

[18] *Responsio Editoris* II, in Schmitt (Note 5), 132.
[19] *Proslogion* II, in Schmitt (Note 5), 101.

> . . . I was trying to prove what was doubtful, to whom at first it was
> enough to show that being to be understood and to be in the under-
> standing in some way, so that it might be considered subsequently
> whether it was in the understanding alone, as false things are, or also
> in reality, as true things are. For if false things and doubtful things are
> understood and are in the understanding in this way, that when they are
> spoken of, the hearer understands what the speaker signifies, nothing
> prohibits what I have spoken of from being understood and being in
> the understanding.[20]

There is one all-important exception to this latter doctrine, according to
Anselm, and that is in the case of God. What establishes God's existence is not
that we admit that the being than which nothing greater can be conceived has
some properties or other—Pegasus has properties, but does not, for all of that,
exist. God's existence is established by the logically unique properties involved
with the being than which nothing greater can be conceived. Such a being cannot exist only *in intellectu,* for then a greater being can be conceived—one who
in addition, exists *in re.* This case is the exceptional one. For any other being,
real or imaginary, it is never self-contradictory to deny its *in re* existence,[21]
but in the case of the being than which nothing greater can be conceived, it is
self-contradictory.

Now we are in a position, hopefully, to see why Russell's theory of descriptions is unsuitable for Anselm's purposes. For Russell, to assign a predicate to
a description-term is to presume that the description-term designates an entity
in re.[22] For Anselm, this presumption has an important qualification. To assign a
predicate to a description-term is to presume that the term designates, but not
necessarily anything *in re.* In cases where a thing is known not to exist *in re,* or
where its existence is moot, the receptacle of predicates is something *in intellectu.*
What keeps Anselm's argument from being blatantly circular is his distinction
between modes of existence. Russell's theory fails in fairly reproducing Anselm's
argument not only because it intentionally ignores the notion of modes of existence, but, more basically, because it proceeds upon a rather stringent view concerning the connection between predication and existence.

---

[20] *Responsio Editoris* VI, in Schmitt (Note 5), 136.

[21] Although it may be "existentially self-defeating" to deny one's own existence. See Jaakko
Hintikka, "*Cogito, Ergo Sum:* Inference or Performance?" *Philosophical Review* 71 (1962): 3–32.
Repr. in *Philosophical Applications of Free Logic,* ed. Karel Lambert (New York: Oxford University
Press, 1991), chap. 7.

[22] See especially *PM* ˙14.01. The language of *Principia Mathematica* does not recognize modes of
existence; in particular, the existential quantifier is univocal.

IV

A formal language like L, supplemented with Russell's theory of descriptions, does not produce a very happy result for Anselm's argument. Can we supplement L with another theory of descriptions and hope to do any better? If we remember that for Anselm, to talk about something, and to ascribe properties to it, is not to assume that the thing exists *in re*, it would seem natural to turn to a theory of descriptions that is free of such existential presuppositions. A discussion of such theories arises from an interest in developing a "free" logic, which is basically a language like the classical first-order predicate calculus, but with an important modification. The requirement that every singular term (i.e., either individual constants or definite descriptions) have a denotation is waived. Any singular term, from a purely formal standpoint, may or may not have a denotation in a free logic.

One such theory of descriptions has been formulated by Jaakko Hintikka.[23] As the basis for his theory, he puts forth the following contextual definition schemata:

$$(\text{SA}) \quad a = (\imath x)(Fx) \ \equiv (Fa \ \& \ (x)(Fx \supset x = a))$$

and

$$(\text{SB}) \quad y = (\imath x)(Fx) \ \equiv (Fy \ \& \ (x)(Fx \supset x = y))$$

Consider these examples:

(1) Russell = the author of "On denoting" if and only if Russell authored "On denoting" and nobody else did.
(2) Homer = the author of *The Iliad* if and only if Homer authored *The Iliad* and nobody else did.
(3) Pegasus = the winged horse ridden by Bellerophon if and only if Pegasus was a winged horse ridden by Bellerophon and nothing else was a winged horse ridden by Bellerophon.
(4) God = the being than which nothing greater can be conceived if and only if God is a being than which nothing greater can be conceived and nothing else is a being than which nothing greater can be conceived.

---

[23] Jaakko Hintikka, "Towards a Theory of Definite Descriptions," *Analysis* 19 (1958–1959), 79–85. See also his "Existential Presuppositions and Existential Commitments," *Journal of Philosophy* 56 (1959): 125–137; "Definite Descriptions and Self-Identity," *Philosophical Studies* 15 (1964): 5–7; "Studies in the Logic of Existence and Necessity," *The Monist* 50, no. 1 (1966): 55–76.

Clearly, (1)–(4) are all translations of substitution instances of (SB). Moreover, in Hintikka's system, there are no existential presuppositions involved in the singular terms; an individual constant or definite description may or may not have a denotation. Thus, if we transcribe (4) into a statement of the form of (SA), symbolizing "God" by an individual constant of L and "the unique x such that nothing greater than x can be conceived" by a definite description, it does not follow that we have presumed the existence of anything at all. It is because of this that Hintikka's theory is more amenable to Anselm's argument than Russell's.

It is natural to ask how one does indicate existence in Hintikka's system. That is, how do we show that some particular individual constant, "a," has a denotation? Hintikka argues that the formal counterpart to "a exists" is "$(\exists x)(x = a)$."[24] Given that this serves to show that a exists, we can use the same method to claim that "$(\iota x)(Fx)$" has a denotation—"$(\exists y)(y = (\iota x)(Fx))$." From (SB), by substitution, we now have a schema that explicates what it means for the unique x such that x Fs to exist:

$$(\text{SC}) \quad (\exists y)(y = (\iota x)(Fx)) \equiv (\exists y)(Fy \ \& \ (x)(Fx \supset x = y))$$

Employing Hintikka's theory, we turn back now to Berg's (A1′), and modify it to produce the following argument:

$$(\text{A1}'')$$

(P1′) God $= (\iota x)(Gx)$	Presupposition
(P2′) $- (\exists y)(y = (\iota x)(Gx)) \supset -(G(\iota x)(Gx))$	Presupposition
(P3) $G(\iota x)(Gx)$	Presupposition
(1′) $(\exists y)(y = (\iota x)(Gx))$	(P2′), (P3), Modus tollens
(2′) $(\exists y)(y = \text{God})$	(P1′), (1′), Substitution

A curious feature emerges from using Hintikka's theory in this argument. It turns out that presupposing (P3) is otiose, and that it can be derived from (P1′). The derivation is as follows. As an instance of (SB) we have

$$(\text{K}) \quad \text{God} = (\iota x)(Gx) \equiv (G(\text{God}) \ \& \ (x)(Gx \supset x = \text{God}))$$

(P1′) and (K) yield

<hr>

[24] See, esp., "Existential Presuppositions and Existential Commitments," 133–134; "Studies in the Logic of Existence and Necessity," 63–64, 70–73.

(L) $G(\text{God})$ & $(x)(Gx \supset x = \text{God})$

from which, by simplification, we get

(M) $G(\text{God})$

By a substitution licensed by (P1$'$) we get, from (M),

$G(\iota x)(Gx)$

which is (P3).

At any rate, it appears that we now have a valid, noncircular argument for the existence of God. No longer are we bothered with the presuppositions (P1) or (P1$'$), which, in the framework of Russell's theory, shipwreck Anselm's aspirations. For in Hintikka's theory, there is no presupposition that the terms in (P1$'$) designate anything *in re*.

Our hopes are short-lived, however, Lambert has shown that, if we accept the unconditional validity of "$(\iota x)(Fx) = (\iota x)(Fx)$," where "$F$" is any predicate whatsoever, then Hintikka's system for free description theory is inconsistent. Schema (SB) yields

(SD) $y = (\iota x)(Fx) \supset (Fy \,\&\, (x)(Fx \supset x = y))$

Truth-functionally, (SD) gives us

(SE) $y = (\iota x)(Fx) \supset Fy$

If we allow that "$(\iota x)(Fx) = (\iota x)(Fx)$" is true whether "$(\iota x)(Fx)$" designates or not, then by substituting into (SE), we obtain

(SF) $(\iota x)(Fx) = (\iota x)(Fx) \supset F(\iota x)(Fx)$

and by modus ponens,

(SG) $F(\iota x)(Fx)$

But as indicated in Note 4, having (SG) as a theorem results in a contradiction when "F" is interpreted as the predicate "$(\lambda x)(Fx \,\&\, - Fx)$."[25]

---

[25] See Lambert (Note 4), 53–54. In his reply to Lambert, "Definite Descriptions and Self-Identity," Hintikka suggests that we ought not to accept the universal applicability of "$(\iota x)(Fx) = (\iota x)(Fx)$." For a critique of Hintikka's proposal, see Karel Lambert, "Definite Descriptions and Self-Identity: II," *Philosophical Studies* 17 (1966): 35–43.

Lambert has investigated the possibility of remedying this theory, while still cleaving to a free logic, and has offered the following alternatives. We can avoid the difficulty engendered by Hintikka's theory by basing a free description theory on the two axiom-schemata,

$$(\text{SH}) \ (y)(y = (\imath x)(Fx) \equiv ((x)(Fx \supset x = y) \ \& \ Fy))$$

and

$$(\text{SI}) \ \ y = (\imath x)(x = y)$$

in conjunction with a modified rule of universal specification. We replace "From $(x)(Fx)$ to infer Fy" with "From $(x)(Fx)$ and $(\exists y)(y = z)$ to infer Fz."[26] We can effect a reduction in this system by introducing one contextual definition schema, viz.,

$$(\text{SJ}) \ \ (\imath x)(Fx) = y \equiv (z)(y = z \equiv (Fz \ \& \ (x)(Fx \supset x = z)))$$

from which (SH) and (SI) are derivable.[27]

If we inspect (A1″) in terms of Lambert's theory, we will find that (P3) is no longer deducible from (P1′), for we are not allowed to treat

$$\text{God} = (\imath x)(Gx) \equiv ((x)(Gx \supset x = \text{God}) \ \& \ G(\text{God}))$$

as an instance of (SH) unless we know that

$$(\exists y)(y = \text{God})$$

is true, which is just what (A1″) is attempting to prove. Of course, (P1′) carries no existential presuppositions for Lambert, and it appears now that we have secured a valid, noncircular argument for Anselm. In fact, we have more than one, for (A4) also seems to meet the test, as does (A3). Concerning (P3b) in (A3), Lambert is willing to allow the unconditional assertability of a statement of its form,[28] although, as we have seen, Russell and Hintikka are not.

If these arguments are valid, it is up to a detractor of them to challenge their soundness. But certainly that task is more than I promised in this paper.

[26] See Lambert (Note 4), 52, 57–58.

[27] See Karel Lambert, "Notes on E! IV: A Reduction in Free Quantification Theory with Identity and Descriptions," *Philosophical Studies* 15 (1964): 85–88.

[28] See Lambert, "Definite Descriptions and Self-Identity: II" (Note 25), 39–40.

11

The Ontological Presuppositions of the Ontological Argument

The most recent stage in the analysis of St. Anselm's Ontological Argument is the modal-logical stage: if one wants to get clear as to what is wrong (or right) with it, one should phrase it in S5.[1] I have misgivings about this maneuver, if it is claimed in the name of historical exegesis. While I think that the connections between the Ontological Argument and modal logic are insightful and exciting, I also think that the arguments presently offered in Anselm's name, even though they might be better than his, are revisionary or revolutionary. What I wish to do in this paper is reactionary. I shall first set out what I take to be the argument contained in *Proslogion* II. I shall then point out that the argument rests on a set of assumptions which reveal a conceptual scheme different from that of the sober, twentieth century modal logician. Finally, I shall show that the assumptions in question lead to a novel criticism of Anselm's argument, a criticism that does not require of us, for instance, that we deny that "exists" is a predicate.

I

Here is the crucial passage from *Proslogion* II:

> Thus even the fool is convinced that something than which nothing greater can be conceived is in the understanding, since when he hears

---

[1] I have in mind the following articles: Robert Merrihew Adams, "The Logical Structure of Anselm's Arguments," *The Philosophical Review* 80 (1971): 28–54; David Lewis, "Anselm and Actuality," *Noûs* 4 (1970): 175–188; and an unpublished paper by Alvin Plantinga, "God and Possible Worlds." The latter two explore the alleged connections between Anselm's argument(s) and the "possible worlds" semantics for quantified modal logic.

this, he understands it; and whatever is understood is in the understanding. And certainly that than which a greater cannot be conceived cannot be in the understanding alone. For if it is even in the understanding alone, it can be conceived to exist in reality also, which is greater. Thus if that than which a greater cannot be conceived is in the understanding alone, then that than which a greater cannot be conceived is itself that than which a greater can be conceived. But surely this cannot be. Thus without doubt something than which a greater cannot be conceived exists, both in the understanding and in reality.[2]

I offer the following argument as a reconstruction of the passage:

(1) Whatever is understood is in the understanding.

(2) If that than which nothing greater can be conceived is understood, then that than which nothing greater can be conceived is in the understanding. (Instance of (1))

But: (3) That than which nothing greater can be conceived is understood.

Thus: (4) That than which nothing greater can be conceived is in the understanding. (From (2) and (3))

Suppose: (5) That than which nothing greater can be conceived is in the understanding only, and does not exist in reality.

(6) For whatever is in the understanding only, and does not exist in reality, something greater than it can be conceived.

(7) If that than which nothing greater can be conceived is in the understanding only, and does not exist in reality, then something greater than that than which nothing greater can be conceived can be conceived. (Instance of (6))

Thus: (8) Something greater than that than which nothing greater can be conceived can be conceived. (From (5) and (7))

Thus: (9) That than which nothing greater can be conceived exists in reality. (From (4), (5), and (8))

Note that the argument is comprised of two sub-arguments. Steps (1)–(4) purport to establish the *in intellectu* existence of that than which nothing greater can be conceived. Steps (5)–(9) purport to establish, in reductio fashion, the *in*

---

[2] St. Anselm, *Proslogion* II, my translation. The Latin edition from which this and subsequent translations are based is *S. Anselmi Cantuariensis Archiepiscopi Opera Omnia,* edited by Franciscus Salesius Schmitt, O.S.B. The edition is now reissued in two tomes at Stuttgart-Bad Cannstatt by Friedrich Frommann Verlag (Günther Holzboog), 1968. The Latin text for *Proslogion* II is in tome I, vol.1, 101–102.

re existence of that than which nothing greater can be conceived by showing that the contrary hypothesis, (5), leads to a contradiction, (8). Each sub-argument has its own characteristic axiom—(1) and (6), respectively. About (6) I shall have little to say in this paper, except to point out that it is more modest in its claims than other similar principles which have been ascribed to Anselm on occasion, for example:

> For whatever is in the understanding only, everything in reality is greater than it.[3]
> For anything of kind *K*, if it is in the understanding only, then there is something of kind *K* greater than it.[4]

(1), however, is intriguing, and an exploration of (1) will lead us into the heart of Anselm's conceptual scheme.

II

Let us begin, then, by marking one feature of Anselm's thought, the existence of which cannot be gainsaid. Anselm distinguishes between a thing's existing *in intellectu* and its existing *in re*. Two questions are important concerning the distinction. First, exactly what is the distinction, and how does it work? Second, what is the point or purpose of the distinction? I shall consider these questions in turn.

Consider (1). Anselm regards (1) as obvious,[5] but it is not as innocent as it may at first appear. Anselm is indifferent as to whether it is linguistic entities or

---

[3] Adams thinks that Anselm "would probably have assented" to this principle, although he acknowledges that the argument of *Proslogion* II does not require it. See Adams, "Logical Structure of Anselm's Arguments," 30. I know of nothing in Anselm's writings that would indicate his acceptance. But see fn. 13.

[4] See Alvin Plantinga, *God and Other Minds* (Ithaca, NY: Cornell University Press, 1967) 67–79, for a discussion of some other (6)-like principles.

[5] "Observe, then, that since it is understood, it follows that it is in the understanding. For just as that which is conceived is conceived by conception, and that which is conceived by conception, just as it is conceived is thus in conception, so that which is understood is understood by understanding, and that which is understood by understanding, just as it is understood is thus in the understanding. What is clearer than this?" St. Anselm, *Quid ad haec respondeat editor ipsius libelli,* in *S. Anselmi . . . Opera Omnia* I, I, 132 (Chapter II).

Anselm did not think, however, that (1) held in the case of "indefinite nouns," such as "not-man," and words that signify the absence of something, such as "injustice" and "nothing." See his fragment on "Aliquid" in Franciscus Salesius Schmitt, O.S.B., *Ein neues unvollendetes Werk des hl. Anselm von Canterbury,* in *Beiträge zur Geschichte der Philosophie und Theologie des Mittelalters* 33/3 (1936): 42–43.

ontological entities that are understood,[6] but it is clear that the things that are in the understanding are things, and not words or phrases. Here we begin to see part of the character of Anselm's thought. A necessary condition for one's understanding something is that that *something* be in the understanding: if it were not the case that something is in the understanding, then it would seem to follow that nothing is understood. Thus, although (1) may have the appearance of a tired truism, it is metaphysically loaded. It tells us that whenever anything is understood, that thing has a mode of being: it exists *in intellectu.*

For Anselm, there is no difference between a thing's being in the understanding and its being conceived.[7] We can express the connection in terms of two alternative principles:

(A) A thing is in the understanding if and only if it is conceived.

Or:

(A′) A thing is in the understanding if and only if it can be conceived.

(A) tells us that a thing is *in intellectu* if and only if it is being conceived or thought of by someone, while (A′) tells us that a thing is *in intellectu* if and only if it *can* be conceived, irrespective of whether anyone is in fact conceiving of it. I do not claim that Anselm ever distinguished between (A) and (A′), although, as we shall see, (A′) fits nicely with another feature of Anselm's thought.

According to (A′), the class of beings *in intellectu* is identical to the class of conceivable beings. The class of *in re* beings is a subclass of the class of *in intellectu* beings. An *in re* being is a being that actually exists. It follows, then, that one and the same being can exist both *in intellectu* and *in re.* The pattern of the argument of *Proslogion* II presupposes that fact: it is one and the same being which is first shown to be in the understanding and then to exist *in re.*[8] These facts, along with the tendency to gloss conceivability in terms of logical possibility, make it tempting to translate the argument of *Proslogion* II into the language(s) of modal logic. That temptation, as I hope to show, ought to be resisted.

---

[6] "But if it were true that that than which a greater cannot be conceived cannot be conceived or understood, it nevertheless would not be false that 'that than which a greater cannot be conceived' can be conceived and understood." St. Anselm, *Quid ad haec respondeat editor ipsius libelli,* in *S. Anselmi . . . Opera Omnia* I, I, 138 (Chapter IX)

[7] This needs to be argued for, and I do so in Chapter 3 of my PhD dissertation, *The Logic of Saint Anselm's Ontological Argument* (University of Minnesota, 1971).

[8] See Adams, "Logical Structure of Anselm's Arguments," 34.

III

Perhaps we are now clear enough as to the distinction between beings *in intellectu* and beings *in re* to ask for the point of the distinction. Why does Anselm talk of two realms of entities? One will search in vain for a direct answer from Anselm himself. I should like to speculate on one sort of philosophical concern which may well have motivated the distinction, and for which the distinction provides one kind of answer. It is illuminating to see the distinction as an attempt to deal with the problems that beset negative existential sentences. Here is one version of a conundrum that shares its antiquity with *The Way of Truth* and *The Sophist:* suppose one alleges that Typhon does not exist. Then, if the sentence "Typhon does not exist" is true, there is no referent for "Typhon," the subject term of the sentence. If that is so, the sentence is not about anything, and hence, it is meaningless. If, on the other hand, the subject term does have a referent—which it must have in order to be meaningful—then the sentence "Typhon does not exist" is patently false. In either case, the sentence cannot be true. It turns out to be meaningless or false. The conundrum is perfectly generalizable to all negative existential sentences, including ones that attempt to deny the existence of species or classes of things.

Our present purpose is not to record all the different responses that have been made to the conundrum. Instead, we may note that Anselm's distinction between beings *in re* and beings *in intellectu* provides him with an answer to it. To say that Typhon does not exist is to say that Typhon does not exist *in re*. But, if the sentence "Typhon does not exist" is to be counted as meaningful, then its subject term must be meaningful. It is correct to say that there is an intimate connection between meaningfulness and understandability, such that if a term is meaningful, it can be understood. But in virtue of Anselm's principle (1), if "Typhon" (or Typhon) can be understood, then Typhon is in the understanding. So if the sentence "Typhon does not exist" is meaningful, Typhon must exist *in intellectu*. Hence, Anselm's distinction enables him to say that in the case of a meaningful and true negative existential sentence, its subject does not exist *in re* but does exist *in intellectu*. Its *in intellectu* existence accounts for the meaningfulness of the sentence, while its *in re* nonexistence accounts for the truth of the sentence.[9]

I shall not dwell on the difficulties that have been urged against any philosophical theory which separates out different-modes of being.[10] It will have to

---

[9] See William E. Mann, "Definite Descriptions and the Ontological Argument," reprinted as Chapter 10 of this volume.

[10] The difficulties receive attention from Anthony Kenny, et al., "Descartes' Ontological Argument," in Joseph Margolis, ed., *Fact and Existence* (Oxford: Basil Blackwell, 1969), 18–62.

suffice here to point out that the argument of *Proslogion* II does presuppose a distinction of modes of being. If the distinction is indefensible, a redeployment of the argument would be required, to say the least.

IV

I want now to explore another feature of Anselm's thought, to which too little attention has been paid. Anselm distinguishes between conceiving a thing and conceiving it to exist. The distinction is presupposed in the exchange between Gaunilo and Anselm in *Quid ad haec respondeat quidam pro insipiente* 7 and *Quid ad haec respondeat editor ipsius libelli* IV. One clear example of Anselm's awareness, acceptance, and use of the distinction occurs in Chapter I of his reply to Gaunilo:

> Moreover, you think that from the fact that something than which a greater cannot be conceived is understood, it does not follow that it is in the understanding, nor that if it is in the understanding, it therefore exists in reality. I emphatically assert that *if it can even be conceived to exist, it is necessary that it exist.* For that than which a greater cannot be conceived cannot be conceived to exist except without a beginning. Moreover, whatever can be conceived to exist and does not exist, can be conceived to exist through a beginning. Therefore, that than which a greater cannot be conceived cannot be conceived to exist and yet not exist. Therefore, *if it can be conceived to exist, out of necessity it exists.*
>
> Furthermore, *if it can even be simply conceived, then it is necessary that it exist.* For no one who denies or doubts that there is something than which a greater cannot be conceived, denies or doubts that were it to exist, it could fail to exist neither in actuality nor in the understanding. For indeed otherwise it would not be that than which a greater cannot be conceived. But as to whatever can be conceived and does not exist: were it to exist, it could fail to exist either in actuality or in the understanding. Thus *if it can even be conceived, that than which a greater cannot be conceived cannot fail to exist.*[11]

This passage is a very rich one indeed: it deserves more attention than I shall presently give it. The only point relevant to our present concerns is that Anselm

---

[11] St. Anselm, *Quid ad haec respondeat editor ipsius libelli*, in *S. Anselmi . . . Opera Omnia* I, I, 130–31 (Chapter I); italics added.

talks exclusively of conceiving to exist in the first paragraph, and exclusively of conceiving *simpliciter* in the second.

Finally, the distinction between conceiving and conceiving to exist is crucial to the success of Anselm's argument. Recall steps (6) and (7) of our reconstructed argument. Consider some being *in intellectu* only, and of modest greatness—say, the first stop light in Northfield, Minnesota. (6) guarantees us that something greater than it can be conceived. (6) leaves it an open question whether some of the beings that are greater can be *in intellectu* only. It is also mute on the question whether the first stop light in Northfield would be greater if it existed *in re*. It may or it may not be, as far as we can tell from (6). Hence, (6) does not tell us that to conceive of an existent first stop light in Northfield is to conceive of something greater than the first stop light in Northfield, not conceived to exist.

Notice what happens, however, when what is conceived is the being than which nothing greater can be conceived, and it is claimed that that being does not exist *in re*. Anselm needs to say that, in that case, something greater can be conceived, and thus generate the contradiction revealed in the consequent of (7). But what could possibly be greater than that than which nothing greater can be conceived, were that than which nothing greater can be conceived not to exist? It is not clear how one might want to answer, but Anselm's answer is immediate. "For if it is even in the understanding alone, it can be conceived to exist in reality also, which is greater." One thing that would be greater than that than which nothing greater can be conceived, were it not to exist, is that than which nothing greater can be conceived, existing *in re*. Therefore, to conceive of something greater than the being than which nothing greater can be conceived, supposed not to exist, one can conceive of that same being, existing *in re*. And Anselm does not provide any other instructions as to how else to conceive of something greater than that than which nothing greater can be conceived, supposed not to exist. It is evident, then, that the distinction between conceiving and conceiving to exist undergirds the argument of *Proslogion* II.

V

It is the distinction between conceiving and conceiving to exist, along with the crucial role that it plays in the argument of *Proslogion* II, that makes it difficult to see how the argument readily accommodates itself to the modern apparatus of modal logic. For the accommodation to work, Anselm's language of conceivability must translate without residue into the language of logical possibility. But the language of logical possibility, exemplified by modal logic, is insensitive to the distinction between conceiving a thing and conceiving it to exist.

Let us note first that in modal logic, the modal operators of necessity and possibility are operators on propositions. That is, it is *states of affairs* which are said to be possible, impossible, or necessary. However, Anselm's distinction between conceiving and conceiving to exist, along with his *in intellectu–in re* distinction, applies to *beings,* or *things,* not states of affairs. And although Anselm says that there is a difference between conceiving a thing and conceiving it to exist, there is no difference between one's saying that a state of affairs is logically possible and one's saying that it is logically possible for that state of affairs to exist. Thus, if we attempt to tailor the argument of *Proslogion* II to fit the mold of modal logic, we shall be required (a) to shift from talk of conceivable beings, etc., to logically possible states of affairs, etc., and (b) to obliterate the crucial distinction between conceiving and conceiving to exist. One might regard these two changes as desirable, on philosophical grounds, but the fact remains that they are changes, and hence not faithful to Anselm's thought.[12]

VI

The Anselmian claim that there is a difference between one's conceiving of a thing simpliciter and one's conceiving it to exist is an extraordinarily difficult claim to assess. What exactly is the relation between conceiving of a thing and conceiving a thing to exist? Surely the following seems to be correct: it is a (logically) necessary condition for one's conceiving of a thing as existing that the thing be conceived simpliciter. This seems to be a conceptually necessary conditional:

If a thing is conceived as existing, then it is conceived.

To conceive of a thing as existing requires conceiving of it; if one were not conceiving of it, then a fortiori one would not be conceiving of it as existing.

Once the above principle is accepted, there is no difficulty in one's subscribing to a modalized version of it:

If a thing can be conceived to exist, then it can be conceived.

---

[12] It is true that given the "possible worlds" semantics for quantified modal logic, one can make sense of talk about possible beings; and thus one might think that the change mentioned in (a) is not so significant as it first appears. There is some merit to this method, I think, but even so, (b) still holds. For no sense can be given to a distinction between something's being a possible being and its being such that it is possible that it exist.

What about the converse of the modalized version? Recall that in the argument of *Proslogion* II, Anselm says that "if it is even in the understanding alone, it can be conceived to exist." He appears to regard the claim as unexceptionable.[13] It is reasonable, then, to attribute the following thesis to him:

> If a thing is in the understanding, then it can be conceived to exist.

But (A′) allows us to infer, in conjunction with the above thesis,

> If a thing can be conceived, then it can be conceived to exist.

We may now combine this result with our earlier modalized conditional to obtain

> (B) A thing can be conceived if and only if it can be conceived to exist.

Hume, of course, denied that there was any distinction between conceiving a thing and conceiving it to exist:

> The idea of existence, then, is the very same with the idea of what we conceive to be existent. To reflect on any thing simply, and to reflect on it as existent, are nothing different from each other. That idea, when conjoin'd with the idea of any object, makes no addition to it. Whatever we conceive, we conceive to be existent. Any idea we please to form is the idea of a being; and the idea of a being is any idea we please to form.[14]

If (B) is a correct representation of Anselm's thought, it seems to play into Hume's (and the modal logician's) hands, for (B) tells us that the class of things which can be conceived is extensionally equivalent to the class of things which can be

---

[13] Note that Anselm can consistently maintain that everything in the understanding can be conceived to exist, and that it is not in general true that to conceive of a thing as existing is to conceive of a greater being than the same thing not conceived as existing. If he were to hold the latter doctrine, he would in effect be espousing a principle stronger than (6). Thus, I am suggesting that the passage cited above should be interpreted as a particular instance of a general principle, but that the addition of "which is greater" to it should only be applied to the case at hand, namely, that than which nothing greater can be conceived. My reason for suggesting this interpretation is due to a desire to give Anselm a charitable run for his money. If a principle significantly stronger than (6) is ascribed to him, I believe it will result in special difficulties with regard to Gaunilo's "Perfect Island" objection. But that is beyond the scope of this paper.

[14] David Hume, *A Treatise of Human Nature*, ed. L. A. Selby-Bigge (Oxford: Clarendon Press, 1888), 66–67.

conceived to exist. Hence, an attempt to analyze the difference between conceiving and conceiving to exist in terms of their respective objects is misguided.

What can the difference be? What is it to conceive of something as existing, as opposed simply to conceiving it? I shall suggest two ways of understanding the distinction. The first may well have been the model in terms of which Anselm thought, but as we shall see, it suffers from a serious incoherency. The second is a modified version of the first; and while it avoids the incoherency of the first, it, when applied to Anselm's argument, strips the argument of most of its persuasiveness.

VII

According to the first model, to conceive something to exist is simply a particular case of the more general phenomenon of conceiving something to have some property or other. Suppose Jones is asked to conceive of a 1949 Hudson. Suppose then he is asked to conceive of a red 1949 Hudson. One way of representing the difference between these two requests is that in the latter case Jones is asked to append redness to the object of his earlier conception. If the object of Jones' original conception was a yellow 1949 Hudson, he must now change the color. If he had not thought of any color at all initially, he must now make the object of his conception more determinate with respect to color. If Jones had originally conceived of a red 1949 Hudson, then he need do nothing more to fulfill the second request. Nevertheless, the two requests are different requests. By parity, the difference between conceiving of a 1949 Hudson and conceiving of an existent 1949 Hudson is that in the latter case, one appends existence to the object of his earlier conception.[15]

---

[15] There are two sorts of puzzles, beyond the scope of this paper, that arise with regard to conceivable beings and one's conception of them. First, what criteria might we employ to individuate them? Is the conceivable fat man in the doorway identical with, or distinct from, the conceivable bald man in the doorway? (Apologies to Willard Van Orman Quine, "On What There Is.") Or, what individuates two conceivable beings with exactly the same non-relational properties?

Second, when I change one of the properties in the object of my conception, am I now conceiving of the same thing, somewhat altered, or am I conceiving of a different thing? Apply the question to Anselm's argument. Suppose I first conceive of God simpliciter, and then I conceive him to exist. Am I conceiving of the same being? Anselm's argument requires an affirmative answer, and in *Proslogion* III, he argues that God cannot be conceived not to exist. It follows then that to conceive of God simpliciter is possible only if one does not conceive of God as not existing. Indeed, the task of *Proslogion* IV is to show that the fool of the Psalms, who denied God's existence, was not really conceiving of God at all.

We may call this model, for the sake of convenience, the *property model* of conceiving to exist. It presumes that existence is a property, and it explains the difference between conceiving and conceiving to exist in terms of the appending of the property of existence. The property model, although not entailed by the doctrine that existence is a property, might nevertheless be naturally suggested by that doctrine.

There is no conclusive evidence to the effect that Anselm subscribed to the property model of conceiving to exist. There is some indication that he did regard existence as a property, however. In Chapter I of *De casu diaboli*, Anselm says:

> However, if you consider those things which exist and which are passing into nonexistence, [you will see that] God Himself does not make them not to exist. For not only does a thing exist in no other way than by His causing it, but also it cannot remain to any extent that which it was made to be, without His thus preserving it. When God Himself ceases to preserve that which He has made, it does not return to nonexistence (in which it used to be) because He Himself makes it not to exist, but rather because He ceases to make it to exist. For even when He, as if in anger, removes the existence of something by destroying it, it is not by means of that [action of His] that it does not exist. On the contrary, He takes back as His own that which He had supplied, by which act it was preserved as it was. It returns to nonexistence, not because of that [action of His], but because it had nonexistence before it was made.[16]

A thing can pass from existence to nonexistence, and from nonexistence to existence. It had nonexistence before it was made, and when it was made, it acquired existence. If we take Anselm's mode of expression seriously, two things are strongly suggested in the above passage. The first is that a thing can in some sense *be*, even though it does not exist, or lacks existence. Anselm has no qualms about saying that *it* had nonexistence before *it* was made. The pronominal usage here indicates the tendency. This feature is hardly unexpected if one remembers Anselm's earlier distinction between beings *in intellectu* and beings *in re*. The second doctrine is that existence is a property which some things possess and others lack. (I shall assume for our purposes that to have nonexistence is tantamount to lacking existence.) When a thing is made, it acquires the property of existence; and when it passes back into nonexistence, it loses the property of existence.

---

[16] St. Anselm, *De casu diaboli, in S. Anselmi . . . Opera Omnia* I, I, 234 (Chapter I).

It would carry us too far afield to consider the arguments for and against the view that existence is a property of things. It will have to do for the present to say that if the refutation of the Ontological Argument depends upon the denial of the doctrine that existence is a property, it is not at all clear that all versions of the Ontological Argument have been refuted. Moreover, my present task is to show that preoccupation with the question of whether existence is a property has distracted attention away from more serious difficulties with Anselm's version(s) of the argument.

Return for a moment to Anselm's distinction between beings *in intellectu* and beings *in re*. One way of characterizing the difference between an *in intellectu* being and an *in re* being is that those *in intellectu* beings not *in re* lack the property of existence, while those, and only those, beings *in re* possess the property of existence. Thus, to predicate existence of anything is to affirm that it exists *in re*.

Now recall that a conceived being is simply a being *in intellectu* (from (A)). On the property model of conceiving to exist, to conceive of a being as existing is to add existence to an *in intellectu* being. But that is precisely what makes an *in intellectu* being an *in re* being. The upshot is disastrous. For, when the property model of conceiving to exist is conjoined to the *in intellectu–in re* distinction, Anselm can give no coherent account of the difference between a thing's existing *in re* and its being conceived to exist. To exist *in re,* an *in intellectu* being must possess existence. To be conceived to exist, an *in intellectu* being, as the object of conception, must possess existence (just as to be conceived to be red, it must possess redness). What then, on this scheme of things, could be the difference between a thing's actually existing and its merely being conceived to exist? The answer seems to be—none. But such a result is preposterous.

The problem is perfectly general, but we can discuss the specific case of that than which nothing greater can be conceived. It has been argued that it is essential to the argument of *Proslogion* II that that than which nothing greater can be conceived be conceived to exist. On the property model of conceiving to exist, that amounts to appending existence to that than which nothing greater can be conceived, which is at least *in intellectu*. But that would be exactly what would make that than which nothing greater can be conceived exist *in re*. In this case, the conclusion is hardly welcome, for it serves only to underscore a fundamental flaw in the conceptual scheme we have developed on Anselm's behalf. The flaw, to repeat, is that the *in intellectu–in re* distinction, in conjunction with the property model of conceiving to exist, obliterates the obvious difference between a thing's existing and its being conceived to exist.

VIII

Let us investigate one attempt to escape the quandary. Surely, it will be claimed, Anselm could not be guilty of such an egregious error. The error is due, rather, to a misinterpretation of the property model of conceiving to exist. The property model should be construed in the following fashion: to conceive of a being (which is ipso facto *in intellectu*) as existing *in re* is not tantamount to predicating existence of that being. Instead, the new property it acquires, when it is conceived to exist, is the property of being-conceived-to-exist. Let us call this the *revised property model* of conceiving to exist. Once the revised property model is accepted, one can retain the *in intellectu–in re* distinction without generating the difficulties that the property model raises. For now we shall be able to mark the difference between an *in intellectu* being's existing *in re* and its being conceived to exist. In the former case, it has the property of existence; in the latter, it has the property of being-conceived-to-exist (although it may also have the property of existing *in re,* just in case it exists *in re*).

If the revised property model is to lose its ad hoc flavor, it will require a general revamping of the property model. We will have to say, for example, that to conceive of a 1949 Hudson as red, the property of being-conceived-to-be-red, and not the property of being red, must be appended to the 1949 Hudson *in intellectu.*[17] Perhaps one would be willing to allow that sort of general revision. It seems, however, that there are at least two difficulties involved when the revised property model of conceiving to exist is brought to bear on Anselm's argument.

First, if one were genuinely puzzled about the distinction between conceiving of a thing and conceiving a thing to exist, and really skeptical about the legitimacy of such a distinction, he is not likely to be mollified by the present account. For the old problem reappears in a different guise. What is it for a thing to be conceived without its having the property of being-conceived-to-exist, and how does it differ from a conceived thing that does have the property of being-conceived-to-exist?

---

[17] One may be puzzled as to how to go about appending a property to an *in intellectu* being. I suppose a defender of the original property model might say that all talk about "appending" can be eliminated by means of the following schema (where "*x*" ranges over conceivable beings and "*P*" over properties):

If *x* is conceived to be *P,* then *x* is *P.*

It is obvious how the original property model runs afoul of the *in intellectu–in re* distinction, once the schema is made explicit.

On the revised property model, the schema becomes

If *x* is conceived to be *P,* then *x* is (has the property) conceived-to-be-*P.*

Even if we agreed to overlook this puzzle about the revised property model, a second, more serious difficulty results when the model is applied to the argument of *Proslogion* II. Let us recall once more that the argument relies on the assumption that to conceive of that than which nothing greater can be conceived as existing *in re* is to conceive of something greater than that than which nothing greater can be conceived, when not conceived as existing *in re*. If this were not accepted, there would be no reason to accept step (7) of the reconstructed argument. However, on the revised property model, the assumption translates into the following claim: that than which nothing greater can be conceived, with the property of being-conceived-to-exist, is greater than that than which nothing greater can be conceived, without the property of being-conceived-to-exist.

Yet the latter claim is far from obvious. Why is there any reason to think that that than which nothing greater can be conceived is somehow greater if it has the property of being-conceived-to-exist than if it does not have that property? There seems to be no reason at all. Consider an analogous situation. Few would question that God would be greater if he were omnipotent than if he were not. Hence, few would question the assertion that to conceive of God as omnipotent would be to conceive of a greater being than to conceive of God as not being omnipotent. But suppose someone claimed that God would also be greater if he had the property of being-conceived-to-be-omnipotent than if he lacked that property. Would the addition of that property actually make God greater? It hardly seems that such a property would count as a "great-making" property. Yet that is what would follow on the revised property model. Good gas mileage might have made the 1949 Hudson a better automobile than it would have been if it had lacked good gas mileage, but being-conceived-to-have-good-gas-mileage would simply be an irrelevant property to the assessment of the merits of the 1949 Hudson. Similarly, to conceive of that than which nothing greater can be conceived as existing may be to conceive of a greater being than that than which nothing greater can be conceived, when not conceived to exist. But it does not follow that that than which nothing greater can be conceived is greater if it has the property of being-conceived-to-exist than if it does not.

We may note in passing that the argument of *Proslogion* III also fares ill by the revised property model. Its crucial premise is that if that than which nothing greater can be conceived can be conceived not to exist, then something greater than it can be conceived. What would this greater something be? That than which nothing greater can be conceived, which cannot be conceived not to exist. The revised property model transforms the above claim into the following: that than which nothing greater can be conceived, which cannot lack the property of being-conceived-to-exist, is greater than that than which nothing greater can be conceived, which can lack the property of being-conceived-to-exist. Again, the result appears dubious. Although it may be true that God would be greater if he could not lack omnipotence than if he could, it seems odd to say that God would be greater if he could not lack the property of being-conceived-to-be-omnipotent than if he could lack the property of being-conceived-to-be-omnipotent. It seems, in conclusion, that the revised property model of conceiving to exist is of no help to Anselm in his effort to produce a tempting Ontological Argument.

IX

What I have tried to do in this paper is to uncover some of the presuppositions of Anselm's thought, presuppositions which, for the most part, have been unduly neglected. The presuppositions play a role in his argument in that his argument proceeds by showing that a certain being *in intellectu* must also exist *in re*, since it can be conceived to exist *in re*, which is greater. Anselm is thus not arguing, for instance, that the concept of God must necessarily contain the concept of existence; for, although this sounds paradoxical, he is not talking about the *concept* of God at all.[18] He is rather talking about *God*, that than which nothing greater can be conceived, who exists *in intellectu* and *in re*.

I have attempted to meet Anselm's argument on its own grounds, by provisionally granting him his presuppositions—namely, the *in intellectu–in re* distinction, the distinction between one's conceiving of a thing and one's conceiving it to exist, and the doctrine that existence is a property. Many philosophers have, of course, argued that one or more of these presuppositions is false. The problem with that line of attack is that each of the presuppositions, *taken singly*, is not utterly indefensible. Indeed, that fact is probably the chief contributing cause of the perennial philosophical fascination with the Ontological Argument. What I have tried to show, however, is that *taken together*, the presuppositions still yield no convincing proof for the existence of God.

---

[18] Jerome Shaffer has argued convincingly that one may let existence be a part of the concept of God, so that it is a necessary truth that God exists, and yet there may still be no God! See Jerome Shaffer, "Existence, Predication, and the Ontological Argument," *Mind* 71 (1962): 307–325. To see how this is possible, consider that a concept can be viewed as a set of properties which may or may not be instantiated by any object. Shaffer's point is that even if we allow existence to be a property, and part of the *intension* of the concept of God, there is still no guarantee that the concept of God has any *extension*, or applies to any thing.

If my analysis of Anselm's thought is correct, then Shaffer's point is irrelevant as a criticism of the historical Anselm.

12

The Perfect Island

There is an objection to the Ontological Argument which is almost as old as the argument itself. In his critique of St. Anselm's *Proslogion,* Gaunilo claims that by using the same argument that Anselm uses to prove the existence of God, one can prove the existence of a perfect island.[1] Gaunilo evidently intends his objection to be a kind of reductio by counterargument: Anselm's argument, if it worked, would admit into existence all sorts of perfect things which we all know do not exist. Thus there is something wrong with Anselm's argument.

Anselm did not say much by way of reply to Gaunilo. In this paper I shall offer a defense of Anselm. I shall argue that whatever other faults his version of the Ontological Argument may have, it does not let a host of perfect things into existence.

I

It would be nice if we had Anselm's argument before us, so we could tell whether Gaunilo's objection is well-taken. I believe that the argument contained in *Proslogion* II is best represented as follows:

(1) Whatever is understood is in the understanding.
(2) If the being than which nothing greater can be conceived is understood, then the being than which nothing greater can be conceived is in the understanding. (Instance of (1)).
But: (3) The being than which nothing greater can be conceived is understood.
Thus: (4) The being than which nothing greater can be conceived is in the understanding. (From (2) and (3)).

---

[1] See Gaunilo, *Quid ad haec respondeat quidam pro insipiente* 6. The text is contained in *S. Anselmi Cantuariensis Archiepiscopi Opera Omnia,* edited by Franciscus Salesius Schmitt, O.S.B. (Stuttgart-Bad Cannstatt: Friedrich Frommann Verlag, 1968), tome I, vol. 1, p. 128.

Suppose: (5) The being than which nothing greater can be conceived is in the understanding only, and does not exist in reality.

(6) For whatever is in the understanding only, and does not exist in reality, something greater than it can be conceived.

(7) If the being than which nothing greater can be conceived is in the understanding only, and does not exist in reality, then something greater than the being than which nothing greater can be conceived can be conceived, (Instance of (6)).

Thus: (8) Something greater than the being than which nothing greater can be conceived can be conceived. (From (5) and (7)).

Thus: (9) The being than which nothing greater can be conceived exists in reality.(From (4), (5), and (8)).

I shall not pause here to justify this reconstruction; I have done so elsewhere.[2] Nor shall I discuss (1), although I think its apparent innocence is only apparent. Instead, I would have us focus on (6). (6) is the runt of a litter of principles which have been ascribed to Anselm. Some of the stronger siblings of (6) are:

(A) For whatever is in the understanding only, anything in reality is greater than it.

(B) For anything of any kind K, if it is in the understanding only, then any actual thing of kind K is greater than it.

(C) For whatever is in the understanding only, there is at least one thing from each kind K of things greater than it.

(D) For anything of any kind K, if it is in the understanding only, then there is at least one thing of kind K greater than it.

Since they bear directly on the Perfect Island objection, we shall return to these principles shortly.

If one were to essay a counterargument against Anselm's argument as represented in steps (1)–(9), one would do well to pick a descriptive phrase that matches Anselm's "the being than which nothing greater can be conceived." Had Gaunilo been a bit more astute, he would have seen that purely on syntactic grounds, there are two different phrases worth considering—"the island than which *nothing* greater can be conceived" and "the island than which *no greater island* can be conceived."

---

[2] William E. Mann, "The Ontological Presuppositions of the Ontological Argument," *The Review of Metaphysics* 26 (1972–73): 260–277. Reprinted as Chapter 11 of this volume.

Suppose we take "the island than which nothing greater can be conceived" first. In my reconstruction of Anselm's argument, steps (1)–(4) represent Anselm's attempt to show that the being than which nothing greater can be conceived is at least a conceivable being. I shall assume that for Anselm, a being is a conceivable being only if its description contains no contradictory predicates, and that inconceivable beings cannot be in the understanding. Hence if the island than which nothing greater can be conceived is an inconceivable island, it cannot be *in intellectu,* and if that is so, then steps (5)–(9) cannot be invoked to show that it exists *in re.*

How can it be shown that the island than which nothing greater can be conceived is an inconceivable island? Anselm has the ingredients of an answer in the following passages:

> Similarly for a thing, [some of] whose individual parts do not exist where or when [other] parts exist: all its parts and thus the whole itself can be conceived to exist at no time or in no place. . . . Moreover, that which is made up of parts can be dissolved in conception and can fail to exist.[3]
>
> However, whatever can be conceived not to exist, [even] if it exists, is not that than which a greater cannot be conceived.[4]

It is reasonable to extract from the first passage the principle that any conceivable thing that has spatial or temporal parts can be conceived not to exist. And it is reasonable to extract from the second passage the principle that any conceivable thing that can be conceived not to exist is not such that nothing greater than it can be conceived. But of course the second principle can also be located earlier in Anselm's thought: its contrapositive is the message contained in the notorious *Proslogion* III.

Give Anselm a third principle—that any conceivable island is a conceivable thing that has spatial or temporal parts—and he can demonstrate that the island than which nothing greater can be conceived cannot be *in intellectu*. The argument would proceed along these lines: to conceive of the island than which nothing greater can be conceived would be to conceive of something that has spatial or temporal parts (from the third principle). As such, the island than which nothing greater can be conceived could be conceived not to exist (from

---

[3] St. Anselm, *Quid ad haec respondent editor ipsius libelli* I, in *S. Anselmi . . . Opera Omnia,* I, I, p. 131 (my translation). See also Chapter IV of Anselm's response.

[4] St. Anselm, *Quid ad haec respondent editor ipsius libelli* V, in *S. Anselmi . . . Opera Omnia,* I, I, p. 135 (my translation). See also Chapter III of Anselm's response.

the first principle). And as such, the island than which nothing greater can be conceived would not be such that nothing greater than it can be conceived (from the second principle). Hence, the island would have contradictory properties, and would thus be inconceivable.

The third principle, which seems obviously true, could be regarded as an instance of a more general principle—that any conceivable physical object is a conceivable thing that has spatial or temporal parts—which Anselm could use to thwart all sorts of other Gaunilonian counterarguments. (Thus the three principles in combination would apply not just to islands but to a host of attempted counterexamples.) But I have imputed this third principle to Anselm. Do we have any reason, other than its obvious truth, to think that Anselm would accept it? Here is one indirect consideration. Suppose that Anselm had thought that some conceivable island had no spatial or temporal parts. If there were such a conceivable island, it could be perfect; at least it would not be ruled out by dint of the first and second principles. But since such an island would have no spatial or temporal parts, Anselm could have regarded Gaunilo's counterargument as simply providing a transcendental deduction for one of the Platonic Forms. But it is clear that Anselm wants no part of that, and I take that as evidence for his holding the third principle.

II

Now let us turn to "the island than which no greater island can be conceived." The first thing to notice is that the three principles invoked to show the inconceivability of the island than which nothing greater can be conceived are ineffectual here. The most that those principles will yield is that the island than which no greater island can be conceived is not such that nothing greater than it can be conceived. Gaunilo can be perfectly content with that result.

But in fact, Anselm does not need to show that the island than which no greater island can be conceived is *inconceivable*. All he has to do is show that even if such an island is conceivable, the pattern of argument he uses to prove the existence of the greatest conceivable being will not prove the existence of the greatest conceivable island. Consider my reconstruction of Anselm's argument, and replace every occurrence of "the being than which nothing greater can be conceived" with "the island than which no greater island can be conceived." Instead of step (8) we will have

(8') Something greater than the island than which no greater island can be conceived can be conceived.

Whereas (8) is self-contradictory, allowing Anselm to prove by reductio the *in re* existence of God, it is obvious that (8′) is not. Thus Gaunilo's counterargument does not work, because it is not parallel to my reconstruction of Anselm's argument.

Why, then, would anyone think that the island than which no greater island can be conceived is a problem for Anselm? Most likely because of a confusion about what principle Anselm needs for his argument. All he needs is (6). If any of (A), (B), (C), or (D) is used in place of (6), then the resultant pattern *will* prove the *in re* existence of the greatest conceivable island, a fact which can easily be verified.[5] Thus the greatest conceivable island would be an embarrassment for Anselm only if (6) entailed any of (A) through (D).

But it does not. To see that it does not, let us formalize (6) and (A) through (D), and provide an interpretation under which (6) is true and all of (A) through (D) are false. Let "U" be assigned to "is in the understanding," "R" to "exists in reality," "G" to "is greater than," and let "K" be a predicate variable ranging over kinds. Then, *in a domain consisting of all conceivable beings,*[6] the logical forms of (6) and (A) through (D) are, respectively:

(6′) $(x)((Ux \mathbin{\&} {\sim}Rx) \supset (\exists y)(Gyx))$
(A′) $(x)((Ux \mathbin{\&} {\sim}Rx) \supset (y)(Ry \supset Gyx))$
(B′) $(x)(K)((Kx \mathbin{\&} Ux \mathbin{\&} {\sim}Rx) \supset (y)((Ky \mathbin{\&} Ry) \supset Gyx))$
(C′) $(x)((Ux \mathbin{\&} {\sim}Rx) \supset (K)(\exists y)(Ky \mathbin{\&} Gyx))$
(D′) $(x)(K)((Kx \mathbin{\&} Ux \mathbin{\&} {\sim}Rx) \supset (\exists y)(Ky \mathbin{\&} Gyx))$.

Now consider the following interpretation of (6′) and (A′) through (D′). Let the domain be the positive integers from 1 to 10, and let "U" be interpreted as "is less than or equal to 9," "R" as "is prime." "G" as "is greater than," and consider the case where the kind of thing that "K" stands for is an odd number. Then (6′), so interpreted, says that for every non-prime positive integer less than or equal to 9, there is a positive integer (in the domain 1–10) greater than it, an obvious truth. On this interpretation, however, (A′) through (D′) are all false. (A′) is false, for example, when the value for "x" is "8" and the value for "y" is 3. (B′) is false when the values for "x" and "y" are 9 and 3, respectively. And (C′) and (D′) are false when the value for "x" is 9.

Therefore (6) does not entail any of (A) through (D). The pattern of argument exemplified by steps (1)–(9), then, will not admit the island than which

---

[5] In the case of (A) and (B), an additional premise to the effect that at least one island actually exists is required.

[6] There are Quinean scruples against the coherence of such a domain. But I shall not exercise those scruples here.

no greater island can be conceived into existence. But if (6) is replaced by any of (A) through (D), the argument pattern will admit such an island into existence. Hence, it is crucially important to sort out these different principles, and to take care not to ascribe the wrong one to Anselm, especially if that ascription is unwarranted. To take two recent examples: M. J. Charlesworth tells us that "[on] St. Anselm's premises, of course, an actually existing island will be greater or more perfect than one merely thought of. . . ."[7] According to Charlesworth, one of Anselm's premises appears to be (B). And Robert Merrihew Adams claims that Anselm "would probably have assented" to the principle that "anything which exists in reality is greater than anything which does not. . . ."[8] Adams thus ascribes (A) to Anselm. In neither case is there any clear textual warrant for these attributions, and in both cases, the principles ascribed to Anselm would validate Gaunilo's counterargument.

I conclude, then, that the Perfect Island objection, no matter how it is construed, does not provide a counterargument to Anselm's Ontological Argument. Of course this does not show that Anselm's argument is sound; I have argued elsewhere that it is not.[9] But it does rule out one more bogus objection.

[7] *St. Anselm's* Proslogion *with* "A Reply on Behalf of the Fool" *by Gaunilo and* "The Author's Reply to Gaunilo," translated by M. J. Charlesworth (Oxford: Oxford University Press, 1965), 94.

[8] Robert Merrihew Adams, "The Logical Structure of Anselm's Arguments," *The Philosophical Review* 80 (1971): 30. Later in the same paragraph, Adams acknowledges that a weaker principle is all that is needed for his reconstruction of the argument in *Proslogion* II.

[9] Mann, "Ontological Presuppositions of the Ontological Argument."

13

Locating the Lost Island

Philosophers have now had nine and one-third centuries to dwell on Anselm's ontological argument in the *Proslogion*. Recent literature on the argument indicates that there is vigorous and sophisticated disagreement about what the argument presupposes, what the argument's logical structure is, and even where the argument is best located.[1] The disagreement persists in spite of, perhaps even because of, the fact that during Anselm's lifetime, Gaunilo criticized the *Proslogion* argument and Anselm replied to that criticism. What I propose here is to examine Gaunilo's most famous criticism to see what we can learn about Anselm's argument in light of it. Anselm's argument has fired up Gaunilo's critical engine, but he lacks the sophistication to express his objection magisterially. His prose needs to be tightened; his argument needs to be articulated more carefully; his logic needs to be brought to the surface for inspection. If we do that on his behalf, we will find that his criticism by counterexample puts significant pressure on Anselm's claim to have discovered a "single argument" for God's existence, and on recent attempts to refurbish Anselm's argument.

I

Before proceeding further, we should note that on one interpretation of the Anselm-Gaunilo exchange, Anselm did a disservice to Gaunilo and the subsequent history of philosophical understanding by writing *Proslogion* 2. According

---

[1] I have in mind Gareth B. Matthews, "The Ontological Argument," in *The Blackwell Guide to the Philosophy of Religion*, ed. William E. Mann (Malden, MA: Blackwell Publishing, 2005), 81–102; Sandra Visser and Thomas Williams, *Anselm* (Oxford: Oxford University Press, 2009); Lynne Rudder Baker and Gareth B. Matthews, "Anselm's Argument Reconsidered," *The Review of Metaphysics* 64, no. 1 (September 2010): 31–54; Nicholas Wolterstorff, "In Defense of Gaunilo's Defense of the Fool," in Nicholas Wolterstorff, *Inquiring about God* (Cambridge: Cambridge University Press, 2010), 68–90; Peter Millican, "The One Fatal Flaw in Anselm's Argument," *Mind* 113 (2004): 437–476.

to Sandra Visser and Thomas Williams, on this occasion Anselm expressed his reasoning "in language so compressed as to be elliptical and indeed misleading." For example, they say, "Anselm famously contrasts 'existing in the understanding' with 'existing in reality,' as though he had some metaphysical doctrine about two modes of existence. As we shall see, he has no such doctrine; such a thing never entered his mind. He clearly just thought the phrasing sounded nice and made the argument memorable."[2] For Visser and Williams *Proslogion* 2 is a misfired and misleading mess, made worse by its being placed strategically as the first chapter of philosophical substance in a thoroughly philosophical work. They argue instead that Anselm does a better job of elucidating his argument in his reply to Gaunilo.

We should be reluctant to join in this judgment, especially in light of Visser and Williams's earlier acknowledgment that "Anselm was not the kind of philosopher who writes to get his thoughts in order. Anselm tended to work everything out in his head first and only then write it down."[3] Moreover, if his reply to Gaunilo presents a more considered revision of an argument badly presented in *Proslogion* 2, then it is puzzling that he persists in invoking the distinction between existing in the understanding and existing in reality. Visser and Williams have reasons for discounting *Proslogion* 2, chief among them the fact that Anselm so curtly dismisses Gaunilo's most vivid objection rather than respond to it. However, from the fact that Anselm's dismissal fails to respond satisfactorily to Gaunilo's criticism it does not follow that Anselm had a completely new or different argument in mind. I will examine Anselm's dismissal below.

Here is the core of Anselm's argument as presented in *Proslogion* 2:

We believe you [Lord] to be something than which nothing greater could be conceived. Or is there then not something of such a nature, since the fool has said in his heart, "There is no God" [Psalms 14:1; 53:1]? But surely this same fool, when he hears this very thing that I speak—"something than which nothing greater can be conceived"— understands that which he hears, and that which he understands is in his understanding, even if he does not understand it to exist. . . . And surely that than which a greater cannot be conceived cannot be in the understanding alone. For if it is in the understanding alone, it can be conceived to exist in reality also, which is greater. Thus if that than which a greater cannot be conceived is in the understanding alone, then that than which a greater cannot be conceived itself is that than which a

---

[2] Visser and Williams, *Anselm,* 74.

[3] Visser and Williams, *Anselm,* 5.

greater can be conceived. But surely this cannot be. Therefore without doubt something than which a greater cannot be conceived exists both in the understanding and in reality.[4]

Gaunilo's strategy in response to the *Proslogion* 2 argument is to produce an argument whose structure is identical to Anselm's, but with a conclusion that is patently false. If Gaunilo is successful, the only difference between the two arguments will be a difference in content. In that case Gaunilo will have produced a counterexample: the obvious unwarrantedness of his counterargument will show that Anselm's argument is similarly unwarranted. It is therefore unfortunate that Gaunilo's presentation of his counterargument is sloppy. He begins by considering a "lost island" which, he supposes, does not exist but which some have thought to exist. Soon thereafter the description is refined to apply to an island "more excellent than all things on earth" (*terris omnibus praestantiorem*). Described in this way, and on the assumption that nothing is more excellent than itself, the phrase guarantees the earthly nonexistence of the island. In similar fashion, Gaunilo repeatedly renders Anselm's description, "that than which a greater cannot be conceived," with the phrase, "that which is greater than all things" (*maius omnibus*).[5] That phrase, if taken literally, logically precludes the existence of any such being. A dose of charity suggests that the descriptions be modified into something like "the island more excellent than all other things on earth" and "that which is greater than all other things," respectively. A second dose of charity prescribes that Gaunilo use a phrase that matches as closely as possible Anselm's description, namely, "that island than which no greater island can be conceived." We can then construct a parody of Anselm's *Proslogion* 2 argument that Gaunilo might have written but did not:

> We believe the lost island to be something than which no greater island could be conceived. Or is there then not something of such a nature, since explorers have said, "There is no lost island"? But surely these same explorers, when they hear this very thing that I speak—"some island than which no greater island can be conceived"—understand that which they hear, and that which they understand is in their

---

[4] The Latin text is in *S. Anselmi Cantuariensis Archiepiscopi Opera Omni*, ed. Franciscus Salesius Schmitt, tome 1, vol. 1 (Stuttgart-Bad Cannstatt: Friedrich Frommann Verlag [Günther Holzboog], 1968), 101–102 (hereafter Anselm, *Opera Omnia*). All translations are mine. Gaunilo's reply (commonly known as *Pro Insipiente*) along with Anselm's response to Gaunilo (*Responsio Editoris*) are also in this volume. Reconstructions of the argument can be found in William E. Mann, "The Ontological Presuppositions of the Ontological Argument," *The Review of Metaphysics* 26, no. 2 (December 1972): 261; and Visser and Williams, *Anselm*, 75–76.

[5] The text of Gaunilo's lost island objection can be found in Anselm, *Opera Omnia*, 128.

understanding, even if they do not understand it to exist. And surely that island than which a greater island cannot be conceived cannot be in the understanding alone. For if it is in the understanding alone, it can be conceived to exist in reality also, which is greater. Thus if that island than which a greater island cannot be conceived is in the understanding alone, then that island than which a greater island cannot be conceived itself is that island than which a greater island can be conceived. But surely this cannot be. Therefore without doubt some island than which a greater island cannot be conceived exists both in the understanding and in reality.

In this parody Gaunilo would have preserved everything essential to the structure of Anselm's argument. The only change is in its content: "that than which a greater cannot be conceived" (the GCB) and its variants are replaced throughout with "that island than which no greater island can be conceived" (the GCI) and its variants. How could that simple replacement make a difference?

Here is the only help we get from Anselm:

> (S1) But, you say, it is as if someone were to allege than an island in the ocean, outstripping all lands in its fertility (which through the difficulty—or rather, the impossibility—of finding that which does not exist, is called the lost island), for that reason cannot be doubted truly to exist in reality, since one easily understands the words describing it. (S2) I say quite confidently that if anyone finds something for me, existing either in reality itself or only in conception—besides that than which a greater cannot be conceived—to which he soundly applies the structure of my argument, I will find and give to him that lost island, no longer to be lost. (S3) However, it now appears clearly that that than which a greater cannot be conceived cannot be conceived not to be, since it exists with such certain, reasoned truth. (S4) For otherwise it would exist in no way.[6]

Nicholas Wolterstorff describes this response as so much "bluster," signaling that Anselm had no response to offer to Gaunilo: "the reason Anselm failed to point out the disanalogy [between the two arguments] is that he realized there was no disanalogy to point out."[7] Visser and Williams concur, pointing out that worse yet, Gaunilo's example generalizes: "If we tidy up Gaunilo's formulation,

---

[6] *Responsio Editoris,* in Anselm, *Opera Omnia,* 133; sentence numbers added.

[7] Wolterstorff, "In Defense of Gaunilo's Defense of the Fool," 89, see also 68–71.

it seems we have an argument exactly parallel to Anselm's . . . And there is nothing special about islands, of course: we could equally well prove the existence of a live oak than which a greater cannot be thought, a cockroach than which a greater cannot be thought, you name it."[8]

It is evident that Anselm made his reply too telegraphic. If he deliberately presented the barest bones of a defense, leaving the fleshing out as an exercise for the reader, it appears that he overestimated the reader's intelligence. Let us begin with (S2). It not only stakes out the claim that Anselm's argument cannot be soundly replicated for any putative entity other than the GCB. It also challenges the reader to try to find a counterexample. Anselm obviously believes that Gaunilo did not succeed in meeting the challenge.

In (S1) Anselm uncharitably attributes this inference to Gaunilo:

(1) We understand the phrase, "the GCI."

Thus:

(2) The GCI exists in reality.

That inference is a non sequitur. But then, it would seem, so is this one:

(3) We understand the phrase, "the GCB."

Thus:

(4) The GCB exists in reality.

The success of Anselm's argument depends on filling the gap between (3) and (4). The constraint on his gap-filling activities is not to rely on principles that will at the same time allow Gaunilo to fill in the gap between (1) and (2).

Look now at (S3) and (S4). (S3) claims that the GCB cannot even be conceived not to exist.[9] (S4) underscores the modal status of Anselm's conclusion: the existence of the GCB cannot be contingent; it is either necessary or impossible. The proximity of (S3) to (S2) suggests that Anselm thinks that the GCI can be conceived not to exist. It is not accidental that the sequence of (S1) through (S4) is sandwiched between affirmations of the following claims that connect conceivability with spatiotemporality and parthood: "Whatever does not exist at some place or at some time . . . can be conceived to exist at no place

---

[8] Visser and Williams, *Anselm,* 77.

[9] That of course was the message of *Proslogion* 3.

and at no time." "But what is composed of parts can be dissolved in conception and can fail to exist." "For if [something] could be conceived not to exist, it could be conceived to have a beginning and an end."[10] All Anselm needs to add is that anything that can count as an island must have parts spread out in space and time, and thus can be conceived not to exist.

Anselm thus supposes that his argument, supplemented with some principles about conceivability, establishes the existence of a being that cannot be conceived not to exist, while Gaunilo's counterargument, similarly supplemented, delivers at most a being that can be conceived not to exist. What of it? Gaunilo has no stake in the existence of the GCI. Quite the opposite: the more obvious it becomes that the GCI does not exist, the stronger his counterargument. His complaint is that Anselm's pattern of argument is overly promiscuous. It should not be delivering any island, necessary or contingent, solely by a priori means. It appears, then, that the overt response to Gaunilo's counterexample, codified in (S1)–(S4), defends where Gaunilo need not attack.

II

So far, then, Anselm has insufficient reason to fault Gaunilo's counterargument. Recall that Anselm needs to fill the gap between (3) and (4) in a way that prevents Gaunilo from moving from (1) to (2). There are other elements in the *Proslogion* 2 argument that may hold more promise for Anselm. One of those elements is what we may call a "greatness principle." However, there is disagreement about what that principle is. Let us begin with the Latin text, as established by F. S. Schmitt:

> (GP) *Si enim vel in solo intellectu est, potest cogitari esse et in re, quod maius est.*[11]

A straightforward translation of (GP) is the translation I gave it earlier:

> (GP′) For if it is in the understanding alone, it can be conceived to exist in reality also, which is greater.[12]

---

[10] *Responsio Editoris,* in Anselm, *Opera Omnia,* 131, 133.

[11] Anselm, *Opera Omnia,* 101.

[12] Variations on (GP′) can be found in M. J. Charlesworth, *St. Anselm's* Proslogion *with "A Reply on Behalf of the Fool" by Gaunilo and "The Author's Reply to Gaunilo"* (Oxford: Clarendon Press, 1965) 117; Jasper Hopkins, *A New, Interpretive Translation of St. Anselm's Monologion and Proslogion* (Minneapolis, MN: Arthur J. Banning Press, 1986), 227; and Thomas Williams, *Anselm: Monologion*

According to G. E. M. Anscombe and others who follow her, (GP′) is a mistranslation of Anselm's Latin, encouraged by Schmitt's editorial placement of commas in a text that originally had none. Anscombe's rationale goes by the reader very quickly. Perhaps she thought that deleting the comma between *re* and *quod* reduces the temptation to think that *quod maius est* is a comparative relation holding between a being conceived to exist only in the understanding and the same being conceived to exist in reality. Perhaps Anscombe then thought that *quod maius est* could function as a substantive, "what is greater" or "that which is greater," in which case the English counterpart can migrate inward upon translation:

> (GP*) For if it exists in the understanding alone, that which is greater can be conceived to exist in reality also.[13]

Let us begin with (GP′). English accentuates what is less syntactically prominent in Latin, namely, that the conditional sentence displays what appears to be a case of anaphora. If it is anaphora the two occurrences of the pronoun "it" would be coreferential; the second occurrence of "it" would have to refer to the same thing referred to by the first occurrence. Both occurrences of "it" stand in for "the GCB." But one might wonder how the pronouns and their associated noun phrase can be coreferential without being referential. And if they are referential, one might be forgiven for suspecting that Anselm's argument has begged the question of the GCB's existence from the beginning. The suspicion is fueled by the disposition to regard "to refer" as a success verb. On this view one has failed to refer if the singular term one employs—a putative proper name, pronoun, or definite description—does not apply to or identify anything that exists.

It is useful to sketch three views about the reference of singular terms, with an eye to seeing how they affect the interpretation of Anselm's greatness principle. The first view is *Parmenidean*. It is rooted in two theses. One is that singular terms must refer: a singular term with no reference yields not so much a

---

and Proslogion with the Replies of Gaunilo and Anselm (Indianapolis, IN: Hackett Publishing Company, 1996), 100.

[13] Anscombe's version: "For if it is only in the intellect, what is greater can be thought to be in reality as well"; G. E. M. Anscombe, "Why Anselm's Proof in the *Proslogion* Is Not an Ontological Argument," *The Thoreau Quarterly* 17 (1985): 37. Although Millican uses the Charlesworth translation, he parts ways from it when it comes to (GP), substituting this sentence, attributed to Alexander Broadie: "For if it exists solely in the mind, something that is greater can be thought to exist in reality also." Millican, "The One Fatal Flaw in Anselm's Argument," 439. The case for translating (GP) as (GP*) has not been made convincingly. Visser and Williams claim that "it seems to us to require an impossible construal of Anselm's Latin." Visser and Willams, *Anselm*, 263. For trenchant criticism, see Hopkins, *New, Interpretive Translation*, 26–33.

contradiction as it does gibberish. The other is that there is only one mode of being, namely, actual existence. As is well known, the Parmenidean view makes it impossible to understand negative existential claims made about individual things, for example, "Sherlock Holmes does not exist." (The same goes for the fool of the Psalms, who says "There is no God.")

Let us call the second view *modism*. Modists agree with Parmenideans that singular terms must refer. But they dissent from the thesis that reference is confined to what actually exists. "Julia Stoner's murderer" refers no matter what, even if it should turn out that Stoner was not killed. There are at least two varieties of modism. One maintains that in the case in which Stoner was not killed "Stoner's murderer" refers to an object that *subsists* but does not exist: subsistence is a mode of being distinct from existence in reality. The other variety maintains that "Stoner's murderer" refers to an "object of thought," something that does exist but not in the public arena. On this view some mental attitudes are *objectual*, having as their content not propositions but things, "Stoner's murderer" being one of them. I suggest that we cast the net of modism wide enough so that it extends over objects that not only do *not* exist but cannot exist. In doing so our net captures the full variety of Lynne Rudder Baker and Gareth B. Matthews's objects of thought, some of which "physically cannot exist in reality (for example, the first perpetual motion machine)," and some of which "logically cannot exist in reality (for example, the first impossible staircase that Escher drew)."[14]

The third and final view, the *supposition-free* view, denies that legitimate singular terms must always have a reference. On the supposition-free view, a legitimate singular term might refer to nothing—nothing in reality, nothing subsisting, no object of thought, *gar nichts*. Sherlock Holmes can conjecture that Stoner had a murderer without knowing who the murderer is, or even whether his conjecture is correct. In order not to bias his thinking he can suppose as little as possible about the attributes of Stoner's murderer. Suppose that Holmes's conjecture is mistaken, that Stoner died of natural causes. In that case we can fault Holmes's sleuthing powers and acknowledge that "Stoner's murderer" lacks reference. We need not default the term itself. It performed its function in Holmes's calculations as well as the terms that did refer, such as the place-names "Leatherhead" and "Surrey."[15]

---

[14] Baker and Matthews, "Anselm's Argument Reconsidered," 36. The first sort of modism is associated with Meinong, but things get complicated very quickly. Meinong apparently reserved the notion of subsistence for abstract objects, things such as numbers and propositions. See Terence Parsons, *Nonexistent Objects* (New Haven, CT: Yale University Press, 1980), 10. It will be convenient for purposes of this paper to extend the notion of subsistence over nonexistent concrete objects, such as Sherlock Holmes, the fifty-first American state, and the hamster asleep under your chair.

[15] The instrument of Stoner's death was a so-called swamp adder. Her killer was Grimesby Roylott. See Arthur Conan Doyle, "The Adventure of the Speckled Band," in *The Complete Sherlock Holmes* (Garden City, NY: Doubleday and Company), 257–273. If examples from fiction seem

Return now to (GP′). How should we understand the reference of its two pronouns, working under the assumption that they are coreferential? It is clear that the Parmenidean view scuttles Anselm's project. Anselm's point is that it takes an argument to demonstrate that "the GCB" refers to something in reality. He must use the phrase in order to do that. If his bare use of the phrase requires that it have a real referent, then his carefully crafted argument is nugatory. Moreover, it hard to see, from a Parmenidean standpoint, how the fate of "the GCI" can differ from that of "the GCB."

Some versions of the modist view appear to be more hospitable to (GP′) and the role it plays in Anselm's argument. The modist view allows one to suppose that the GCB exists in the understanding without thereby conceding that the GCB exists in reality. But recall the pronouns in (GP′), along with the supposition that they are coreferential. On a subsistence version of modism, the pronoun in the antecedent of (GP′) refers to a being that merely subsists. If the pronoun in (GP′)'s consequent is coreferential, then it refers to the same, merely subsistent being referred to in the antecedent, now having the property, not of existing in reality, but of being conceived to exist in reality. It does not help to point out that the realms of subsistence and existence are not mutually exclusive, that one and the same being can inhabit both realms. The pronoun in the antecedent picks out a being that merely subsists. To insist that it must pick out a being that actually and necessarily exists, as subsequent argument shows, is to abandon what is supposed to be distinctive about subsistence modism. It may be that the antecedent describes an impossibility, because the GCB cannot merely subsist. But subsistence modism tolerates the subsistence of *impossibilia*.[16] Given coreferentiality, the two pronouns in (GP′) must match. If the first one picks out something that merely subsists, so must the second one. If the second one picks out something that necessarily exists, so must the first one.

Perhaps the culprit here is subsistence modism. Among the many scholarly disputes about Anselm there is disagreement about whether he holds such a view about reference. Wolterstorff claims that "Meinong is the Anselm of the twentieth century, Frege the Gaunilo."[17] Responding to this claim, Visser and Williams say it is "completely mistaken."[18] Baker and Matthews offer reasons for distancing their objects-of-thought modism from Meinongian subsistence modism.[19] Under these circumstances it would be nice if we could find a way of

---

compromised, consider Mendeleev's postulation of the existence and properties of the element eventually to be called gallium, four years before it was discovered.

[16] See Parsons, *Nonexistent Objects,* 21–22.

[17] Wolterstorff, "In Defense of Gaunilo's Defense of the Fool," 87.

[18] Visser and Williams, *Anselm,* 89; see also the observation on page 74 cited above.

[19] Baker and Matthews, "Anselm's Argument Reconsidered," 41.

representing Anselm's *Proslogion* 2 argument that does not depend on subsistence modism.

We have just seen that there is a problem with the supposition that the pronouns in (GP′) are coreferential. Matthews, in "The Ontological Argument," interprets the greatness principle, (GP), in such a way that it does not require pronominal coreferentiality. The interpretation reappears in Baker and Matthews, "Anselm's Argument Reconsidered," modified somewhat to fit their objects-of-thought version of modism:

> (G) For anything x that existed only in thought, an otherwise same thing that existed both in thought and in reality would be greater (not just greater in thought) than x.[20]

Baker and Matthews's (G) certainly does not look like Anselm's (GP). It nonetheless does for Anselm something that (GP′) does not do. Anselm wants to be able to say that the GCB would be greater if it existed in reality than if it did not. But no being is greater than itself![21] One thing can, however, be greater than another. More to the point, an enhanced version of a thing can be greater than its unenhanced doppelgänger. (G) employs a greater-than relation, but it is, as it should be, a relation with two nonidentical relata.

Still, it might seem that Gaunilo can appeal to (G) to establish the existence of the GCI. Not so, say Baker and Matthews:

> If it did exist in reality, it would be a complete object (with so-many palm trees, such dimensions, and so forth). In that case we could conceive of a greater island—one with another palm tree, or a little larger. However, now we have a contradiction: we can conceive of an island greater than the island than which none greater can be conceived. Nothing that is the island than which no greater island can be conceived can exist in reality—on pain of contradiction.[22]

Suppose that Gaunilo dubs the GCI with "I_1," and appeals to (G) to argue that I_1 must exist both in thought and in reality. Baker and Matthews reply that

---

[20] Baker and Matthews, "Anselm's Argument Reconsidered," 46. Matthews's earlier version is, "(G3) Anything that exists both in the understanding and in reality is greater than the otherwise exact same thing, if that thing exists merely in the understanding." Matthews, "The Ontological Argument," 91.

[21] One thing can *become* greater than it once was. I take it that Anselm's commitment to God's timeless eternality precludes any kind of becoming from belonging to God. See *Proslogion* 18–19 in Anselm, *Opera Omnia*, 113–115.

[22] Baker and Matthews, "Anselm's Argument Reconsidered," 39–40.

they can conceive of island I_2, exactly like I_1 except for containing one more palm tree and the additional space to accommodate it. I_2, then, is a conceivable island greater than I_1, which was supposed to be the GCI. Suppose then that a dogged but somewhat obtuse Gaunilo attempts to avoid the contradiction, acknowledging that as it turns out, I_2, by dint of (G), is really the GCI. Alas, he will not have outstripped the imaginative powers of Baker and Matthews, who have, I suppose, a whole hierarchy of conceivable islands, I_{n+1}, each of which is greater than its predecessor, I_n. Either the hierarchy is infinite or it terminates at some I_k. If it is infinite, then the GCI does not exist. If it should turn out that some I_k is the GCI, then by (G) I_k would exist in reality, vindicating Gaunilo. In "The Ontological Argument" Matthews is explicit in choosing the first alternative on Anselm's behalf:

> If Gaunilo did characterize his lost island as an island than which no greater island can be conceived, we could reply that islands, like natural numbers, are inherently limited entities. For any specified island, it could be argued, one might conceive one that is bigger and better—perhaps one that has even more palm trees, or bigger beaches, or whatever.[23]

Gaunilo and his skeptical successors are not yet vanquished. For if Anselm were to choose to fault the GCI on grounds that there is no upper limit to greatness in conceivable islands, then it would be fair for Gaunilo to point out that the same lack of an upper limit might be true of conceivable beings. Gaunilo does in fact complain that Anselm's phrase, suitably regimented to match Anselm's own phraseology, gives him no guidance in forming a conception of such a being, because it identifies no genus or species known to Gaunilo under which such a being might fall.[24] Gaunilo seems to think that it is as if he has been told to conceive of the [blank] than which no greater [blank] can be conceived; he claims not to know how to proceed.

Anselm's attempt to provide in reply some pointers on divine concept formation is significant for what it does not say. We can raise our thoughts "from lesser goods to greater goods," and thus "on the basis of things than which a greater can be conceived we can gather many inferences about that than which nothing greater can be conceived."[25] The example Anselm uses to illustrate the ascent from good to greater to greatest involves beings and their relation to time. Any ephemeral being has some measure of goodness even though it begins to exist

<hr>

[23] Matthews, "The Ontological Argument," 92.

[24] See *Pro Insipiente* in Anselm, *Opera Omnia*, 126–127.

[25] *Responsio Editoris*, in Anselm, *Opera Omnia*, 137.

and ceases to exist in time. Any being that begins to exist but then never ceases to exist is better than any ephemeral being. Better still is a temporal being that has neither beginning nor end. The best of all would be a being that is immune to the infections of time and change, a being that "in no way needs or is compelled to be changed or moved."[26]

The exercise of this process of intellectual ascent may have unwelcome consequences for other attributes alleged to be essential to the GCB. If any one of those attributes has no upper limit—no ultimate degree that is the perfection of that attribute—then Anselm's descriptive phrase will be vulnerable in the same way that Gaunilo's is. For example, if one can always think of a being more powerful than any given being, then either omnipotence is not essential to the GCB or there is no such being. A similar problem may be in store for infinite love. But instead of pursuing directly the dialectical intricacies attendant on those examples, we can examine the implications of a case much closer to Gaunilo's case. Let us suppose that Gaunilo ambitiously chose as his counterexample nothing so trifling as an island, but rather the universe, the whole shebang, supposing further that it is essential to its existence that it be created by the GCB.[27] Now to fault Gaunilo's counterargument by arguing that there is no limit to greatness in conceivable islands is to invite the parallel consideration that there is no limit to greatness in conceivable universes. In that case, the GCB cannot create the greatest conceivable universe. Perhaps even more unsettling, there would be infinitely many conceivable universes greater than any universe the GCB could create. And one might then wonder whether this situation tells against the creator's unlimited power or unlimited love.[28]

This is the beginning of a conversation that, though charming in itself, would take us far afield from present matters. Before we turn our attention to (GP*) and the supposition-free view of reference, I want to call attention to a worrisome feature of Baker and Matthews's objects-of-thought modism as applied

---

[26] *Responsio Editoris,* in Anselm, *Opera Omnia,* 137. This passage harks back to Anselm's depiction of God's eternal nature that begins in Chapter 13 of the *Proslogion*: "But all that which is enclosed in any way by place or by time is less than that which no law of place or of time confines." (Anselm, *Opera Omnia,* 110.)

[27] See *Monologion* 7–8, in Anselm, *Opera Omnia,* 20–24. It is important not to confuse the claim being made with the claim that the GCB of necessity had to create something.

[28] It would be ironic if it should turn out that two of the greatest archrationalists in the history of philosophy were in polar opposition on this point. Leibniz famously asserted that this world is the best of all (the infinitely many) possible worlds; were there no best world, God would not have created any world. Leibniz's assertion rests on his imputation of perfection to God, an imputation grounded in his adherence to a version of the ontological argument! For texts and discussion, see my "The Best of All Possible Worlds," in *Being and Goodness: The Concept of the Good in Metaphysics and Philosophical Theology,* ed. Scott MacDonald (Ithaca, NY: Cornell University Press, 1991), 259–268.

to Anselm's argument. As we have seen, Baker and Matthews specify that their objects of thought include *impossibilia*. They have reason for the inclusion. Suppose I tell you that I propose to work on a theorem that will prove that the circle can be squared. You know that the theorem is impossible. You inform me that my theorem will have to contain a flaw. I insist that when I finish it, it will be flawless. Baker and Matthews want to be able to say that our disagreement is about the same thing, my theorem—otherwise, we would be talking past each other. In similar fashion, Anselm and the fool of the Psalms should be in genuine disagreement about the existence of God, even if it should be that God's existence is impossible.

Now Baker and Matthews claim to have produced a variation on Anselm's argument that "is sound: it is valid, has true premises, and does not beg the question against the atheist."[29] Suppose that is so: I propose not to challenge the claim here. My worry lies elsewhere. Because Baker and Matthews admit impossible objects into the domain of objects of thought, it might be that the GCB is one of those impossibilities. In that case we would have a sound argument with a contradictory conclusion, which is to say that we would have an unsound argument.

Baker and Matthews attempt to allay that worry by arguing that "in the absence of an argument that demonstrated that there could not exist in reality that than which nothing greater can be conceived, such an objection would have no weight." In amplification, Baker and Matthews claim:

> In contrast to the "perfect island" case—in which we showed that a contradiction follows from the assumption that the described object of thought exists in reality—no one, in our opinion, has succeeded in demonstrating that there could not exist in reality an object of thought denoted by "that than which nothing greater can be conceived."[30]

This attempt at shifting the burden of proof is not persuasive. The seeds of doubt have been planted by Baker and Matthews. Extensions of the maneuvers used by them to motivate and defend Anselm—allowing for impossible objects of thought and infinitely ascending sequences of greater and greater objects—can be employed to undercut confidence in their argument. Leibniz faulted Cartesian versions of the ontological argument on grounds that they failed to show that God is a possible being. Visser and Williams regard their own modal reconstruction of Anselm's argument as vulnerable because Anselm "does not have an adequate argument for the claim that God is a possible being."[31] There

---

[29] Baker and Matthews, "Anselm's Argument Reconsidered," 33.
[30] Baker and Matthews, "Anselm's Argument Reconsidered," 45.
[31] Visser and Williams, *Anselm*, 92.

is something to this criticism that does not require pointing out a logical flaw. A valid, sound, non-question-begging argument can be a lovely thing to behold, yet not improve its beholders' epistemic status. Skeptics about such an argument need not have a demonstration of its unsoundness: if they did they would not be skeptics. It is enough that they have reasons to doubt the argument's soundness; defeasible reasons, one presumes, but reasons nonetheless.

Cases of reasonable doubt concerning the logical possibility of the GCB come from two families of sources, both alluded to above. First, two or more attributes essential to the identity of the GCB might be *incompossible*; the possession of one of them would logically preclude the possession of the other(s). To take an example from nearby, Anselm devotes three chapters of the *Proslogion* to an attempt to reconcile God's supreme justice with God's supreme mercy.[32] It would seem that to be merciful is to remit punishment in a case in which justice demands it. How, then, can one and the same agency dispense both what justice requires and what mercy advocates in one and the same case? It is clear that Anselm struggles with the problem. It is also clear that he does not resolve it fully in the *Proslogion*.[33] Second, one or more attributes essential to the GCB may lack an intrinsic maximum. One can reasonably doubt, for instance, whether there is an upper limit to attributes like power or loving-kindness, and thus wonder whether for any conceivable being, one can always conceive of another being more powerful or more loving.

III

We have yet to consider the supposition-free view about reference and the (GP^*) interpretation of (GP). I propose considering them in tandem. Recall that on the supposition-free view, singular terms can function legitimately without referring to anything. In a *free logic,* for example, one can operate in a formal language with individual constants like "g" and definite descriptions like "$(\imath x)(y)(y \neq x \rightarrow Gxy)$" without thereby presupposing that they refer, respectively, to God and the being greater than all other beings.[34] This sort of freedom from existential commitment has the virtue of allowing one to choose the domain of interpretation, whether it be the set of actual beings, possible beings, or conceivable beings. The choice of domain will then determine whether to understand $(\imath x)(y)(y \neq x \rightarrow Gxy)$

---

[32] See *Proslogion* 9–11 in Anselm, *Opera Omnia,* 106–110.

[33] See Visser and Williams, *Anselm,* 107–108, who suggest, as have others, that Anselm resolves this issue in his *Cur Deus Homo.*

[34] See the essays in *Philosophical Applications of Free Logic,* ed. Karel Lambert (New York: Oxford University Press, 1991).

as the greatest actual, possible, or conceivable being, without begging the question of the existence of $(\imath x)(y)(y \neq x \rightarrow Gxy)$. An attractive feature of the supposition-free view is that it allows one to postpone and perhaps even sidestep entirely the issue of whether Anselm was a modist.

To recall, (GP*) interprets (GP) as:

(GP*) For if it exists in the understanding alone, that which is greater can be conceived to exist in reality also.

The case for regarding (GP*) as a translation of Anselm's (GP) is controversial. Might we nonetheless be doing Anselm a favor by attributing (GP*) to him? In particular, would it help him to dismiss Gaunilo's counterargument? Note first that in its favor, (GP*) raises no puzzles about anaphoric reference. Note second that (GP*), like its rival (GP'), is tacitly general. Anselm's surrounding text makes it clear that (GP) is a claim about a particular being, the GCB. Even so, (GP) and its rival siblings, (GP') and (GP*), gain credence only if they are general, applying to anything that exists only in the understanding. Note third that because (GP) and company are general and allow for things that exist only in the understanding, the domain for interpreting them must be very wide. Let us assume that the domain includes all actual and conceivable beings, including those conceivable beings that are impossible.[35] Note fourth that as it stands, (GP*) is ambiguous in spread. It might be that everything existing in reality is greater than anything that exists in the understanding alone. Or it might be that something existing in reality is greater than anything existing in the understanding alone. Because the latter, particular interpretation seems to stake out a more modest claim, let us begin with it:

(GP*P) For any conceivable being, x, if x exists in the understanding alone, then there is at least one conceivable being, y, such that y exists in reality and y is greater than x.

Apply (GP*P) first to Anselm's description and then to Gaunilo's description, under the assumption that both descriptions apply to conceivable beings:

(GP*P$_{Anselm}$) If the GCB exists in the understanding alone, then there is at least one conceivable being, y, such that y exists in reality and y is greater than the GCB.

---

[35] Visser and Williams allege that "[w]e cannot, however, think something that is impossible." See *Anselm*, 81; reaffirmed on page 99. For them, the set of conceivable but impossible beings is empty. As we have seen, Baker and Matthews disagree.

$(GP^*P_{Gaunilo})$ If the GCI exists in the understanding alone, then there
is at least one conceivable being, y, such that y exists in reality and y is
greater than the GCI.

Armed with (GP^*P_{Anselm}) Anselm can easily complete the *reductio* that establishes the actual existence of the GCB. $(GP^*P_{Gaunilo})$, however, is cold comfort
to Gaunilo. $(GP^*P_{Gaunilo})$ generates no contradiction in the way that (GP^*P_{Anselm})
does. $(GP^*P_{Gaunilo})$ does debar, on pain of contradiction, any actual island from
being greater than the GCI. But $(GP^*P_{Gaunilo})$ is otherwise powerless to prevent
a host of actual beings from asserting their credentials as superior to the GCI.

It might thus seem as though Anselm can finally navigate his argument away
from the treacherous waters surrounding the lost island. Yet (GP^*P) is vulnerable. Advocates of Gaunilo's position can embark on a two-stage strategy to
exploit the vulnerability. The first stage offers the observation that Anselm himself seems committed to a universal version of (GP^*), and continues by arguing
that this version appears to be less arbitrary. The second stage shows that the
universal version of (GP^*) reinstates Gaunilo's counterexample.

(GP^*P)'s surface modesty lends a measure of plausibility to it, inasmuch as it specifies that only one thing in reality need be greater than anything solely in the understanding. (GP^*P) thus appears to be less venturesome than its universalized cousin:

(GP^*U) For any conceivable being, x, if x exists in the understanding
alone, then for every conceivable being, y, if y exists in reality, then y is
greater than x.

There are two reasons to think, however, that Anselm is or should be receptive
to (GP^*U).

First, there is some textual evidence that Anselm accepted (GP^*U). At the beginning of Gaunilo's reply to Anselm, Gaunilo recapitulates Anselm's argument by
ascribing to him the principle that "it is greater to exist also in reality than only in the
understanding," from which Gaunilo immediately infers, "if this being [the GCB]
exists in the understanding alone, then whatever existed also in reality would be
greater than it."[36] Although Anselm is more than willing to point out Gaunilo's mistaken interpretations of his argument, he does not take exception to this ascription.

Second, we can point out that Anselm is in an uneasy quandary vis-à-vis
(GP^*P) and (GP^*U). The virtues of (GP^*P) are its modesty and its success in

---

[36] . . . *[Q]uia mains est esse et in re quam in solo intellectu, et si illud in solo est intellectu, maius illo erit
quidquid etiam in re fuerit . . . . Pro Insipiente,* in Anselm, *Opera Omnia,* 125; emphasis added. Gaunilo
presents a curtailed version applied to the GCI on p. 128: "if it [the GCI] did not exist, any other land
whatsoever in reality would be greater than it."

allowing him to develop the *reductio* that is central to his argument (on the assumption that (GP*) reflects his thinking more accurately than (GP′). Its vice is its modesty, especially when it is compared to (GP*U). Suppose that Anselm accepts (GP*P) but rejects (GP*U). His rejection of (GP*U) would commit him to holding that there are some things in reality that are not greater than the GCB that exists only in the understanding. So if Anselm rejects (GP*U) while accepting (GP*P), a critic like Gaunilo can rightly press him to give an account of what makes some but only some things in reality greater than the GCB that exists only in the understanding. What rational principle(s) can Anselm employ to differentiate the wheat from the chaff? The project of attempting to answer that question is best left to wits more forward than mine. Notice, however, how Anselm's quest for a "single argument" would ramify into many quests if he were to pursue the option of accepting (GP*P) while rejecting (GP*U). Anselm can avoid this particular project simply by accepting (GP*U).

The acceptance of (GP*U) introduces a new project: to explain now why everything existing in reality is greater than the GCB that exists only in the understanding. Baker and Matthews offer an appealing strategy. For them the difference between Pegasus existing only in thought and a Pegasus doppelgänger existing in reality is that the Pegasus in reality has "unmediated causal powers," powers that do not depend on how Pegasus is thought of or represented in myth. Pegasus in thought does not have unmediated causal powers. In general, they claim, "something's having-in-reality unmediated causal powers is greater than an otherwise same thing's having-in-reality only mediated causal powers that depend on thoughts of people who exist in reality."[37]

Baker and Matthews are overtly committed only to the thesis that for any pair consisting of object-of-thought and doppelgänger in reality, the doppelgänger is always greater than the thought-object, as befits their adherence to (GP′). Thus, for example, no matter how many talents and strengths I confer on my image of myself, I end up with good news and bad news. The good news is that I am greater than my image. The bad news is that I am still the same old me. Baker and Matthews may be receptive to an extension of their thesis. In a later paper they have Anselm saying, in reply to the point that people could tell stories about how he sprouted wings and flew:

> Alas, if it were only in stories that I could do that, then flying would not be an unmediated causal power of mine. I would still have unmediated causal powers all right, *and so would be greater than Pegasus.*[38]

[37] Baker and Matthews, "Anselm's Argument Reconsidered," 47.

[38] Gareth B. Matthews and Lynne Rudder Baker, "Reply to Oppy's Fool," *Analysis* 71 (2011): 303; emphasis added.

In virtue of his unmediated causal powers, the real Anselm is greater than the mythical Pegasus. Is he, simply in virtue of those unmediated causal powers, also greater than the GCB that exists only in the understanding? And does everything in reality have unmediated causal powers? If the answer to both questions is yes, then we are well on our way to the thesis that everything's having in reality unmediated causal powers is greater than anything's having in reality only mediated causal powers, which would supply a rationale for (GP*U).[39]

Now comes the Gaunilonians' second stage, to show that (GP*U) reinstates the GCI. Assume that at least one island exists in reality; call it Isla. (GP*U) entails that if the GCI exists only in the understanding, then Isla is greater than the GCI.[40] It is easy to complete a reductio that parallels Anselm's.

Thus there is a quandary for Anselm: (GP*P) without (GP*U) allows him to discriminate against Gaunilo's counterargument, but leaves behind the unfinished agenda of specifying in a rationally convincing way which things in reality are greater than the GCB that exists only in the understanding. (GP*U), supplemented with the distinction between mediated and unmediated causal powers, holds out the promise of helping to complete the agenda, but refuels Gaunilo's counterargument.[41]

IV

Gaunilo shows no interest in trying to repair Anselm's argument; perhaps he thought it was beyond repair. Wolterstorff, along with Visser and Williams, claims that Gaunilo's counterargument to the *Proslogion* 2 argument is unanswerable. Baker and Matthews disagree, arguing that the GCI is logically impossible while at the same time claiming that there is a presumptive case in favor of the logical possibility of the GCB. I have suggested that the presumptive case is less presumptive than they believe: the success of their argument hinges on the resolution of a series of projects in philosophical theology. The discussion

[39] Millican is a champion of the stronger, universal version, applied to individual "natures," claiming that "among the various criteria for greatness (power, wisdom, goodness, etc.), real existence 'trumps' all others, so that any nature which has a real archetype, however lowly its characteristic properties may be, will on that account alone be greater than any nature, however impressively characterized, which does not." Millican, "The One Fatal Flaw in Anselm's Argument," 451.

[40] The assumption of at least one island existing in reality is essential for the contradiction. There are no unicorns. So if the unicorn than which no greater unicorn can be conceived exists only in the understanding, then (GP*U) entails that anything existing in reality is greater than it. No reductio ensues.

[41] This conclusion reverses an opinion I once held; see my "The Perfect Island," *Mind* 85 (1976): 417–21. Reprinted as Chapter 12 of this volume.

has been embedded in a scaffolding of disagreement about how best to understand Anselm's greatness principle and how best to understand the semantics of conceivable beings. I would like to think that there is one thing about which all parties to the dispute can agree: there are very few texts in the history of philosophy that pique philosophical activity more than *Proslogion* 2. It all begins with Gaunilo.[42]

---

[42] An earlier version of this paper was read at a memorial symposium in honor of Gareth B. Matthews, sponsored by the Society of Christian Philosophers. Fellow symposiasts were Lynne Rudder Baker and Edward Wierenga.

‖ 14 ‖

Anselm on the Trinity

One of the central mysteries of the Christian faith is the doctrine of the Trinity. According to it, there is but one God, yet that one God is threefold in nature: there is the Father, the Son, and the Holy Spirit. That God is triune in nature is a "mystery" in a special, theological sense of the term: it is communicated to humans by divine revelation; it is beyond the powers of natural human reason to demonstrate; and so if it is to be accepted, it must be accepted as an item of religious faith. Skeptics in their polite moments might call the doctrine a "mystery" in the more usual sense of the term. They will claim that the doctrine flouts elementary principles of counting, confusing one with three. For skeptics the only mystery to be explained is how Christians can think they remain faithful to monotheism while courting polytheism.

Anselm investigates the doctrine of the Trinity extensively in three of his treatises. Roughly two-fifths of the *Monologion* is devoted to it, and it is the sole center of attention in *On the Incarnation of the Word* (*De Inc. Verbi*) and *On the Procession of the Holy Spirit* (*De Proc.*). Despite operating under a number of constraints that may appear to us to preclude successful completion of his project, he proceeds self-assuredly, confident that reason can demonstrate, not that the doctrine is true (for then it would not be a mystery) but that it is free from contradiction—more than that, that It All Makes Sense. I shall begin by describing briefly some of the constraints by which Anselm takes his investigation to be governed. I shall then examine selectively and in more detail the more noteworthy features of his investigations. Most of my attention will be devoted to the *Monologion*, which lays the foundation for Anselm's position. *On the Incarnation of the Word* and *On the Procession of the Holy Spirit* amplify but do not deviate from the *Monologion*.[1]

---

[1] Excellent overviews of *On the Incarnation of the Word* and *On the Procession of the Holy Spirit* can be found in Jasper Hopkins, *A Companion to the Study of St. Anselm* (Minneapolis: University of Minnesota Press, 1972), chap. 4. All translations of Latin texts in this essay are my own.

Authority

Most importantly, because the doctrine of the Trinity is in the domain of revealed theology, Anselm takes his enterprise to be guided necessarily by authority, the authority of Scripture (the revealed word of God), the authority of confessional creeds formulated by Church councils (in particular, the Nicene Creed), and the authority of the Church Fathers (in particular, Augustine). It would require a book to document all these influences. Here are examples of each of these kinds of authority, however, that figure prominently in Anselm's writings.

The first three verses of the first chapter of the Gospel according to John say that "In the beginning was the Word, and the Word was with God, and the Word was God. He was in the beginning with God; all things were made through Him, and without Him was not anything made that was made." The passage anchors Anselm's identification of the Son with the Word (*Monologion* 29–48), while simultaneously raising the question of what the point could be of saying, given that the Word *was* God, that the Word was also *with* God.

Here are excerpts from the Nicene Creed, as Anselm understood it:

> I believe in one God, the Father almighty, maker of heaven and earth, and of all things visible and invisible. And in one Lord Jesus Christ, the only-begotten Son of God, begotten of his Father before all worlds, God of God, light of light, very God of very God, begotten, not made, being of one substance with the Father, by whom all things were made . . . And I believe in the Holy Spirit, the lord and giver of life, who proceeds from the Father and the Son, who with the Father and the Son together is worshiped and glorified . . .

A significant bone of contention during Anselm's lifetime was the claim that the Holy Spirit proceeds from the Father *and the Son* (*filioque*). Although the Western or Latin church affirmed the language of *filioque*, the Eastern or Greek church denied it, maintaining that the Holy Spirit proceeded from the Father *through* the Son. In 1098 Anselm attended the Council of Bari to defend the *filioque* conception of procession before delegates of both Latin and Greek churches. *On the Procession of the Holy Spirit* is Anselm's record of the views he expounded at the council.

Anselm was familiar with Augustine's monumental work *On the Trinity*. In it Augustine had argued that among created things we can find images of the Trinity, traces, as it were, of the triune nature of their creator. Star examples are provided by the human mind: one is the mind itself, its self-love, and its self-knowledge (Book 9); another is the mental faculties of memory, understanding, and will (Book 10). Anselm reworks these Augustinian images in *Monologion* 46–67.

Simplicity

Augustine also bequeathed to Anselm a remarkable metaphysical doctrine, the doctrine of God's *simplicity*. Augustine gives partial expression to the doctrine in *On the Trinity*:

> God indeed is truly spoken of in many ways as great, good, wise, blessed, true, and whatever else is seen as not unworthily said [of Him]. But He is the same as His greatness, which is wisdom (for He is not great by means of bulk, but by means of power) and the same as goodness, which is wisdom and greatness, and the same as truth, which is all these. And in Him it is not one thing to be blessed and another to be great, or wise, or true, or to be good, or to be altogether Himself. (6.7.8)

To say of a person that she is good and wise is to say two different things about her, and the two things thus said are distinct from the thing about whom they are said. A person is one thing, her goodness another, and her wisdom a third. She might have been good without being wise, or wise without being good, and in any event, her goodness and wisdom are accidental to her: she was born without them and, having acquired them, she might still lose them. But to say that God is good and wise is not to identify three things, or rather, it *is* to *identify* three things, for God just is goodness itself and wisdom itself (see also *On the Trinity* 15.5.7). To put it in the formal mode, the terms, "God," "goodness itself," and "wisdom itself" necessarily refer to the same thing, just as, on theories of direct reference, "Hesperus," "Phosphorus," and "Venus" are rigid designators necessarily referring to the same heavenly body. Thus even though "Gloria is good" and "God is good" have the same surface grammar, their deep structure is different. The "is" in "Gloria is good" is the "is" of predication. The sentence picks out a subject, Gloria, and predicates the property of goodness of that subject. In the case of "God is good," however, the "is" signifies identity; the sentence is to be understood as "God is identical to goodness itself." Although Gloria is good, Gloria is not goodness itself.

As so far put forward by Augustine, the doctrine of divine simplicity seems to supply a way of regimenting all predicates that apply necessarily or essentially to God, such as "is good," "is wise," and the like: convert the predicate, "is F," into "is identical to F-ness itself," and reconstruct the sentence according to the form "It is necessarily the case that God is identical to F-ness itself." In the first twenty-five chapters of the *Monologion* [hereinafter *Mon.*] Anselm presents a remarkable discussion of the doctrine of divine simplicity and extends it to cover other cases of predication. I shall concentrate on the aspects of Anselm's discussion that are directly relevant to the doctrine of the Trinity.

It turns out to be crucial to Anselm's discussion that we pay attention to a principle that he enunciates early on, a principle called *Aseity* (from the Latin *a se*, in or of itself):

> *Aseity*: God is the only being that exists and is what He is entirely through Himself. (*Mon.* 3. I use the term "God" where Anselm uses terms like "supreme essence.")

The intuitive idea behind *Aseity* is that while every other being is a dependent being (dependent at a minimum, as Anselm argues in the same chapter, on God), God depends on nothing other than himself. *Aseity* will resurface shortly in this discussion.

Now one kind of claim that one can make about God that need not be a claim about God's essence or nature is a relational claim. One can say, for example, that God is greater than all creatures (*Mon.* 15). Anselm has no quarrel with the claim; he regards it as true. But, Anselm insists, its truth says nothing about God's essence. In order for "God is greater than all creatures" to be true, there have to be creatures to which the comparison is made. But if those creatures were to cease to exist, nothing would thereby have changed in God essentially. (Note that Anselm's argument does not rely on the claim that God might not have created anything. Consistent with this argument, Anselm could maintain that God's nature is such that He must create something.) An earthly parallel may help. "Homer is taller than all Arians" presupposes that there are some Arians. Upon the death of the last Arian the sentence would become false, but nothing need change regarding Homer's height. Thus the existence or nonexistence of Arians tells us nothing about how tall Homer is, or even what kind of thing Homer is. ("Homer" might be the name of a radio tower.) The following general principle seems to be at work here:

> *No-rel.*: No relational term ascribed to any being refers to that being's essence. (*Mon.* 15.)

Anselm agrees with Augustine that subject-predicate sentences that specify what God is essentially, such as "God is just," must be recast. In fact, the *Monologion* has been crafted to supply a theoretical justification for the recasting. If Gloria is just and God is just, then they are just "through" justice. Gloria is just in virtue of her participating in the quality of justice. But if God is just through justice and if, by *Aseity*, God is whatever He is through Himself, then God does not participate in justice, as if justice were a quality apart from God; God Himself *is* justice. The identities entailed by Augustine's remarks on divine simplicity receive, in Anselm's hands, their theoretical underpinning by way of *Aseity*.

Anselm presses on further with the doctrine of divine simplicity. In *Monologion* 17 he enunciates this principle about composite things:

> *Comp.:* If *x* is a composite thing, then *x* has its existence and nature through its components, and *x*'s components do not have their existence and nature through *x*.

Comp. and *Aseity* entail there being no composition in God. Anselm apparently thinks that *Comp.* is too obvious to require justification. How obvious it is may depend on what is covered by the notion of a component. The context and subsequent discussion indicate that Anselm means to claim that God has no physical or metaphysical components whatsoever. Thus *Monologion* 18–24 are given over to a discussion about how God exists everywhere and always even though he lacks spatial and temporal parts. On analogy to the principle that any spatially extended thing has spatial parts (e.g., a left side and a right side), and is thereby composite, Anselm thinks that any temporally extended thing has temporal parts (e.g., a past or a future), and is thus similarly composite.

We have seen Anselm argue that God's essential "properties" are not components or parts of God, but just different ways of specifying what God is. But heretofore Anselm has not ruled out explicitly the claim that God has accidental properties. It is not obvious that *Aseity* and *Comp.* rule out divine accidental properties, for it does not appear that an accidental property must affect its bearer's very existence or nature. Yet if God has accidental properties, then it would seem that to that extent, God is metaphysically complex, not simple.

In *Monologion* 25 Anselm tackles the issue of accidental properties. Properly speaking, an accidental property is always an indicator of a thing's mutability: something a thing acquires after not having it, or loses after having it, or has modified over time by augmentation or diminishment. These processes occur only in beings that have a temporal career, divisible into temporal parts. But if God has no temporal parts, then He is not the subject of accidents properly speaking. But we do not always speak properly. Sometimes we describe individuals in ways that appear to imply change in them but really do not. Anselm notes that he is presently neither taller than, shorter than, nor the same height as someone who will be born next year. After that person, Gloria, is born, it may be true at different stages in Gloria's growth that Anselm is taller than, subsequently the same height as, and finally shorter than Gloria. We can say, if we like, that Anselm has *become* shorter than Gloria. But we can at the same time suppose that this change is grounded entirely in Gloria, not Anselm. Similarly, Anselm maintains, whenever we use language that suggests a change in God, we will find that the locus of change is really in mutable creatures.

The example that Anselm supplies is relational. If all putative cases of accidental properties in God are relational in character, it might appear that they are ruled out by *No-rel.* But *No-rel.* requires only that no relations refer to God's essence. *No-rel.* does not pronounce on whether God has relational properties that would be candidates for the status of accidental attributes. Moreover, *No-rel.* would not help Anselm in the event that some putative cases of accidental properties in God are nonrelational in character. Despite initial appearances to the contrary, Anselm's case against accidental properties in God is based on *Aseity* and *Comp.*, along with a thesis that emerged in the *Monologion* 18–24 discussion, namely, the thesis that beings with temporal careers are thereby composite. This thesis, *Aseity*, and *Comp.* entail God's being essentially non-temporal. Together with the *Monologion* 25 claim that accidental properties can belong only to temporal beings, they yield the result that God has no accidental properties.

Triplicity

One can be pardoned for wondering whether and how the doctrine of God's simplicity is consistent with the doctrine of the Trinity. How can God have no parts or composition of any kind yet be threefold in nature? The wonderment might increase when one sees that in the *Monologion* Anselm begins his delineation of the doctrine of the Trinity almost immediately after his defense of simplicity.

One might think that at a minimum, the doctrine of the Trinity must maintain that for some interpretation of "*P*" and "*Q*," God is three *P*s but only one *Q*. Anselm follows the Latin church in saying that God is three *persons* in one *substance*. He acknowledges that the Greek church uses a formulation that can be translated as three *substances* in one *person*, but he is inclined to regard the difference as merely terminological; although the Greek church does differ from the Latin church in doctrine, the doctrinal difference is not located here. (See *Mon.* Prologue and *De Inc. Verbi* 16.) His toleration here may be brought about by his own perplexity about how to fill in the "*P*" place in the above schema. Speaking of the Father and the Son, he says that although they are two, he cannot say what they are two *of.* They are not "two equal spirits or two equal creators or two of anything that signifies either their essence or their relation to creation." (That is, they are not two supreme beings or two omnipotent beings, or two beings who said "Let there be light.") Nor are they two Words: only one of them is the Word; the other is the one who utters the Word (*Mon.* 38; see also *Mon.* 79).

Anselm realizes that there is deeper philosophical puzzlement than this. The most pressing challenge can be illustrated in the following way. *Arianism* had been identified by the formulators of the Nicene Creed as a heretical view, maintaining, among other things, that the Son (and perhaps also the Holy Spirit) is an impressive but nonetheless subordinate being created by the Father. The creed's language describing the Son, for instance, as "very God of very God, begotten, not made, being of one substance with the Father," was directed against Arianism. In insisting on the radical ontological equality of the three persons, however, the creed can be (mistakenly) interpreted as an endorsement of *tritheism*, the position that if there really are three coequal divine persons, then there are three Gods, not one. *Modalism*, on the other hand, maintains that there is only one God, but unlike Arianism, does not discriminate in favor of the Father against the Son and the Holy Spirit. "Person" comes from the Latin *persona*, whose root meanings include a mask or a character in a play. Modalism can exploit the etymology by maintaining that Father, Son, and Holy Spirit are three roles that the one God assumes or three functions—for example, creation, redemption, inspiration—that the one God discharges. A modalist might supplement such an account with an explanation of how humans can understandably come to think that there must be three agencies behind these different types of divine activity when in reality there is but one, just as early stargazers thought there must be three celestial bodies, the planet Venus, the morning star, and the evening star. Here is the challenge: from Anselm's point of view, tritheism and modalism are both heretical positions, as heretical as Arianism. But is there a possible interpretation of the doctrine of the Trinity that avoids Arianism, tritheism, and modalism and that is also consistent with the doctrine of divine simplicity?

Father and Son. Let us begin by examining the *Monologion.* Recall, first, that the opening verses of John had identified the Son with the Word, or the *logos.* Harking back to a preliminary discussion in *Monologion* 10–12—a discussion interrupted by the digression on divine simplicity—Anselm describes the Son as God's *locutio,* through which all things are made. The choice of *locutio* is initially curious; one might have expected *verbum* for *logos.* In fact, Anselm also uses *verbum.* But *locutio* conveys more clearly than does *verbum* an aspect of the Son that is important to Anselm. A *locutio*—henceforward, I will use the English "locution"—is a speech act. But Anselm includes in the notion of a speech act something that may be surprising to modern sensibilities. Thinking is a kind of speaking, an inner speaking: concepts function as inner words in the language of thought (*Mon.* 10). Thus there are mental locutions. Some of them take the form of plans for action. A craftsman first conceives of what he will produce and how he will produce it. The craftsman's conception is a mental locution. Similarly, the world is the result of God's locution.

The craftsman's locution is merely an idea or a concept. Anselm confidently identifies God's locution with the second person of the Trinity. Surely the Son cannot be merely an idea or concept in the divine mind; the very suggestion would make an Arian blush. That suggestion is based, however, on an illegitimate extension of the craftsman's way of formulating locutions to God's way. To illustrate the points that I believe Anselm wants to make, let us suppose that our craftsman is a violin maker who wishes to replicate an Amati. The violin maker's plan or locution is an amalgam of images of Amatis that he has acquired from experience. Success in his execution is determined by two measures of likeness. How accurately does the violin maker's locution represent a genuine Amati? How closely does the finished violin resemble the violin maker's locution? Failure of match between the genuine article and the locution is primarily a kind of cognitive failure. Perhaps the violin maker has not done enough research on Amatis or has paid insufficient attention to their details. Slippage between the locution and the violin produced is more likely due to a failure of power. Perhaps the violin maker's skill is insufficient, or perhaps he was unable to obtain the right raw materials.

Anselm insists that neither sort of liability can affect God's act of creation. Let us take the second one first. Qua omniscient and omnipotent, God does not lack the skill required to realize the content of His locution. Nor is His creative activity confined, as the violin maker's is, to acquiring and rearranging pre-existing material; in creating, God brings that material into existence (*Mon.* 11).

Anselm's dismissal of the applicability of the first sort of liability to God sheds some light on the notion of God's locution. To suppose that God's locution could fall short of some ideal of created reality is to put things precisely backwards. Return, for the sake of contrast, to the violin maker. There were two resemblance relations involving locution and objects here. The locution should resemble the archetypal object, and the object produced should resemble the locution. If both resemblances are sufficiently high, then the object produced resembles the archetype. The images constituting the violin maker's locution represent and thus are measured by a preexisting archetype, namely, the family of Amati violins. But there is no archetype against which God's locution is to be compared. On the contrary, God's locution *is* the archetype against which created things are compared. Whereas the violin-maker case involves two resemblance relations, the case of divine creation involves just one, and even it is a one-way resemblance. Created things are good to the degree to which they resemble this supremely excellent locution, not the other way around (*Mon.* 31). Thus for Anselm, "*x* resembles *y*" need not entail "*y* resembles *x*." Although he does not elaborate on why or when this is so, a plausible hypothesis is that he thinks that *y* need not resemble *x* in cases in which *x* is causally parasitic on *y*. Two peas in a pod can resemble each other, because neither is causally dependent on the other. But on the hypothesis I am attributing to Anselm, a person does not resemble her mirror image or portrait even if her mirror image and portrait resemble her.

This reversal of normal expectations concerning locution, archetype, and object produced is intimately connected with another reversal. In the normal course of events a concept or a mental word depends for its intelligibility on its bearing a resemblance to that for which it is a concept or word. In the beginning was the thing; the word comes later. There would still be a divine locution, however, even if God had decided not to create anything. In the absence of a created world there would be no created world for God to understand. Even so, supremely wise God would be aware of and understand something, namely, Himself. The doctrine of divine simplicity allows Anselm to infer that God's eternal self-awareness and self-understanding just is God's eternal locution. Thus the Word is coeternal with the Word's source (*Mon.* 32). But Anselm is not content to leave matters here. To put it in Johannine terms, he has shown that the Word was with God, but he has not shown—at least not to his obvious satisfaction— that the Word was God. A second appeal to divine simplicity might appear to be all that is required. If, however, the doctrine of divine simplicity converts essential predications about God into necessarily true identity statements, then it is exactly the wrong thing for Anselm to use for the present task. Anselm does not want to conclude that it is necessarily the case that the Father is identical to the Son; that leads to modalism. To borrow a term from discussions of the Nicene Creed, Anselm presents the following argument to show that the Father and the Son are *consubstantial*, not identical.

Whenever a mind tries to understand something, it forms a conception of that thing. The more accurate the conception, the better the understanding. Consider now the special case of a mind trying to understand itself. If it succeeds, the conception it forms not only perfectly matches itself, it *is* itself: in understanding itself it understands itself as understanding itself. There is no room in this case for a distinction between ontologically superior subject and ontologically inferior image. The distinction here between subject and object of understanding is not ontological but rather a distinction discernible solely by reason (*Mon.* 33).

Because God is eternally omniscient, God cannot fail to have perfect, eternal self-understanding. This self-understanding is His locution. But we have just seen Anselm argue that in the case of perfect self-understanding, there can be no ontological difference between the self that understands and the vehicle that delivers self-understanding. That is, God's Word is consubstantial with God. And yet the Word is also what God understands about Himself. The English verb "to conceive," which means both to become pregnant and to understand, would suit Anselm's purposes quite well. The Word is the act, object, and *offspring* of God's conceiving. The relation that holds between the Father and the Son, as the language of the Nicene Creed specifies, is the relation of *begetting* (*Mon.* 41–42). A relation is *asymmetric* if and only if for everything, x, and everything, y, if x bears the relation to y, then y does not bear the relation to x. The relation of *being taller than* is asymmetric: if x is taller than y then y is not taller than x. Anselm regards the *begetting* relation as asymmetric. The clearest evidence is provided in *On the Procession of the Holy Spirit* 1: "It is impossible for a father to be a son of him whose father he is, and for a son to be a father of him whose son he is."

One can show that if a relation is asymmetric, then it is *irreflexive*, that is, that nothing bears that relation to itself. Consider, for example, the asymmetric *being taller than* relation. Suppose now that for some *x*, the *being taller than* relation were not irreflexive. In that case *x* would be taller than *x*. But since the relation is asymmetric, it would follow that *x* is *not* taller than *x*. Thus the supposition leads to its own denial. To apply this result to the case of *begetting*, the asymmetry of the relation entails the result, that Anselm certainly accepts, that nothing begets itself. "Indeed, nature does not permit, nor does the intellect grasp, that something existing from something *is* the being from whom it exists, or that the being from whom it exists exists from itself" (*De Proc.* 1). The Father, then, begets the Son, but the Son does not beget the Father. Moreover, the Father does not beget Himself. Nor, as it turns out, does the Holy Spirit beget the Father. Since no other being is apt to beget the Father—that would be a violation of *Aseity*—it follows that the Father is unbegotten.

Perhaps because Augustine had used the notion in one of his images of the Trinity, Anselm introduces *memoria* in *Monologion* 48, immediately before beginning his discussion of the third person of the Trinity. If we translate *memoria* and *meminisse* as "memory" and "to remember," respectively, we are saddled with some puzzling Anselmian assertions, chief among which is the claim that "Since a human mind is not always thinking of itself, as it is always remembering itself, it is clear that when it is thinking of itself, its word is born from memory." Anselm infers from this that if a mind were always thinking of itself, its word would always be born from its memory. But God always thinks of Himself, so His word or locution, that is, the Word, is born from His eternal memory. The stumbling-block is the first premise. It is hard to know what Anselm means when he says that the human mind always remembers itself, especially when he has just granted that it does not always think of itself. And even if we get clarification on this issue, there is a further problem of seeing how the results would apply to God's mind. Inasmuch as there are no temporal stages to God's existence—in particular, nothing is *past* to God—it would seem that God has no need of nor capacity for memory.

I suggest the following way of understanding what Anselm intends. Like the English "memory," *memoria* can refer to the mental faculty of recollection or the content retained therein. *Meminisse* can mean to recall actively, but it can also mean simply to retain in mind, not to have forgotten. We can interpolate various of these elements into a gloss on Anselm's claim: "Since a human mind is not always thinking of itself, as it is always remembering itself [that is, always retaining its capacity to focus its attention on itself], it is clear that when it is thinking of itself, its word [in this case, its concept of itself] is born from memory [that is, is brought to consciousness by its faculty of recollection accessing its storehouse of concepts]." The rest of Anselm's argument now goes smoothly enough. We can ascribe *memoria* to God as a faculty presupposed by self-reflection, even divine self-reflection. Divine *memoria* differs from human memory in these respects. In humans, memory is an on-again, off-again sort of faculty, always present but finite in its capacity, sometimes dormant, sometimes active, and sometimes, when active, faulty at retrieving what it seeks. One source of its spotty retrieval record is the gradual decay or distortion of memory traces over time. Another source is internal to the metaphysics of human memory. The contents of human memory are likenesses or images of the things (*Mon.* 36 and 62), caused, one presumes, by the things of which they are the likenesses. But the process of causal transmission can result in distorted images, due, perhaps, to imperfections in the medium of transmission or in the human recipient. In contrast, divine *memoria* is infinite in its capacity, never dormant, and never faulty. Nor is it timebound. If Anselm is right, memory is prior to self-reflection, but in the divine case the priority is only logical, not temporal. The Father, or *memoria*, is that from which the Son, the Word, or perfect image of the Father (an image in which the relation of resemblance is symmetric), is coeternally begotten. Finally, divine *memoria* does not contain images of created things, but rather, through the activity of the Word, the perfect essences of those things (*Mon.* 36), of which the things themselves are images.

Holy Spirit. In *Monologion* 49 and 50 Anselm lays the foundation of an argument for the third person of the Trinity. The argument proceeds in two stages, each stage depending on a principle connecting memory and understanding to love. In *Monologion* 49 the principle is this:

> *Utility*: An agent's memory and understanding of a thing are useless unless the thing itself is loved or rejected to the degree required by reason.

If we apply *Utility* reflexively, to the agent himself, we get the result that an agent's self-memory and self-understanding are of no use if the agent does not love or reject himself to the right degree.

Anselm does not expatiate on the notion of loving something "to the degree required by reason." He could—and perhaps did—find ample authority for the notion in the writings of Augustine.[2] According to Augustine, everything that exists is good, because everything that exists either is perfectly good God or was created by perfectly good God. But not everything is equally good; some things are more excellent than others (see *Mon.* 4 and 15), and their excellence resides in their being better images of God. So, for example, rational, perceptive,

---

[2] See the sources mentioned in William E. Mann, "Augustine on Evil and Original Sin," in Eleonore Stump and Norman Kretzmann, eds., *The Cambridge Companion to Augustine* (Cambridge: Cambridge University Press, 2001), 40–48. Reprinted as Chapter 5 of this volume.

animate beings are better than nonrational, perceptive, animate beings, which in turn are better than nonperceptive animate beings, which are better than inanimate beings (*Mon.* 31). In light of these Augustinian considerations, I shall risk imputing to Anselm a principle according to which love should track excellence:

Track: A thing deserves to be loved to the extent to which it is excellent.

(I have chosen to phrase *Track* in this way rather than, for example, "One's love for a thing should be proportionate to the thing's excellence," because *Track* leaves open the possibility of *grace*, understood as the notion of love that exceeds the merits of the beloved.)

Now I can expand, on Anselm's behalf, the compressed argument in *Monologion* 49. *Utility* requires that God's memory and understanding are useless if He does not love Himself to the degree that reason requires. Divine simplicity requires that God is His memory and understanding. Thus, God would be useless were He not to love Himself to the degree that reason requires. Anselm would regard that conclusion as absurd. Therefore, God loves Himself. This is the conclusion that ends *Monologion* 49, but we can extend the argument to capture a claim that Anselm makes in a subsequent chapter. *Track* entails God's deserving to be loved to the extent to which He is excellent. But God is supremely excellent. Thus God would be remiss if He failed to love himself to a degree equal to His supreme excellence. Since God cannot be remiss in anything, it follows, as Anselm puts it, that "His love is as great as He Himself is" (*Mon.* 52).

The second of the two principles connecting memory and understanding to love appears in *Monologion* 50:

Prior: Any rational being that loves itself does so because and only because it remembers and understands itself; it does not remember and understand itself because it loves itself.

Prior makes a claim about the explanatory priority of self-memory and self-understanding over self-love. *Prior* gives us a conception of rational love, a kind of love that presupposes memory and understanding at a minimum. Yet memory and understanding are not sufficient. Anselm observes that there are many things we remember and understand but do not love. *Prior* is restricted in two ways, dealing only with self-love and only with rational beings who love themselves. Anselm immediately endorses, however, a less restricted principle, one that applies to all cases of love, namely, that *nothing* is loved without its being an item of (the lover's) memory and understanding. But even the less restricted principle does not imply that every rational being loves itself. For all that *Prior* says, there may be rational beings whose self-memory and self-understanding are such that they do not love themselves. Borrowing an idea from *Track*, we can say that it may be that such beings recognize their own conspicuous lack of excellence.

Because divine self-love must be coeternal with God—indeed, must turn out, for Anselm, to be consubstantial with the Father and the Son—it is important for Anselm's purposes that explanatory priority need not involve temporal priority. Even among timebound creatures, explanatory priority is compatible with simultaneity: a pendulum's length explains its period, not vice versa. So Anselm has grounds for holding that God's self-love follows from His self-memory and self-understanding, even though the "following" cannot imply a temporal sequence.

Anselm relies on the consubstantiality of the Father and the Son to establish to his satisfaction that this divine love proceeds equally from both, who love each other and themselves to the same extent—an extent compatible with their supreme excellence and independent of their creating anything—with one love that proceeds as a whole from each of them (*Mon.* 50–54).

In *Monologion* 55 Anselm stakes out a major claim, for which he offers two arguments. The claim is that divine love is not the offspring of the Father or the Son. That is, the asymmetric, irreflexive begetting relation that holds between the Father and the Son does not hold between them, singly or collectively, and divine love. Here Anselm is conforming to the demands of the Nicene Creed, which specifies that the Son is "only-begotten." The second of the two arguments consists of an attempt to reduce to absurdity the offspring hypothesis by ringing the changes on which of the first two members of the Trinity would be the mother. It cannot be that one is the father and the other the mother, since love proceeds from both the Father and the Son in exactly the same way. And it cannot be that both are father and mother; no nature could be both. The argument is less than overwhelming. Anselm has already conceded that there are no sexual distinctions to be found between the first two members of the Trinity. We regard them as male because of the gender of the nouns in Latin (*pater* and *filius*) and on the basis of sexist biology (*Mon.* 42). So to utilize generalizations about sexual reproduction in creatures is out of place. Moreover, if those generalizations are loosened up enough so that the Son can be begotten by the Father parthenogenetically, so to speak, without benefit of a mother, then it would seem not to be much more of a feat to have love begotten by both.

The first of the two arguments is more intriguing. Although the Son is the perfect image of the Father, Anselm asserts that divine love resembles neither the Father nor the Son. From this premise we are to conclude that divine love is not begotten. I presume that we are to fill in the argument by supposing that if divine love were begotten, as the Son is, it would resemble its parent(s). Therefore it must proceed from its source in some different way. What is intriguing about the argument is the lack-of-resemblance assertion. What could justify it?

There was the pressure of authority from Augustine, who had pronounced that "The Son alone is the image of the Father" (*On the Trinity* 6.2.3). But that confers a pedigree, not a justification. I suggest that the reason why Augustine and Anselm converge on this assertion is grounded in the analogy of Trinity to memory, understanding, and will. Memory and understanding are essential to *cognition* or *contemplation* (liberally construed). We are entitled to impute the following picture to Anselm. Understanding is an intellective process or state, represented in thought by mental locutions. The possibility of forming these locutions, and thus the possibility of understanding itself, depends on the understanding agent having in memory the relevant concepts, or inner words, from which the mental locutions are formed. A necessary condition for the agent's understanding is that the agent's mental locutions correctly image the connections that exist among the relevant concepts. The transfer of this picture to the first two members of the Trinity is reasonably straightforward. The Father is the primordial memory, as it were, that is perfectly imaged by the Son's locution.

If, however, the third member of the Trinity is analogously identified with will, then we shift from the realm of cognition and contemplation to the arena of *desire* and *action*. It can seem natural to say that the process of coming to understand something resembles the process of recalling something, natural enough to lead Plato to assimilate all cases of genuine learning to recollection of what one already knows. But there is no similar obvious affinity between recalling or understanding something and desiring or doing something. In particular, love and love-motivated actions do not immediately resemble cognitive states and feats. I suspect that it is considerations like these that lead Anselm to assert the lack-of-resemblance thesis. Anselm never puts it this way, but it can be said on his behalf that if he had confined himself solely to a consideration of the first two members of the Trinity, without the dimension of divine love, he would have been left with a conception of God as a purely contemplative being, unconcerned about creation, unconcerned about Himself, unconcerned even about contemplation.

Divine love, then, is not the offspring of the Father or the Son but nevertheless proceeds from both of them. Although proceeding from them, it is uncreated, coeternal, and consubstantial with them. In traditional trinitarian terminology, the relation that describes this mode of proceeding is *spiration*, a kind of divine exhaling or sighing that produces—and *is*—the *Spirit* (identification of divine love by that term is postponed by Anselm until *Mon.* 57). Like the begetting relation, spiration is an asymmetric and irreflexive relation.

Following Augustine, Anselm models his conception of the Trinity on memory, understanding, and will. The model is fueled by the thought that among the created things that we ordinarily encounter, the human mind bears the clearest traces of its creator. Yet in the human mind, memory, understanding, and will are three separate faculties, each responsible for a separate domain of human competence and each operating semi-autonomously from the others. In *Monologion* 57–61 Anselm argues, in effect, that this feature of human mental life cannot be ascribed to God. Divine memory, understanding, and will are not encapsulated. The Father, the Son, and the Holy Spirit are "equally in one another," in such a way that, for example, the Father does not understand solely through the instrumentality of the Son and love solely through the Spirit. Each person of the Trinity is fully endowed with all the abilities of the others. Yet it is not as if each were a separate, free-standing module backed up with the capacities of the others. That would be tritheism.

Taking Stock

We have, then, the following results. The Father, the Son, and the Holy Spirit are associated, respectively, with memory, understanding, and will. Each of these mental functions was introduced by means of its self-reflective capacities, self-memory (adjusted to extend to a being for whom nothing is past), self-understanding, and self-love. In humans memory, understanding, and will are encapsulated or modular. In God they are not: the doctrine of God's simplicity entails there being no separate "components," mental or otherwise, in God. Anselm is thus insulated against a charge of tritheism. In order to avoid lapsing into modalism Anselm must find a way in which God is threefold that does not collapse into merely ascribing three different roles or functions to God. In service of that goal, Anselm relies on the two relations, begetting and spiration. The Son is distinguished from the Father by being begotten; the Holy Spirit is distinguished from the Father and the Son by being spirated from both.

But recall *No-rel.*, the principle that no relational term ascribed to any being refers to that being's essence. Anselm invoked *No-rel.* to support his thesis that no relational term ascribed to God refers to God's essence. But the terms, "begets" and "spirates," are relational and ascribed to God. Now Anselm faces a dilemma. Take the case of begetting; analogous remarks apply to spiration. Either the Father begets the Son essentially or not. If the former, then *No-rel.* is false. If the latter, that is, if the Father does not beget the Son essentially, then it would seem that the Son's existence is as contingent as the existence of any creature. But that consequence flies in the face of everything that Anselm has said about the Father and the Son, in particular, that the Father's existence is necessary and that the Father and the Son are coeternal, coequal, and consubstantial. Anselm is in danger here of capitulating to Arianism.

If Anselm cannot have *No-rel.* along with essentially existing, coequal members of the Trinity, then perhaps he should jettison *No-rel.* The principle seems false for independent reasons. The proposition that the number 4 is even specifies part of 4's essence. But that proposition is irreducibly relational: to be even is to be divisible by 2. We have already seen that *Aseity* and *Comp.* suffice without *No-rel.* to ground an argument against ascribing accidental properties to God. My conjecture is that *Aseity* and *Comp.* are sufficient to allow Anselm to argue for a robust doctrine of God's simplicity.

Still, we are left with the question whether Anselm's doctrine of the Trinity falls prey to a charge of modalism, a question made all the more poignant by Anselm's candid admission that he cannot say what the Father, the Son, and the Holy Spirit are three *of.* In *On the Incarnation of the Word* Anselm presents an arresting analogy that sheds light on this issue. An analogy like it had originally been employed by Augustine in *On Faith and Creed.* I shall first discuss Augustine's version of it, then Anselm's.

How is it possible, Augustine asks, that the Son is not the Father, and neither the Father nor the Son is the Holy Spirit, yet the Father is God, the Son is God, and the Holy Spirit is God, without there being three Gods (*On Faith and Creed* 9.16)? It will help to dispel a sense of logical impropriety if we can find similar patterns of claims made about things found in nature. Think of a spring, the headwaters of a river. The spring is not the river itself. Nor is drinking water obtained from the spring or the river identical to the spring or the river. But the spring is water, the river is water, and the drink is water. We do not say that there are three waters; there is only one water (*On Faith and Creed* 9.17). Augustine is quick to point out that the analogy is not perfect; for the same water might at one time be in the spring, later in the river, and still later in the drink. God, is not, however, at one time the Father, at another the Son, and at still another the Holy Spirit. But that kind of slippage can be attributed to the difference between temporal and eternal entities. Augustine suggests a second analogy involving the roots, trunk, and branches of a tree all being *simultaneously* the same wood, not three woods.

"Water" and "wood" are *mass nouns,* nouns whose paradigm cases refer to stuffs. Mass nouns resist pluralization, numerical modifiers, the indefinite article, and the degree determinatives, "many" and "few." In some obvious ways, assimilating "God" to a mass noun should be attractive to monotheists. Even so, Augustine's analogies ignore a distinction that is critical in this context. Consider the two claims:

(1) The spring is water.
(2) The river is water.

Set aside worries about temporal successiveness. Focus instead on the copula, "is," and ask the question: What is the logical structure of (1) and (2)? Since "water" is a noun, the sentences cannot have a subject-predicate structure. Nor can the "is" express identity, for if it did, then (1) and (2) would be represented as:

(1′) The spring = water.
(2′) The river = water.

(1′) and (2′) entail the falsehood that the spring = the river. Moreover, if the spring is supposed to be the analogue to the Father, the river the analogue to the Son, and water the analogue to God, we get the result, inimical to the doctrine of the Trinity, that the Father = the Son.

A more promising approach to (1) and (2) is to view them as elliptical for sentences that include a non-count quantificational noun applicable to water:

(1*) The spring is a portion of water.
(2*) The river is a portion of water.

Since the portion of water constituting the spring need not be identical to the portion constituting the river, the analogy gives no reason to think that the Father is identical to the Son. Nevertheless, the analogy implies that the Father and the Son are portions of God, which, insofar as it is intelligible at all, probably implies tritheism and certainly contravenes divine simplicity.

At first glance Anselm's reworking of the Augustinian analogy appears to be a trivially different variation of it.[3] We are to envision the Nile, flowing from spring into river and from river into lake. (Ignore your knowledge of actual African geography.) The spring is not the river and neither the spring nor the river is the lake. Yet spring, river, and lake are all called the Nile; there are not three Niles but only one (*De Inc. Verbi* 13). One may be inclined to object that the analogy is more obviously inept than that of Augustine. The spring, river, and lake are *parts* of the Nile; thus Anselm's analogy even more overtly leads to tritheism or the denial of divine simplicity.

Anselm anticipates this objection: his response to it takes us well beyond the resources proposed by Augustine. We are to suppose that "the Nile" names something that exists from *where* it begins to where it ends and from *when* it begins to when it ends. It appears as though Anselm is advocating a view

---

[3] For another analysis of Anselm's Nile analogy, see Christopher Hughes, *On a Complex Theory of a Simple God* (Ithaca, NY: Cornell University Press, 1989), chap. 5.

according to which "the Nile" names a four-dimensional entity, occupying a certain region, not just of space, but of the spatio-temporal continuum. (It is not too farfetched to think of this use of "the Nile" applying to the Nile as perceived by God, *sub specie aeternitatis*.) Now Anselm claims that if we think of the Nile in this way, we will realize that "the whole Nile is the spring, the whole Nile is the river, the whole Nile is the lake," even though the spring, river, and lake are not identical with each other. Anselm's move from supposition to conclusion is not brokered by any intermediary steps, so, in addition to trying to decipher what the conclusion means, we need to understand why Anselm believes it to be a consequence of his four-dimensionalistic premise about the Nile.

Let us suppose that Anselm would agree that what holds for "the Nile" holds for all proper names. In that case, for example, "Anselm" names a seventy-six-year-old continuant stretching through years of the eleventh and twelfth centuries and regions of Italy, France, and England. Now suppose that in the late eleventh century Gloria says that she just saw Anselm yesterday. Boso, an acquaintance of Gloria's, seeks to correct her, pointing out that she did not see *Anselm*; strictly speaking, what she saw was just a "time-slice" of Anselm. Boso assures Gloria that her describing her encounter with the time-slice as an encounter with Anselm is a case of synecdoche. It occurs to Gloria that were she to acquiesce in Boso's diagnosis, she would have to acknowledge that she never sees any three-dimensional object: all that she really sees are "space-slices," or surfaces of objects. But why should Gloria accept Boso's diagnosis? She can cling to four-dimensionalism and reject Boso's diagnosis by maintaining that she *did* see the four-dimensional Anselm yesterday. This feat of perception is no stranger than the phenomenon of apprehending a felon by grabbing the felon's ankle.

Anselm may have something like this in mind when he claims that the whole Nile is the spring, the whole Nile is the river, and the whole Nile is the lake. The expression is dramatic, to be sure. But it allows Anselm to preserve an important item of common sense, namely, that people routinely see the Nile, not just a fragment of it. And, finally, it provides Anselm, I think, with a way of rejecting modalism. If the whole of God is the Father, the whole of God is the Son, and the whole of God is the Holy Spirit, then it follows that the Father is the whole of God, the Son is the whole of God, and the Holy Spirit is the whole of God. Where there is wholeness, there is no room for apportioning roles or functions.

Anselm is fond of the Nile analogy. He suggests that it can help us to understand the doctrine of the incarnation (*De Inc. Verbi* 14) and he uses it to argue for the appropriateness of the *filioque* doctrine (*De Proc.* 9). Yet we should bear in mind that when he introduces the analogy, it is designed simply to show how even among spatio-temporal things composed of parts, it is possible to find that "three can be said of one and one of three." If the analogy helps to forestall a charge of modalism, that is to its credit. Anselm hastens to remind us, however, that the analogy, like the other analogies on which he has relied, is just that—an analogy, his best attempt to explicate what must remain inexplicable. The mystery of the Trinity remains a mystery. For now we see in a mirror dimly (*Mon.* 67), a mirror whose act of reflecting is itself a dim reflection of its maker.[4]

[4] An earlier version of this essay benefited from the criticism of Brian Davies and Brian Leftow, hereby gratefully acknowledged.

INDEX

Abelard, citations to works
    Commentary on Paul's Letter to the Romans, 165
    *Dialogues between a Philosopher, a Jew, and a
        Christian,* 151, 153, 163–4, 169, 171
    Ethics (or *Scito te Ipsum*), 151–7, 161–70
Abelard, moral cases discussed
    arson vs. fornication, 168–70
    Hamlet and Claudius, 159–60
    homicide motivated by greed vs. by
        compassion, 170
    hunting accident, 164
    just punishment of the innocent,
        162n16, 168–9
    monkish temptation, 157
    mugger's choice, 156
    persecution of Christ, 162–5, 168
    servant killing master, 154–6
    smothered baby, 167–8
    Sophie's choice, 159
    successful vs. thwarted charitable
        intentions, 166–7
    two executioners, 158, 170
    wealthy donor, widow's mites, 172
Abelard on two senses of "sin," 163–4
Abelard, Peter, 1, 4, 11–2, 26, 119
accidental properties, 233, 235–6, 246
acting in ignorance, 41, 43, 48–9, 83–4,
        101, 108
    of fact, 162–4
    of law, 164
acting on mistaken belief, 162, 165–6
action-consent, 99–100, 113
act-utilitarianism, 126
Adam and Eve's fall, consequences of. *See*
        ignorance and difficulty
Adams, John, 56
Adams, Robert Merrihew, 130n15, 191n1,
        193n3, 194n8, 211
Adeodatus, 12, 134

anaphora. *See* coreference
Anscombe, G. E. M., 218
Anselm, 1, 5–7
Anselm, citations to works
    Cur Deus Homo, 225
    De casu diaboli, 201
    De Grammatico, 178
    Monologion, 6, 178, 184, 223n27, 231–7,
        240–3, 245
    Proslogion, 6–7, 179, 184n17, 185n19, 191–4,
        196–200, 202, 204, 206, 208, 212–4,
        216n9, 217–8, 221, 223n26, 225, 229–30
    On the Incarnation of the Word, 6, 231,
        246, 248
    On the Procession of the Holy Spirit, 6,
        231–2, 239
    Reply to Gaunilo, 179n10, 184–6, 214n4, 215,
        217, 222
Anselm on God's simplicity, 6, 233–7, 239,
        242, 245–7
Anselm's trinitarian principles
    Aseity, 234–6, 240, 246
    Comp., 235–6, 246
    No-rel., 234, 236, 245–6
    Prior, 242
    Track, 242–3
    Utility, 241–2
anticonsequentialism, 102
anti-Manichaeanism, 2–3, 36, 50–1, 74,
        109n28, 135
anti-Pelagianism, 36, 41, 69, 74, 85, 102,
        111–2, 135
Aquinas, Thomas, 13n7, 41n8, 47n19, 80, 83,
        106n26, 110n29, 156n6, 168n19
Arianism, 6, 236–7, 245
Aristotle
    on teaching, 142–4
    on tragedy, 56n12, 57
assumption mode, 135, 137–8, 141–2